**Leon McCarron** is a Northern Irish writer, film-maker and speaker. He is a Fellow of the Royal Geographical Society and specialises in storytelling via long distance, human-powered expeditions. He has cycled from New York to Hong Kong, walked 3,000 miles across China, trekked 1,000 miles through the Empty Quarter desert in Arabia and travelled along Iran's longest river. At the end of 2014 he rode a horse across Argentina, following the Santa Cruz River in the footsteps of Charles Darwin. Most recently, McCarron walked from Jerusalem to Mount Sinai to explore another side of the Middle East. His first book, *The Road Headed West*, described a cycling adventure across North America. McCarron has also produced a TV series, *Walking Home from Mongolia*, for National Geographic and made three independent films. In 2017 he was awarded the Neville Shulman Challenge Award.

'Immensely readable true travel writing in the honourable tradition of Robert Byron, but with a sharp political edge. He informs us about the region of our troubled world we should, perhaps, understand best. The theme throughout is how walking brings solutions to all problems; or *solvitur ambulando*, as St. Augustine said.'

Robin Hanbury-Tenison

'A marvellous adventure and an impressive feat of endurance. This is also a journey that explores the people and landscapes of a misunderstood part of the world with great insight and enthusiasm.'

Ranulph Fiennes

'Informed, engaging and sensitive – Leon makes the perfect companion for the dusty road.'

Benedict Allen

# THE
# LAND
# BEYOND

A Thousand Miles on Foot through
the Heart of the Middle East

## LEON McCARRON

I.B. TAURIS
LONDON · NEW YORK

MIX
Paper from
responsible sources
FSC® C007584

Published in 2017 by
I.B.Tauris & Co. Ltd
London • New York
www.ibtauris.com

ISBN: 978 1 78831 056 7
eISBN: 978 1 78672 284 3
ePDF: 978 1 78673 284 2

A full CIP record for this book is available from the British Library
A full CIP record is available from the Library of Congress

Library of Congress Catalog Card Number: available

Typeset in GaramondPremrPro by OKS Prepress Services, Chennai, India
Printed and bound in Sweden by ScandBook AB

'The land beyond the sea, that is to say, the Holy Land, which men call the land of promise or of behest, is the most worthy of lands [...] for it is the heart and the middle of all the world [...] He that will pass over the sea to go to the city of Jerusalem may go many ways, both by land and sea: many ways come to one end.'

(John Mandeville, *Diaries*, c.1322)

'I have met but with one or two persons on the course of my life who understood the art of Walking, that is, of taking walks [...] sauntering: which word is beautifully derived "from idle people who roved about the country, in the Middle Ages, and asked for charity, under the pretense of going à la Sainte Terre," to the Holy Land, till the children exclaimed, "There goes a Sainte-Terrer," a Saunterer, a Holy-Lander.'

(Henry David Thoreau, 'Walking', 1862)

*To all who create paths, and to those who sustain them
and keep them alive. Walk well.*

# Contents

*List of Plates*                                                              viii
*Preface*                                                                        x
*Map of the Author's Route through West Bank, Jordan and Sinai*    xvi

Part I    The Centre of all the World                                          1
Part II   East of the Jordan                                                  95
Part III  The Path to the Sacred Summit                                      181

*Acknowledgements*                                                           254
*Trail Companions*                                                           256
*Information on the Trails*                                                   258
*Glossary*                                                                   263
*Notes*                                                                      266

# List of Plates

1 The view east towards St George's Monastery in Wadi Qelt between Jerusalem and Jericho – this is said to be the 'Valley of the Shadow of Death' from Psalm 23:4.

2 Looking out east to the mountains of Jordan from an olive grove in the West Bank, just north of Jericho.

3 Anwar making tea over a fire and resting in the shade in Wadi Auja, West Bank (photo by Dave Cornthwaite).

4 Um Fares and members of the women's co-operative in Aqbat Jabr refugee camp near Jericho in the West Bank.

5 The elders of the Samaritan community on Mount Gerizim, above Nablus city.

6 Eisa stopping for one of many tea breaks in the rolling green hills near Ajloun, Jordan.

7 Suleiman, the desert philosopher, watching the sunset in Feynan, Jordan.

8 Author sleeping in a cave near Burbeita, Jordan.

9 Author and Sean Conway walking through the mountains between Petra and Rum.

10 The mouth of Wadi Feid, Jordan.

11 The Monastery at Petra, Jordan.

12 Austin climbing Jebel Milehis, with the view back across the peninsula to the east. In the distance are the mountains of Saudi Arabia, across the Red Sea.

13 Shepherds south of Kerak, Jordan, making tea and camping out while they look after the newly born kids.

14 Musallem and Suleiman sharing stories and cigarettes around a fire in the Sinai Desert.

15 Suleiman and Harboush the camel walking in highlands close to the town of St Catherine.

16 Suleiman and Musallem smoking cigarettes and loading a reluctant Harboush for the day.

17 The final day: (from left) author, Suleiman, Harboush, Musallem, Austin, Nasr.

18 Musallem and Austin walking through the wadis in the coastal range near Nuweiba, Sinai.

Unless otherwise stated, all photos are the author's own.

# Preface

I was drowsy and grumpy, and the red-eye flight to Amman full to capacity. I counted three other non-Arabs on board: a red-faced and intolerant little Scotsman and two loud, blonde American girls whose presence rendered an adjacent row of Emirati men silent and staring. All other space was taken by Jordanian families, squeezed into small seats underneath layers of children, discarded overcoats and mall-branded shopping bags.

I sat by the aisle alongside an Iraqi architect called Sattar, who enjoyed napping with his head on my shoulder. When awake, though, he was great company, throwing out big, toothy grins from under an enormous bushy moustache. He designed office blocks in Iraq, Jordan and the Emirates.

'Baghdad for the heart, Amman for the head, and Dubai for the money [...] all of the money!' he said.

I told him that I was only passing through Amman en route to Jerusalem to begin a four-month journey on foot.

'Very nice,' he nodded, 'walking is good for us. It makes people less fat and more intelligent.'

His conversational style compelled constant attention; regularly he would change topic rapidly and without warning, and in between would be placed bite-sized nuggets of wisdom. He politely asked my thoughts on how to destroy the 'IS, IS' (pronouncing each couplet separately) in Syria and Iraq, and then we segued into philosophy via football; Da'esh to Ronaldo to Nietzsche in one swift movement. I'd never before sat beside a stranger on an aeroplane who could quote by heart Kant, Aristotle and Ibn Arabi ('the greatest Islamic scholar of all', I was assured).

'It's stories,' Sattar said suddenly, after wrapping up a particularly lengthy summation of *Ecce Homo*. 'What you're doing with walking is storytelling, but it's also how the 'IS, IS' are rallying gullible people. The drama of football is a story, and the best philosophers talk in parables. No one wants lectures, but everyone will listen to a good story. You cannot take these things with you to the grave. Storytelling is a way of compressing time – it is how we pass on history, and it is the key to understanding, for everybody.'

The in-flight snacks arrived, and Sattar fell silent; behind me the Scotsman was blustering about the sandwiches.

'This chicken is fucked!' he yelled at blank-faced stewardesses.

Sattar, I realised, had very neatly encapsulated what I hoped lay ahead of me over the following months. I'm still grateful to him for the timely reminder; in that part of the world the minutiae of each moment can make it easy to lose sight of the bigger picture. If that doesn't make sense as you read this now, I hope it will by the end of this book. What follows is the outcome of the concept, my hopes rendered into raw reality. This is the account of my life on the path, or, in Arabic, the *masar*. This is the story of a thousand miles on foot through the heart of the Middle East, a place that is at once confusing, conflicted and utterly compelling.

The first time I saw a Palestinian flag, we had just moved house and I must have been about five years old. In my formative years, the green, white, red and black would regularly be displayed proudly over houses in the village near where I lived. I was acquainted too with the blue and white Israeli colours: they fluttered in different villages, slightly farther away, taking their place in a multifarious line of flags protruding from roofs, windows and lamp posts. This all took place not in the West Bank, but 3,500 miles away on the north coast of Northern Ireland.

The relationship between the Irish and the land of Palestine is a complex one. The Irish Republic is one of the most vocal supporters of the Palestinian cause in all of Europe: many Irish identify with the idea of an oppressed people fighting for liberty and justice against a larger and more powerful aggressor. In Northern Ireland the same feeling is even more prevalent amongst the Republicans,[1] who see parallels between the Israeli government's actions and the Protestant English monarchy's rule of the six counties of Northern Ireland. Meanwhile the Loyalists[2] – many of whom are descended from Protestant migrants from England and Scotland – see their own struggle to defend what they see as a righteous claim to land against a violent uprising reflected in that of the Israelis. Somehow this all led – in a small corner of a tiny island in the North Atlantic – to an appropriation of the colours and rhetoric of the Middle Eastern struggle as another weapon in the sectarian symbolic arsenal.

Since the Good Friday Agreement in 1998, Northern Ireland has lived under an uneasy peace accord, but the cultural and religious divide still remains. Aside from occasional violent flare-ups, the rifts are most obvious in passive-aggressive posturing: the fervent painting of curbstones (red, white and blue versus green, white and gold), parades and marches and shows of 'strength', and above all else the zenith of commitment to the cause: flying the flag. The Northern Irish *love* flags. It has become something of a national joke recently – the sort of joke where you have to laugh to avoid crying.[3]

With disharmony ever present under the surface, ever more need is felt to appropriate other causes and symbols, and the Israeli–Palestinian struggle is the one that remains closest to the hearts of many people in Belfast and beyond (although most of them would struggle to tell you what it's actually about, where Israel and Palestine are and who's fighting who).

It was probably about the same time as the Good Friday Agreement was signed that I realised what the Israeli and Palestinian flags actually represented (or rather, I first established that they weren't just alternative Irish or British flags). For my part I had always preferred the Palestinian colours – in the same way a rookie punter might choose a horse at a racetrack because the jockey is wearing the most appealing shirt – and because the villages around me were predominantly Catholic those were the colours I saw more frequently. For some, that's probably reason enough to hang the flag on a pole outside the front door. I had little interest in the politics of it, but even then – when usually the only topic that could enthuse me was football – I wondered about the places behind the flags. Were they like Northern Ireland? Were the people similar? Did they also like football?

Some 15 years down the line, I was an habitué of the Middle East. I had walked across the largest sand desert on earth, the Empty Quarter, and observed up close the contrasting wilderness and rapid urbanisation of the Gulf. I had followed the longest river in Iran from source to sea and found the Persian countryside full of warm, hospitable people who were dismayed that the world viewed them as terrorists. I had spent time in Egypt, Lebanon and Iraqi Kurdistan, and I moved from London to Muscat, Oman. The Middle East that I had come to know was enormous, diverse and captivating, and each day I spent in any part of it increased my desire to stay.

I began to wonder what the people back home made of it. Some people, of course, know all about the complexities. Others read the *Daily Mail*. I made a film about my time in the Empty Quarter and was surprised that people's reactions to it included a lot of incredulity that my friend and I might be able to travel safely in such a place. A keyword search online shows that the most common associations for the 'Middle East' include: deserts, camels, Islam, burqas, conflict, terrorism.

Until recently, little effort has been made to educate the British (or Irish) public about the Middle East. The culture and history of the region are yet to make it onto most school curricula here and (as indeed in the US and across much of Europe) our impressions are shaped by the mainstream media. What we are presented with is overwhelmingly negative.

And so there is little awareness of the disparate nature of such a huge area, and how much history it shares with the West. The fierce clashes of empires and cultures over the centuries are well known – the Muslim occupation of Europe, the Crusades, British colonisation and more recent battles over oil – but how many people know, for example, that we have the medieval Islamic world to thank for the invention of hospitals, surgery, universities, algebra and stringed instruments?

Over half of Britons now see mainstream Muslims as a threat to Western society.[4] One in three young children think that Islam is 'taking over Britain'.[5] Islamophobia is on the rise, and hate crimes have risen a reported 70 per cent since the summer of 2015.[6]

Perhaps it is wise not to take these polls as absolute truth, but it's certain that now more than ever what happens in the Middle East impacts on the Western world, and our fates are tied together. The rise of ISIS and the flight of millions of desperate refugees to Europe are monumental events that demand international attention. Public perceptions of the region shape Britain's actions and voting patterns, with knock-on effects that could last for generations to come.

My journey and the route that I took were born of my curiosity to delve deeper into the wider region. I would go to Jerusalem, to the hub of the Israeli–Palestinian enigma, and see for myself what it looked like. Needless to say, I was hoping to find, when I got there, at least one Union Jack and one Irish tricolour flying over this holy, ancient city in the centre of the world – for posterity's sake, it seemed only fair.

I settled on a plan to walk through the West Bank, Jordan and Sinai, and to finish atop the sacred mountain just as Moses is said to have done. I would walk because I love walking, and because I have yet to find a more immersive or exploratory way to travel. Many aspects of it that might seem at first to be drawbacks are, to me at least, a large part of its appeal – the minimalism, the endurance, the slowness, the physicality, the time alone. It also seemed the only suitable way to travel in this particular place. Early on in my research I discovered a series of new and audacious hiking trails in the region that would take me through a variety of landscapes, climates and communities. The wadis, shepherds' paths and mountain tracks were to be my guide, and would provide the adventurous backdrop for the stories I sought out. By stitching these trails together, I could travel for a thousand miles on foot through the Holy Land, more or less continuously.

Between them, these territories tell the story of the rise and development of all civilisation west of the Hindu Kush; they are the birthplace of the three Abrahamic religions, and played host to the many empires and dynasties that have tried and failed to control the strategic land masses around the Mediterranean. Geographically too they are diverse, from the fertile lands of Levant to the upper reaches of the Great Rift Valley, connecting the continents and cultures of Asia with Africa.

This is the story of the Holy Land,[7] told by the people who live there. My focus was on communities rather than countries, people rather than politics. The aim, however implausible it may seem, was simply to travel from conversation to conversation. It was a journey intended to focus on the *other* side of the Holy Land and the Middle East, the part that we don't hear about all that often. My looping journey may be a useful metaphor as well – so many discussions involving the Middle East spend a lot of time going around in circles. Writing this book has given me a sense of retrospective clarity that the journey itself could not achieve.

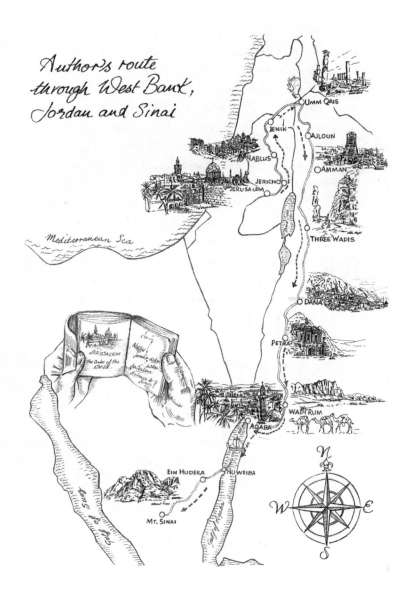

Author's route through West Bank, Jordan and Sinai

Mediterranean Sea

UMM QAIS

JENIN

NABLUS

AJLOUN

AMMAN

JERICHO
JERUSALEM

THREE WADIS

DANA

PETRA

WADI RUM

AQABA

EIN HUDERA    NUWEIBA

MT. SINAI

N
W    E
S

# PART I

# THE CENTRE OF ALL THE WORLD

*I am surrounded by the cultures and memories of the city that are lived everyday throughout their residents' lifestyle. Jerusalem, a magnificent city in all her grandeur, impresses me with every sight I see.*

(Ibn Battuta)

# Leaving Jerusalem

Someday – when I set off on another long journey perhaps – I will begin my travelling in the afternoon, after a long sleep and a lingering breakfast. I would also like to embark without a headache induced by too many 'farewell' beers the night before. Finally – and it doesn't seem too much to ask – I'd like that first day to be an easy one with little to challenge me physically or otherwise so that I might ease into the quest gently. Unfortunately, I have been promising myself these luxuries for years, and they have yet to come to pass. There appears to be an unwritten rule book for expeditions, and feeling thoroughly miserable and exhausted at the outset seems to be absolutely imperative.

An hour before the first rising sun of December breached the barren shale hills beyond the walls of my room in the Jerusalem Hotel, I wrestled myself awake, shrugged an unfamiliar weight onto my shoulders and stepped outside to take the first of 2 million-odd steps. With me were four companions: Dave, a friend from London and a permanent fixture on the journey, and Matt, Hannah and Laurence who, as expats in Jerusalem, would act as auxiliary guides to get us out of the city.

Bleary-eyed, I stumbled past the dawn street vendors with their circular bread and bags of *za'atar*, across a main road where teenage Israeli army conscripts sagged under the weight of their automatic weapons, and finally on to the archway of the Damascus Gate, one of eight remaining openings into the Old City of Jerusalem, the holiest square mile of land on the planet.

Behind the towering stone fortifications of the gateway, the various fractured districts of Jerusalem sprawled out across a plateau on the Judaean Mountains, wedged in between the Mediterranean and the Dead Sea. This was once considered to be the centre of the world[8] – Benjamin Disraeli famously said that 'the view of Jerusalem is the history of the world' – and it tells a story of villains and heroes, heresy and faith, mercy and bloodshed (especially bloodshed). The city has twice been reduced to nothing, has been besieged on over 20 occasions, and captured enough times to make one wonder how it ever remained in existence to this day and age. Above all, the chronicles of Jerusalem are a tale of the vicissitudes and weaknesses of mankind – the building of great empires, their subsequent violent destruction, and our eternal failure to learn from mistakes of the past. It is a city that despite all of this transcends the physical, becoming a celestial symbol: the beating heart of the Holy Land.

Jerusalem's beginnings were inauspicious. The first residents were farmers who, some 6,000 years ago, made a home around the Gihon Spring area, a few miles from the medieval city centre that still survives today. Since then, control of the coveted city has often been wrested but rarely retained, slipping through the hands of each victor in turn like sand through an hourglass. Material remnants of much of Jerusalem's chequered past are long gone, yet in places there is a palpable presence of that which has come before. Nowhere is this more apparent than within the walls of the Old City itself, where glimpses of powers past peek out at those who know where to look, showing how each stratum of history was created from the ruins of the last, in turn becoming a building block for the next and, ultimately, leading to the contemporary cauldron of the modern city.

Below the Ottoman architecture of the Damascus Gate itself is a small and unpretentious triple-arched gateway that has survived since the time of the Emperor Hadrian, nearly 2,000 years ago.[9] The Roman occupation also endures on the market street, the Cardo, which still runs north to south, bisecting the Old City. Much of the rest of the street plan dates from Byzantine times. How do we know? Experts tell us, but even to an untrained eye it is easy to see where 1,000-year-old stone walls have been added to by 200-year-old brickwork, and finished off with a twenty-first-century piece of corrugated iron to act as a shelter for the modern-day bazaar.

Each of the gateways through the great city walls was originally built at an angle, to slow down enemies on horseback. Now those alcoves are home to market stalls and to stony-faced Israeli soldiers. Once through the Damascus Gate our party turned abruptly, and began to wander slowly along narrow streets where hundreds of years of human traffic had worn the cobbles smooth, like rocks sculpted by the sea.

The Old City has traditionally been split into four uneven quarters, and we passed first through the largest, the Muslim Quarter, just as it began to wake. In a few hours the streets would be an ocean of people – locals and foreigners alike – twisting and swirling and colliding in the winding labyrinth of alleyways. The sides of each passage would fill with produce and merchandise – from cabbages to kebabs, and from Christian icons and Arabic carpets to candles, key rings and snow globes. Religious division and sectarianism often take a back seat to business in tourist hotspots like this, and even in the early hours bearded Muslim shopkeepers were offering 'Free Palestine' T-shirts alongside those emblazoned with 'Stand up for Israel'. 'Just Jew It' seemed a bestseller, with a picture of a soldier surrounded by the Star of David.

Each step further, and each minute that passed as the city stirred, brought more life into the *souq*. Heavy aromas of fried food and freshly sliced fruit mixed with the scent of a thousand aftershaves, and, floating underneath all else, the smell of the gutters was mercifully subtle. Elderly Arab women in swathes of black material bent double over cardboard boxes packed tight with vegetables – most of which had come straight from bountiful fields in the Jordan Valley – while sleepy-looking young men crouched on haunches in doorways, hair plastered tight to their heads with gel, fitted polo shirts stretched across their slight frames. In a room above us someone babbled loudly into a mobile phone on loudspeaker. Technology aside, much of this scene felt like it could have been playing out unchanged for hundreds of years.

We turned right on the Via Dolorosa, following the route that Jesus had walked, under the weight of his own cross, on his way to be crucified. An invisible barrier had been crossed and we were now in the Christian Quarter, a disorientating but pleasant warren of pathways with a baffling assortment of churches and hospices peeping out from alleyways and looming down from above. The centrepiece here is the magnificent Church of the Holy Sepulchre, the holiest site in Christendom. Unsure of how else to mark arriving at Calvary itself, I sought my own religious experience through the medium of breakfast: fresh *simit* bread covered in toasted sesame seeds and two warm, steaming falafel.

Towards the end of the third decade of the first century AD,[10] a young Galilean Jew called Jesus – having survived the purge of the Roman king Herod in Bethlehem – began travelling around Galilee and Judaea preaching the word of God. His life was not a long one – at least not in earthly terms – but it was certainly productive. The New Testament places his crucifixion as taking place on a hill at Golgotha, and the Church of the Holy Sepulchre is now built over this original site, also covering the tomb from which Jesus was resurrected. As the Christian sect grew in the centuries after his ascension to heaven, culminating in the Roman emperor Constantine I ending persecution in the fourth century, Jerusalem became the cradle of this new religion – the pivot for an ever-expanding Christian world. The first documented spiritual journey there was made by an unnamed pilgrim from Bordeaux, whose account from AD 333 reads:

> On the left hand is the little hill of Golgotha where the Lord was crucified. About a stone's throw from thence is a vault wherein his body was laid, and rose again on the third day. There, at present, by the command of the Emperor Constantine, has been built a basilica; that is to say, a church of wondrous beauty.[11]

That wondrous beauty is still apparent to all who see the church, and we gazed upon it for a long time from our seat on the cobbles. Fear and loathing are late risers in Jerusalem, and the early morning is perhaps the most tranquil and harmonious time to see the city. A food cart beside us was watched over by a middle-aged Arab in a grey *thobe* and black-and-white keffiyeh, and, as we munched, two young Jews in casual jeans and loose shirts ambled past, knitted *kippot* clinging to the backs of their heads. An ultra-Orthodox Haredi marched along a little way behind, his long black beard and curled *payot* bouncing in rhythm and his long black coat hiding everything but a scuffed pair of pointed dress shoes. Coming the other way, a Greek Orthodox priest in a black tunic with red trim stopped briefly beside us, attracted by the wafting smell of frying chickpeas just as we were. This cast of characters all ignored one another, but not for reasons of fear or discomfort – they were simply on their own missions, and each was unimportant to the other. In Jerusalem, to see mutual disregard is a pleasant departure from witnessing mistrust.

According to the Hebrew Bible, Jerusalem – Yerushalayim in Hebrew – was the site of the first Jewish temple, and since then it has been seen as the spiritual homeland of the Jewish people.[12] In Islam, while the city is not mentioned by name in the Qur'an, other sacred texts mark it as the place where the Prophet Muhammad ascended to heaven.[13] Islam continued to expand rapidly after Muhammad's death in AD 632, soon stretching from Spain in the west to India in the east. Jerusalem – *Al Quds* in Arabic – was quickly conquered by the armies of the converts, and Muslim rule lasted for nearly 400 years, but in the eleventh century the papally ordained zealots of Europe rode on the Holy Land to claim it back for Christendom. In 1099 the Crusaders arrived in the city, slaughtering Muslims, Jews and all others in their path, thus beginning one of the goriest chapters in the already blood-soaked history of Jerusalem.

As a crossroads of faiths Jerusalem has always had devotees of many diverse religions, but now, placed as it is at the heart of the contemporary Israeli – Palestinian question, it is the most high-profile place where Jews and Muslims quite literally rub shoulders on the same city streets. At its best, Jerusalem can embody the hope that two peoples and two states can exist peaceably side by side. At its worst, it becomes a pressure cooker of hatred and animosity and, at the time of travelling, it was experiencing one of the lowest ebbs of mutual suspicion seen in recent years. Throughout the city, soldiers of the Israeli Defence Forces (IDF) patrolled along busy intersections with weapons gripped tightly, and it was not unusual to see Israeli civilians wearing stab-proof vests and carrying handguns on their hips.[14] During my time in the city I had seen three separate Palestinian teenagers being pulled aside by soldiers and roughly patted down for anything that might resemble a knife. All were carrying nothing but cigarettes and mobile phones, and looked truly terrified (as did most of the Israeli civilians in vests, and indeed some of the soldiers).

Jewish immigrants had been trickling into Palestine[15] since the late 1800s, but it was in the aftermath of World War I that their numbers really began to grow, with refugees from the Balkans, the Soviet Union and the Near East fleeing persecution. World War II, and in particular the atrocities of the Holocaust between 1941 and 1945, saw a further movement of Jews towards the perceived safety of the Holy Land. Slowly however, as the demographics shifted, tensions and mutual resentment began to grow among the Jewish and Arab populations. Violence escalated on the streets between old residents and new, forced into increasingly close proximity, and in the corridors of power things were even worse; the British had secretly promised Palestine to both the Arabs and the Jews. In 1947, with the situation dire and seemingly beyond their power to resolve, the British washed their hands of it. When their Mandate ended in May 1948, the state of Israel declared independence and the inevitable happened: war ensued. To Palestinians, and in much of the Arab world, this is known as the *Nakba*, or 'the Catastrophe'.

Ten months of civil war left the land of Palestine and the city of Jerusalem split along physical and ethnic lines. The west of the city belonged to the new Israeli state, and the east was annexed by Jordan. In 1950 Israel declared Jerusalem its capital. In 1967 the 'Six Day War' was fought: Israel launched a pre-emptive strike against its regional enemies Jordan, Syria and Egypt, resulting in the seizure of the Golan Heights, the Sinai Peninsula, the West Bank[16] and East Jerusalem. Sinai was eventually ceded back to Egypt and in 2005 Israel pulled out of Gaza, but Jerusalem has remained divided, with the eastern area of the city annexed. The Israeli parliament, the Knesset, claims Jerusalem as its 'eternal and indivisible capital',[17] but the international community refuses to acknowledge the occupation.

For their part, Palestinians see Jerusalem as the capital city for a future state which they hope will one day soon come into being. As it stands, Palestine (as a political entity) is only partially recognised by the international community. The Palestine Liberation Organization (PLO) emerged shortly before the Six Day War as an umbrella organisation for the various factions that sought to represent those fighting – politically and otherwise – for the Palestinian cause, and it is this national front that has, at the time of writing, been recognised by 136 of the 193 member states of the United Nations. The Palestinian Authority meanwhile – the interim government of the Palestinian territories – has been granted non-member observer status in the UN. What hasn't changed is that 4 million Palestinians living in the West Bank, Gaza and East Jerusalem are still stateless. Tensions between Israelis and Palestinians are today as high as they've ever been, and peace in the region seems farther off than ever before. The city that is the spiritual nucleus for the 3.5 billion followers of the Abrahamic faiths is in danger of self-destructing through religious and ethnic civil war. However, if one thing is clear from the history of Jerusalem it is that nothing lasts forever, and perhaps for once that can be a small source of encouragement.

To reach the southern city walls, we wound our way in and out of the Armenian and Jewish Quarters. Much of the Jewish Quarter has been reconstructed since large areas were destroyed in the Six Day War. The exception was along the Cardo, the main north–south thoroughfare, where a small clump of Roman columns had been excavated and maintained and beside which a busy underground mall sold Judaica to the first tourists of the day. Beyond that to the east, past the mosaics and yeshivas and ornate beauty of domed synagogues,

9

lay the Western Wall compound and, farther still, the Haram ash-Sharif, known to the Jewish people as the Temple Mount.[18]

The Armenian Quarter is the smallest of the four and is distinct from the Christian area (despite Armenians being Christian). Christianity in Jerusalem is full of sects – a cursory walk through the city reveals Greek Orthodox, Greek Catholic, Roman Catholic, Syriac Catholic, Syriac Orthodox, Maronite, Anglican, Armenian Orthodox and Armenian Catholic. The Armenians are the most fiercely independent and have had a presence in the city since the fourth century. The Quarter is a complex of multiple historical sites that have morphed into a self-sufficient community, and our path to the Jaffa Gate – our exit – was lined with small restaurants that smelt of fried garlic and cumin, and shops with big windows and striped awnings offering traditional Armenian ceramics for sale.

We crossed a busy main highway where oversized American-style cars with Israeli number plates idled by a stop light, then climbed the gentle but unrelenting stone staircase that ascends the hillside leading to the Mount of Olives – one of the highest points in the city and a common location for New Testament happenings.[19] A group of about 20 schoolchildren paused on their way to school to examine us; who were these strange creatures who were sweating so profusely at half past six in the morning?

The sun was fighting a losing battle with bulbous grey clouds, but here and there it sliced through in sharp, direct pinpricks of celestial light, illuminating oblivious neighbourhoods of a sleeping city. Not far from where we stood lay the Garden of Gethsemane where Jesus prayed hours before his crucifixion; beyond that was the site of his apparent last footprint on earth – now housed inside a mosque – and beside that thousands of ancient graves on terraces leading back down to the buttressed walls from whence we'd come. The iconic golden dome of the Qubbat Al-Sakhrah, or Dome of the Rock, reflected back a strand of divine sunlight over the Haram ash-Sharif/Temple Mount, connecting heaven and earth, however briefly.

In an academic, historical or religious context, there are many things which can be said to define Jerusalem – these centres of faith and shrines to antiquity are just some of them. To someone on foot, however, and especially someone at the beginning of a long expedition, the main feature of the landscape is much more prosaic. It is a town built on hills. To look out from on high in Jerusalem is to watch an unlikely assortment of white and beige climbing over the hillside; limestone and breezeblocks punctuated by minarets and steeples and the occasional high-rise. It is impossible to travel anywhere in Jerusalem without going up or down, often repeatedly.

Atop the hill I was uncomfortable. Had I been a pilgrim at the end of a lengthy and pious expedition I might have felt differently, but more than ever I was acutely aware that I was just a walker and uneasy about the prospect of so much walking ahead. I wanted to put some miles behind me so that I might begin to enjoy the experience. Perhaps I would return here, *insha'allah*, when I was finished, and perhaps at that point it would have some meaning, but right then the only thing likely to make a real and lasting impression on me was the shoulder strap of my overloaded rucksack.

I began to move once more, now down the other side of the hill towards the desert beyond. Escape was imminent.

My life, or the components for surviving and thriving, was suspended in a 25-kg bag on my back. I had camping gear for sleeping anywhere, warm clothes and a variety of cameras, audio recorders and notepads. I had a rough idea of where I wanted to go and details of local trails that I hoped to follow. I had a well-formed mental checklist to go through in any given scenario to determine whether and how I would react. I had contact details for local guides who knew how to find shepherds' paths and remote wadis, and who would be able to add insight to my wanderings. Finally, I also had my friend Dave Cornthwaite, who planned to walk with me the all the way to Mount Sinai.

Dave and I were both drawn to the Middle East as the latest in a series of individual projects which combine our selfish love for the mystery of adventure (of waking up somewhere new, of meeting crossroads and guessing which way to go) with a desire to explore for ourselves the *real* world – the one in which the majority of the 7 billion people on our planet get on with their lives peacefully and without an excess of conflict or depravity. The world of the mass media machine can seem a nasty, evil place; the one in which we had spent the last ten years travelling was not.

Matt and Hannah – two friends who worked for an NGO in Jerusalem, and our escort out of the city – were American, and both spoke Arabic (Hannah also spoke Hebrew). They were equally fluent in the politics and sensitivities of the region, and they had offered to walk with us on the first day *just in case* – a phrase that we'd hear often on our journey throughout the West Bank. A Belgian filmmaker called Laurence completed our unlikely crew, and the three temporary members of the team strode out ahead while Dave and I staggered slowly behind, bowed backwards by the shock of having so many extra kilograms of weight hanging off our shoulders.

The city of Jerusalem ends where the town of Al-Eizariya begins; while no open space separates the two, they are kept apart by the most physical of barriers. In impressive cement-block uniformity an 8-m high wall struck out across the landscape to the north and south as far as the eye could see, and straight across the road we were on. We had reached the infamous Separation Barrier or, according to the Israeli government who built it, the 'Security Fence'. To call it a fence does not quite seem to do it justice. Maybe that's because I have a rather more parochial understanding of the term but, as the comedian and activist Mark Thomas once noted wryly after walking the length of the structure: 'This is a Wall – if you can't buy it at B&Q, it's not a fence.'

The Barrier, like most things in this part of the world, represents different things depending on who you speak to. According to the Israeli government, and as confirmed by most of the Israelis that I'd met in Jerusalem, it was a security mechanism designed to protect them from terrorism. In 1987 a Palestinian uprising – referred to as the First Intifada – began against the Israeli occupation of the West Bank and Gaza. It took the form of boycotts and strikes on the one hand, and active defiance on the other; stone-throwing and Molotov cocktails became the weapons of choice of a despairing and poorly armed rebellion. The clampdown from the IDF was brutal – initially 80,000 troops were deployed and live rounds fired, killing over 300 Palestinians in the first year[20] – yet the intifada lasted until the Oslo Accord of 1993 brought an uneasy respite. As the resistance movement became increasingly desperate, a deadly new form of violence began to emerge: suicide bombing. Attacks on Israeli buses and road junctions were carried out sporadically over the next decade and a half, continuing as late as 2008. The nadir was reached during the Second Intifada, when 47 separate bombings were recorded in 2002 alone. This prompted the Israeli government to begin work on a physical barrier to regulate entry between Israel and the West Bank, the theory being that this would help stop would-be bombers crossing into Israel to attack.

The Barrier when completed will be over 400 miles long and will completely encircle the West Bank. At the time of writing, around 270 miles had been constructed,[21] and it takes various forms: in some places it is an electronic fence flanked by military roads, barbed wire and trenches, while in Jerusalem and Bethlehem it is the concrete colossus that I had arrived at – twice the height of the Berlin Wall.

While Israelis are overwhelmingly of the opinion that it is a security device – and there have undoubtedly been fewer suicide bombings since its inception – the Palestinian opinion differs radically. The Arabic name for it – *idar al-fasl al-'unsuri* – translates as the 'Apartheid Wall', and it is detested by all, politicians and civilians alike. The Barrier has cut off a significant number of Palestinians from homes, schools and farmland and there is broad agreement that, in emphasising the control of the Israelis and accentuating their squeeze on the West Bank, it breeds discontent that will ultimately add to the security problem rather than diminish it.

If, as some think, the Barrier also constitutes a border for a future Palestinian state, this too poses problems, for 85 per cent of the Barrier is inside the internationally recognised boundary of the West Bank. This boundary is called the Green Line and refers to the 1949 Armistice Line, which demarcated Israel's borders from its Arab neighbour countries after the 1948 Arab–Israeli War. The Barrier consistently crosses it, snaking in and out of the occupied territory, taking land and relocating it onto the Israeli side. Had the Barrier followed the Green Line, its total distance would have been much less. In 2004 the

International Court of Justice ruled that the route of the Barrier was illegal. It recommended that the Barrier be removed and the Palestinians affected be compensated; Israel responded by stating that it did not recognise the authority of the International Court of Justice.

I do not like walls like this – I suspect most people feel the same. After World War II, there were less than five border walls anywhere in the world. Even when the Berlin Wall fell in 1989, there were still only 15. Today, there are at least 70. Standing in its shadow, it was hard not to see the Security Barrier simply as a great prison wall, complete with razor wire and guard towers, separating and enclosing the West Bank from the rest of the world (and perhaps isolating Israelis, too, in a different sense). We would see much more of it in due course. Dave and I packed our cameras deep inside rucksacks (*just in case*) and walked slowly through turnstiles, squeezed sideways with our gear, then into the sheep-pen-like compound of the crossing zone. At that time of the morning, few people were entering the West Bank with us; on the other side, going into East Jerusalem, hundreds of Palestinians with work permits for Israel shuffled noiselessly forward towards a much busier-looking inspection area. The Israeli government are generally less concerned about who goes into the West Bank, but, given the security concerns, they sure as hell want to know who's coming back.

It took just five minutes of winding our way through the maze of metal-railed bollards and we were out, back into the grey light and occasional fat raindrops. The Barrier was behind us, and ahead lay the West Bank.

'*Ahlan wa sahlan!*' – the ubiquitous Arabic 'Welcome!' – shouted a cab driver, right on cue. He offered us all a tour of the area, promising the tomb of Lazarus, the Church of the Nativity in Bethlehem, Shepherds' Fields: the full Holy Package, and at a bargain price of only $20! Matt explained in Arabic that we were walking, and we already had a plan for the day. The price went to $10, and then to $5. He smiled and conceded defeat. '*Ahlan wa sahlan ala Filistine,*' he said. 'Welcome to Palestine.'

# Twenty-First-Century
# Bedouin

Al-Eizariya was not a pretty town. The buildings were grey and in various states of disrepair. Those that weren't at the end of their lives were at the beginning: half-built, featureless concrete blocks with wooden scaffolding lined the road we followed onto the main street. The leaking clouds above gave up the fight and burst, and we cloaked ourselves in the neon-coloured waterproofs that reliably distinguish European hikers from normal people all over the world.

On the high street, small rivers formed in the gutters and we hopped between them, sporadically sprayed by cars that passed us at speeds that seemed to ignore both the rain and laws of physics. I walked at the back of our small group and watched Dave tiptoe ahead of me through the puddles. In the last few years I have walked upwards of 5,000 miles on journeys such as this and I take for granted the feeling of a loaded pack, hiking poles and trousers tucked into socks. To Dave these were all new sensations and as he walked he shrugged his shoulders, still looking for that sweet spot where the weight of the rucksack seems to melt away. So far it had eluded him. He changed gait every few steps, stopping to adjust his hip-belt, lengthening his hiking poles. His movement, ironically given we were simply doing a variation of something we've known most of our lives, was anything but natural. He turned and stopped, sighing dramatically.

He grinned at me. 'I thought you said this would be easy!'

All of this was now second nature to me, I realised. My shoulders still ached, of course, but I was comfortable. Even after just a few miles I felt settled – I knew this stuff. I *liked* this stuff: the sense of being self-sufficient and having an unbroken line of footsteps behind me and myriad options ahead. I could walk all day if I wanted, or I could stop for an hour to drink tea. I could talk to anyone that passed me by and it didn't feel strange or unsolicited. My pack and neon waterproofs served a functional purpose but they also acted as a calling card: 'I am a traveller,' they said. 'I have chosen to visit this place, and I would (probably) appreciate some help.'

We were inevitably cause for comment and laughter, pointing and staring. On the high street alone at least a dozen people stepped out into the rain to shake our hands or make the ubiquitous Middle Eastern gesture of confusion. Imagine the action of turning over a snow globe – hand down with fingers spread out suddenly rotated to face upwards. All over the region this is shorthand for '*What ARE you doing?*' My get-up showed, more than anything, vulnerability. That's what I've come to believe over the years. A hiker climbing a hill in the rain with his head down is unlikely to be a thief or murderer, and the way in which they are exposing themselves to the world around them draws kindness and compassion. It is one of the many reasons to travel on foot.

We were ushered into a small roadside shack for breakfast by a small man in a hooded sweatshirt with 'Florida' on the front. There was no need to make a choice; we were given the same as the handful of other (exclusively male) diners. 'Hummus, falafel, hummus, falafel. Everyone has hummus, falafel,' said Florida in a deep voice, leaving little mystery as to what would follow.

Deep, red ceramic pots with olive oil pooled on top of creamy hummus came first, followed by warm pitta bread and steaming, crispy balls of fried chickpeas. Four men served us in relay. I doubt if any of them worked there, but all were keen to help. Alongside one of the temporary gutter rivers outside walked an elderly, stooped man pushing a glorified cupboard on wheels. It had a homemade roof to cover circular tubes of seeded bread inside, and the man's head swayed from side to side as he walked a fine line between water and traffic.

'*Yemeen, Yemeen!*' shouted one of our auxiliary waiters from under the awning. 'To the right, to the right!'

'He's blind,' said Florida by way of explanation, turning to face me but shouting at full volume. 'Since he was 18 his eyes don't work. But he can't stay at home all day, so we give him this cart and try and stop him getting run over. Would this happen in your country?'

He asked where I came from and I told him I was Irish. (Technically I am Northern Irish, but the further I travel into the crumbled ruins of the British Empire, a funny thing happens – I seem subconsciously to become increasingly more patriotically and holistically Irish.) I suggested that the old man would likely get some government support, but probably not be given a job that involved navigating amongst traffic. 'Ah ha! We look after people here the best!' he smiled, taking my response as an admission of an inferior national system. 'I like the Irish a lot – they're my favourite of all the people who visit. The Irish know suffering too.' We left with those words ringing in my ears. It wouldn't be the last time someone drew a parallel between the Palestinians and the Irish.

The town disappeared behind us and landscape ahead began to open up. We followed a road that cut through small patches of scrub and dwindling concrete facades until finally it felt like we were free – for the first time, we were in the open. We stepped off the road on a small track that led onto a plateau. Ahead, through the haze and the raindrops, were multiple horizons all the same: rounded, lunar, desert hills, leapfrogging each other into oblivion.

It was not, however, an empty landscape, and each mound told two very different stories. As we walked we glimpsed occasional snapshot images below into the valleys and wadis. These played host to small Bedouin communities – visible as small enclaves of corrugated iron, animal pens and sheets of waterproof material flapping in the wind.

Overlooking these at the top of the hills lay the Israeli settlements. 'Settlement' is a rather disarming term for what are essentially fortified towns and cities built in occupied lands, illegal and invasive by an almost unanimous global reckoning. They looked odd and alien here. Ma'aleh Adumim, for instance, which we now passed, was heavily walled and sat high above all else, like some ancient embattled fortress taking up a strategic position to watch for approaching enemy hordes. The houses and apartment blocks were an unvarying homogeny of beige buildings with bright red roofs, stretching off into the distance. That uniformity itself was perhaps the strangest thing of all, followed closely by the deep bottle green of the gardens and parks – well-watered shrubbery and allotments making a mockery of the desert outside.

These settlements, dotted colonies stretching ever eastwards towards the River Jordan, are populated exclusively by Israelis, and are seen by many in the Palestinian and international communities as being a way for the government to grab more land. Ma'aleh Adumim is the third largest settlement in the West Bank, with a population of over 40,000. It felt monumentally big and it was in this vast shadow that we met Ahmad, a Palestinian Bedouin who had agreed to walk with us for the final stretch towards Jericho. There was an Israeli military firing zone close by which we would do well to avoid, and as we tramped the hills we were advised that it was important to identify ourselves clearly to local Palestinians as *not* being a settler. *Just in case.*

These days, a Bedouin guide does not turn up in flowing robes with a donkey or camel in tow. In 2015, in Palestine, a Bedouin like Ahmad turns up in jeans, a leather jacket and with a bachelor's degree in Biology. Ahmad grew up walking these trails. He knew each of the disparate Palestinian encampments intrinsically. He also wore a keffiyeh draped over his shoulders rather than on his head.

'I live two lives sometimes,' he told us as we started walking. 'Maybe my keffiyeh shows this. At university I keep it round my neck like the other students, and back with my family I have it over my head like the other Bedouin.'

His English was good, but not as good as Matt and Hannah's combined Arabic. The three of them chattered away and Laurence skipped alongside at the same speed. Dave and I brought up the rear, in the odd position of being left behind and not really knowing where we were on our own journey.

When we could catch him, Ahmad was good company; he was an animated bridge between the traditional and the modern world. At the top of a particularly steep climb, he quickly and efficiently lit a fire and rested a blackened teapot on top, all the while chatting rapidly into his smartphone. We drank sweet tea and ate handfuls of light, brown bread which we tore from a pile in a plastic bag in the middle of our cross-legged circle. Dave inspected some snails, presumably to ignore the screaming pain in his calves, and the rest of us talked idly about tea, settlements, hiking and weather. Ahmad spoke with a large man on a small donkey who appeared out of nowhere. This would become, though we didn't know it yet, a regular and endearing feature of our journey – there are few places in the Palestinian countryside where one can spend more than a few minutes without seeing a man on a donkey.

'My law brother,' he told us after the man left.

'Brother-in-law?' asked Dave to clarify.

'Family man!' summarised Ahmad.

The sun was low in the sky by the time we reached the community of the Hamedin family and were met by Ahmad's brother, Jameel. The camp was home to about 70 people and spread out as a series of large oblong tents, shipping containers and motor vehicles in various stages of disrepair. We were now at sea level and the next day would descend even further. It was a beautiful scene, but not quite as appealing as the carpeted floor of the nearest tent. We'd done 26 km (just over 16 miles) and were beat.

Matt, Hannah and Laurence now returned to their lives in the city. We hugged them goodbye and apologised for being grumpy and slow. Dave and I eased ourselves onto the floor of the tent, surrounded by members of the Hamedin family who smiled politely as we removed toxic socks and reclined. The tent was large, perhaps 10 m long by 4 m wide, and reserved for visitors. The centre was kept mostly clear, save for a few weight-bearing wooden struts, and the edges were lined with thick rugs to sit on. Every metre or so there was a nest of cushions to lay one's elbows on, encouraging the rest of the body to stretch out to the side. It felt extravagantly comfortable after a day's hiking.

Food was served – a gloriously large plate of *maqluba*[22] – and then, as it was obvious to all around that we were either antisocial or worn out, we were quickly left alone to make our beds in the blankets. In the corner, Jameel and Ahmad talked quietly over cigarettes, and a dusty laptop was produced from a small rucksack. That was my last image as I went to sleep – two Bedouin squinting into a computer screen in a tent in the Holy Land.

Breakfast with the Hamedin community was also something of a feast. It would become apparent in the fullness of time that this was simply the Bedouin way, but for us the novelty was great. Before the sun had breached the pale desert hills, Jameel arrived with a platter stacked full of offerings, all freshly made by the unseen women in the next tent. We'd occasionally hear them giggling, and in the distance some might pass by on their way to or from the trail, but that was about as deep as our interactions got – it was not appropriate for strangers to mix with the female members of the tribe. While we gorged on the boiled eggs, creamy hummus, still-warm flat bread and plump tomatoes, Jameel stuck to the true Palestinian man's breakfast: a cup of sweet coffee and as many cigarettes as possible in a given time window.

As he reclined on the carpet, wispy smoke framing his face, he told us that the Israeli government had imposed a demolition order on his camp. 'On this *tent*!' he said, emphasising the final word. They had fought the order twice but still it stood. The result was that they couldn't move from that spot in case their homes were destroyed during their absence.

'This is important,' he said. 'Our tribe originally came from the Negev, from Beersheba, but after 1948 we came here. We moved seasonally. Now we cannot move, because if you remove your tent, you won't be allowed back to build it again. The name "Bedouin" means *return to the desert*. That is what we *do* – we should move.'

Jameel said that the Israeli plan was to move all the Bedouin tribes together into collective towns and villages – three large ones and one smaller one. The bigger towns would house around 12,000 people each. That would allow the government to consolidate land, he said, and turn it into firing zones, meaning that no one would be allowed to use it, let alone live on it. 'It's all part of the squeeze,' he concluded.

Younger members of the family occasionally toddled in as we spoke to see what was going on. They were all under five, a mixture of boys and girls. At that age they are not yet segregated by gender. The little boys wore tattered football shirts and had big, deep eyes and the girls had their hair knotted in pretty pigtails that bounced around as they trotted around the tent. As they arrived, Jameel scooped them up or shooed them out, smiling and playfully chastising them in Arabic. We prepared to leave and he handed me a printed flyer for Sahari Desert Eco Tourism. This was his tour company, he said. Ahmad and he were owners, and Jameel had been the first West Bank Bedouin to gain certification as a local desert guide by the Palestinian Ministry of Tourism and Antiquities. This, he said, was their future. I asked if he was worried that the demolition order on his community might affect it. 'I cannot worry about that,' he replied. 'We will just continue to do exciting and important things, and see what happens. We are really proud of our company.'

The sun was now well above the rugged rocks that surrounded the Hamedin community, and the sea-level temperature was rising quickly. Dave and I wandered down a small rise, past a pristine looking Portaloo with a shiny blue sticker on it advertising EU funders. From there we crossed a trafficless road – which must have led from nowhere to the Dead Sea – and the Hamedin community was almost immediately swallowed into the crinkles of the papier-mâché hills. We were alone once more, headed for one of the oldest thoroughfares known to mankind.

# The Oldest City

The way from Jerusalem to Jericho is well used by travellers, and always has been.

Marco Polo is said to have passed by, as did the great Arab traveller Ibn Battuta. Jesus and his contemporaries would have made the journey in one or two days using a Roman road which ran along the top of a deep gorge; many thousands of pilgrims and aspiring conquerors have followed in their wake in the centuries since.[23] Mark Twain made the journey and, as with most of his experiences in Palestine, had a miserable time, and Thomas Cook saw in the trip an opportunity to bring tourists in droves to the ancient trail. Dave and I were the latest in a long and varied line of adventurers and pilgrims to walk by way of Wadi Qelt, the original natural thoroughfare between the two hubs.

It is, objectively, one of the most beautiful parts of the West Bank. Ahead of us a narrow but well-worn trail led down the face of the gorge towards a green, blossoming oasis below. The palm trees stretched out in our direction of travel – a green ribbon of life leading the way amidst dramatic, sheer cliff faces. Near the valley bottom we trod lightly on ancient, smooth Roman steps. The layers of history here lay heavy on the land: ahead of us an Ottoman-era aqueduct crumbled into the ground, and not far beyond a simpler Roman one was still channelling water from the three springs at the head of the valley to destinations up- and downstream. Surrounding both were the twenty-first-century offerings to the wadi: landscaping, to allow easier access, and piles of discarded plastic bottles and other garbage.

We passed a tumble of faded rocks, which were said to be the remains of a third-century monastery, the first to be built in the Jerusalem wilderness. Everything around us encouraged regular breaks to take pictures and to sit in the shade of overhanging rocks. Dave seemed stronger, perhaps buoyed by the companionship of the scenery. At one of our rest stops, an elderly Bedouin man passed us on the trail and leant down on his haunches alongside me. I related the catechism that would become so familiar: *We were British and Irish hikers, heading first for Jericho. The Palestinians were very friendly, and we were having a lovely time.* The goal with this was to establish ourselves as trustworthy and likeable, and to get the key information out of the way as blandly as possible so that we could begin the more interesting part of the conversation: interrogating our questioner. I would repeat my story in this form hundreds of times over the coming months and it would eventually take the form of a mantra – my own refrain to recite in the Holy Land.

The Bedouin said that from a distance he had suspected we were Israelis because of our fancy hiking equipment; up close, though, he knew we weren't, because we had 'kindly faces'. The wadi was a protected Israeli nature reserve, he told us. Many Israelis from West Jerusalem and the nearby settlements would come here for day-hikes. This is one of the few places in the West Bank where Israelis and Palestinians meet regularly and must share the same space. Once, he said, he saw a settler swimming naked in one of the natural pools in the gorge. He considered taking the man's clothes, but his son who was with him cautioned against it. They left feeling like they'd done a good deed. He smiled broadly at this story and stood up with a flourish. Perhaps peaceful coexistence was possible, after all.

Our trail was well maintained and blazed with coloured markings – put in place by the Israelis – and we walked along the north side of the wadi. To the south, beyond the ridge, ran a modern-day highway built on the original Ascent of Adumim. It's likely that this is the very road upon which the Good Samaritan was robbed, stripped and beaten, and where Jesus travelled on his way to Jerusalem 'as King' (Luke 19:28). We were a pleasant distance from the modern motorway – so far away, in fact, that we couldn't even hear it. Inside the walls of the valley we were alone with the history and the abundant life all around, which created a lot of noise and vibrancy – the limestone cliffs reverberated with the calls of blackstarts and mourning wheatears, and frogs, fish and dragonflies abounded in the creek. Rock hyraxes – small mammals whose claim to fame is being so genetically unusual that their nearest relative is the elephant – would pop out onto the trail, look up at us with tilted heads and twitching noses and then dash off back into the undergrowth. Herons, falcons and eagles also made a life in the valley, and three distinct ecosystems nurtured numerous lizards, foxes and porcupines.

We followed the Roman aqueduct downhill to the east. In various places it leaked onto the brown earth below and hungry plants grew in giant vertical swathes of green punctuating the monotone of dirt. Dave remarked that we must now be well below sea level. The heat seemed to intensify with this, stifling us in the shadeless stretches.

We walked for just long enough to forget about the one thing that we knew to expect, and so it was a pleasant surprise to round a bend in the wadi and see, clinging precariously to the rocks below, the Monastery of St George. We sat by a wooden cross on the apex of the path and looked down at the labyrinthine structure. Two other hikers – the first we'd seen all day – joined us. Both were Americans, working in Jerusalem. They came here often, they said, to escape the madness of the city. To get to the path they had driven into a small parking lot a few miles back, then braved hordes of donkey-taxis offering rides and snacks to tourists. A lot of visitors would come by car to look at the view, but very few stepped beyond the scenic photo-spot.

The four of us ambled down the hill to the entrance to the monastery only to find that it was closed. I learned from the hikers, instead, that the monastery was the biggest and most enduring legacy of what had once been something of an underground religious retreat.

After the Roman Empire converted to Christianity in AD 312, bringing centuries of persecution to an end, many monks struggled with the new-found ease and freedom. The most disillusioned fled to caves in these hills to live out solitary, holy lives. Around 150 monasteries are said to have sprung up during the fourth to sixth centuries, including veritable cities of the desert such as Mar Saba to the south. The monks lived in the rabbit warren of caves and cells in the cliffs surrounding these monastic centres and it seemed to me that if isolation and asceticism was one's goal, this would be a fine place to seek it.

Upon leaving the wadi we were greeted by a wonderful framed view of the lowest, and perhaps oldest, city in the world: Jericho. Many have written about this same moment – it is one of the great shared experiences of Holy Land travel. Not all, however, relished it as we did. In the early nineteenth century the wild and scandalising Caroline of Brunswick, second daughter of the Duke of Brunswick and estranged wife of the Prince of Wales, travelled through the Holy Land in flagrant defiance of the wishes of her court. Her journey through Wadi Qelt is described thus:

> In the midst of frightful precipices, and on a road, known to be infested by robbers [...] we entered ravines, almost impassable, which appeared to be the effects of a recent convulsion of nature [...] after descending into frightful abysses, we were obliged to climb up sharp rocks, to procure a sight of the plain of Jericho – at present nothing more than an assemblage of huts built of earth and reeds.[24]

From our vantage point, and after a much more enjoyable journey, it was easy to see the appeal of Jericho over the ages. The town is built on a rich oasis, fed by the springs from the wadi and with the River Jordan only a couple of miles away. The fertile soil has always made life here much easier than elsewhere in the desert, and certainly more so than beyond the high cliffs to the east and west.

Modern Jericho sprawled out across the plain – a low-rise, dense jumble of blocky white structures with an occasional minaret or steeple reaching out skywards above the crammed cluster. Beyond those, the mountains of Jordan rose higher still in great tiered majesty above the city. In the margins, buildings gradually seeped out into green and brown fields until there was nothing visible but the patchwork of agriculture. It reminded me of the farming towns in northern California that I'd cycled through on my way across America in 2010. This, though, was different. For a start, I could clearly see a large, flat mount that had once been the winter palaces of the Hasmonean period and King Herod. It was he who, over 2,000 years ago, built the aqueduct to carry water from the spring at Ein Fawwar, at the top end of Wadi Qelt.

Twenty successive communities have survived in Jericho, dating back over 11,000 years. In Herod's time, Jericho was the source of many of the most keenly desired spices and aromatic perfumes of the era, including the single most expensive oil in the ancient world, grown from the opobalsamum plant. Whilst it is still a bustling Palestinian market town, the recent conflicts have shaved away its prominence, leaving it mostly as a reminder of what came before.

Dave and I spent that night on the outskirts of the city in a refugee camp called Aqbat Jabr, built for Palestinians displaced by the 1948 war. There are 58 such camps across Jordan, Lebanon, Syria, Gaza and the West Bank, and another 10 that were set up after the Six Day War. To be officially recognised, the camps must be on land that is given by the host government, and they are administered (though not run) by the United Nations Relief and Works Agency for Palestine Refugees in the Near East (UNRWA). Around 5 million Palestinians are eligible for this support.[25] The UN defines Palestinian refugees as those who lost homes and livelihoods as result of fleeing or expulsion after the 1948 hostilities and, as the situation remains unresolved, those in the camps are stuck in perpetual displacement from their ancestral homes.

Aqbat Jabr was my first experience of one of these camps and, unsurprisingly for a place that has been running for over twice as long as I have been alive, it felt very much permanent and functioning. We were guests of the Women's Union, run by the inimitable Um Fares Intesor who beamed out at us from the behind the gated entrance to the school where we arranged to meet. She was tall and strong, and a tightly bound navy-and-white hijab framed a long and sombre face that would crack regularly into an all-encompassing smile. She wore a long black abaya, as did most other women in the camp, hers with an intricately stitched pattern of silver flowers on the front.

We sat down, joined by two other women in black abayas and colourful hijabs, and rice, chicken and yoghurt appeared before us. Um Fares, Jamile and Hanan watched us closely to make sure we ate enough and then took us outside to sit in a small, enclosed garden to digest. Small black birds sat on the thin branches of newly planted trees, and the soil underneath was ruffled and loose, waiting to be watered and minded. Outside the building much else shared this feeling of anticipation: walls were half-built, roads partly sealed and nearby were empty plots with foundations like afterthoughts.

'This is one of the least densely populated refugee camps in the West Bank,' said Um Fares. 'We're lucky like that, although there are still all the normal problems.' I asked what those were and she laughed. Jamile and Hanan requested a translation of the joke and they too laughed. 'It's hard to know where to start,' said Um Fares eventually. Later, she would mention that nearly a third of the population are unemployed and they suffer severe water shortages in summer. The other major problem comes in winter when it rains and the camp floods because of a lack of drainage. The irony of this was not lost on her.

Um Fares had worked with the women's co-operative for 22 years, setting up adult literacy classes, promoting education on hygiene and applying for funding to provide catering for the children who attended next door. I told her that I thought there must be a lot of challenges for her. 'We face many problems,' she said, 'but so does everyone who tries to do something new. We prefer to focus on the good things, and there are many of those.'

As she spoke she passed us soft, doughy biscuits with dates inside and freshly washed fruits. A conversation with her filled the stomach as much as the brain. Sleep that night came easily, and Dave and I woke the next morning at dawn to competing calls-to-prayer in surround sound. We were now very much in the heart of the West Bank.

We walked out through Aqbat Jabr in the dull half-light of morning, past small groups of old men huddled around bright fires of rubbish and twigs burning in rusted oil barrels. Bare brickwork and semi-constructed structures lined the way; an occasional dash of panache came from periodic pinstriped awnings stretched over the front of a grocery shop and sprawling attempts at graffiti in Arabic across vacant walls. Rubbish piled up in alcoves, and the street itself was covered in a light dusting of plastic packaging and multihued pools of waste water and oil that reflected back the scene around us in kaleidoscopic candour.

I remembered Um Fares's words: some considered the refugees here to be the lucky ones. Looking around the streets as we left, it was hard to see it in such relative terms. During the many miles that lay ahead, Dave and I would pass by other camps like this throughout the West Bank and in Jordan. More still surrounded us in the wider region. Some are notorious – Balata, in Nablus, for example, has developed a reputation for being a particularly fervent bastion of rebellion against the Palestinian Authority as much as Israel – but most exist quietly, offering little cause for attention from the wider world. I wondered if this silence was the worst part of all for the refugees, for whom their plight must at times feels like purgatory. Yet despite this, women like Um Fares were lights in the darkness. She was remarkable, of course, and unwaveringly positive and affirmative and I am sure there are countless others like her who take the initiative to create hope from despair. It was hard not to feel the weight of tragedy and unfulfilled ambitions in the camp, but it was also impossible to leave without carrying onwards the resilience and optimism of Um Fares and her cohort of changemakers.

The road though Jericho was broad and new and it afforded Dave and me our first experience of travelling alongside traffic. Most cars that passed would stop so that a driver or passenger could pop his head out to either welcome, question or scold us. '*Ahlan wa sahlan!*' 'Where you go?' 'Why do you walk?' I have found that in much of the world – especially once I leave behind the cultural norms of western Europe and the USA – it is considered very strange to walk out of choice. In Iran, whilst walking along a small road in the Zagros Mountains in winter,

I was told that it was a stupid thing to do: people should only walk until they can afford a bicycle or a donkey, which they can then replace with a motorbike and finally with a car, which they can continually upgrade in line with their income. When I have been on the road for some time, I am often assumed to be one of those people who cannot afford a bicycle or donkey, but, at the start of a journey such as this one, while my clothes and pack still blush with cleanliness and inexperience of dust and hardship, I am a wandering paradox. Why would someone who can *afford* to buy nice things not travel in a jeep or a taxi?

For this reason perhaps, taxis were the most tiresome. They would try everything they could to secure a ride. We were quite probably the only tourists they would see that day; maybe even that week. Once, not so long ago, West Bank tourism was booming and Jericho would have seen a steady stream of visitors, attracted mostly by the biblical and historical attractions. The city was a permanent fixture on the Holy Land Pilgrimage Tour, available from travel agents on most British high streets. Now the impression is that the West Bank is unsafe, and only the hardiest dare venture. That left Dave and me as the sole business opportunity for the myriad tourist vendors in Jericho, and they were determined to try and extract from us something of worth. One – seemingly a taxi driver, hotelier, restaurateur and tour guide simultaneously – drove along at walking pace for nearly ten minutes offering everything he could think of. The deals he promised sounded wonderful, we said, had we not already got a plan. Politely we declined each offer, to the increasing exasperation of the poor man. Finally, he stopped the car, leaned on the door frame and shouted after us with desperate, hopeful longing, 'But ... I have *aubergines!*'

Jericho itself was bustling with the energy of a city that cares not what anyone thinks. In the centre a large roundabout led to five or six tributary-like market streets where everything from meat to pinstripe suits to beachballs overflowed out of the stores into traffic. Before leaving Jerusalem, a friend advised us to pick up a Palestinian keffiyeh; they were commonplace here, especially among older men who wore them over their heads in a variety of styles. Beyond functionality, they represented pride and solidarity in Palestine and it was suggested to me that a keffiyeh was a useful indicator from a distance that we were not Israeli settlers. This would become exponentially more valuable the farther we got from big towns.

We stopped at the entrance to a long, narrow shop specialising in luggage, lingerie and headwear, where I bought the Palestinian scarf in black and white, and Dave chose the Jordanian version of red-and-white checks. A young man stopped to help Dave choose and handed us each a wrapped Ferrero Rocher chocolate. 'They are from my engagement,' he said by way of explanation, and moved on. In an adjacent store, we bought Israeli SIM cards for our phones. Palestinian SIM cards do exist but are unable to use cellular data. 'It is seen as a security risk,' the store owner told me with a wry smile. Most Palestinians use two phones as a workaround: one with a local SIM to call each other, and the other with an Israeli card to access the internet. I asked if it was frustrating having to pay money to an Israeli company for the service. 'After a while, these things become normal. There is no energy left to be angry,' he said before moving on. 'But tell me, how is England? I really like your Margaret Thatcher. She is such a strong woman, no?' I corrected him, but only on the tense of his statement. I broke it to him that, 'she died a few years ago.' He looked crestfallen. 'We truly do live in a dark world today,' he muttered.

Dave and I walked past the entrance to the archaeological site Tell as-Sultan – the original permanent settlement in this area through which the layers of history can be traced back to the Neolithic period, 10,000 years ago. Not far beyond that, a young man in a wicker armchair beckoned us in to explore the eighth-century ruins of the Umayyad Palace of Hisham. We had already declined invitations to tour the mosaics of the area, which would have featured the 'Tree of Life' at Hisham's Palace in addition to visits to the Shalom al-Israel Synagogue and the Coptic Church of St Andrew. By the time we reached the road to the Monastery of Temptation, it was almost *too much* history. 'I'm not even remotely tempted,' grumbled Dave, and we slumped off the tarmac into the shade of a very modern and pleasantly uninteresting roadside generator station. I was reminded of Mark Twain's grumbles:

How it wears a man out to have to read up a hundred pages of history
every two or three miles – for verily the celebrated localities of Palestine
occur that close together. How wearily, how bewilderingly they swarm
about your path![26]

The yellow hue to the Mount of Temptation marked an almost violent
transition from the palm trees of the oasis, jarring for a traveller moving
from the comforts of the city to the indifference of the mountains.
Somewhere beyond the crags, Jesus is said to have spent 40 days fasting
and meditating, fending off the temptations of the Devil. Throughout
the early Christian era, monks sought refuge to live and pray in the
rabbit-warren-like labyrinth of caves in the face of the mountain, much
as they did in the Monastery of Saint George. As in Wadi Qelt, this
community too eventually became a monastery: first in Byzantine
times and then, after a Persian invasion, when it was repopulated and
expanded by the Crusaders in 1099. The present monastery dates from
the late 1800s and hangs impossibly off the rock face, suspended perhaps
by faith alone. I was never sure of the reasoning behind this type of
architecture – for there is certainly a history of monasteries being
both remote and elevated – except maybe that the only path to true
connection with God is through isolation in places where prayer and
meditation cannot be interrupted by the desires of weaker men.

Dave and I agreed that we'd both make poor monks, though secretly
I thought I'd probably do better than him. (That thought alone almost
certainly means that I wouldn't.) Over our heads, empty cable cars
screeched past in a halting ascent, designed to carry the now-absent
tourists to the top of the mountain with the least possible fuss. The fact
that they continued to run, wheezing ever upwards in batches of three,
seemed particularly futile.

We followed a dirt trail alongside rich, verdant fields and farmers in
faded football shirts and ripped jeans who, to a man (for they were all
men), would wave and, with hand on heart and a slight bow, bid us
hello. We dipped briefly into a shallow coffee-coloured wadi and then,
when it came to an abrupt end, climbed the shallow banks onto a plain
by the foot of the precipitous cliffs.

Our way was enclosed on the other side by a long, high mesh fence, topped with barbed wire. Inside, about half a mile away, a series of greenhouses and a clutch of palm trees clustered together. The space between was dry and rocky scrub, empty but for a couple of outhouses and one rather out-of-place-looking farmhouse. A rusted red car had bricks in the wheel arches, and washing hung on a line from the gable wall. We skirted along the fence wondering who lived inside. Later on I was told that this was a small and relatively new Israeli settlement, and the owner was 'a madman'. The person who told me that – and who requested that I didn't name them (just in case) – said that they'd heard he chased away visitors with an M-16. They had personally seen him driving around with an AK-47 in his pick-up. It seemed a rather wild story, even for a tale about a West Bank settler, but it's hard to know.

# To Know Where
# to Go

Before leaving Jerusalem, Dave and I had visited a man called George Rishmawi to ask about the trails that lay ahead of us. George lived and worked in Beit Sahour, a medium-sized and predominantly Christian town close to Bethlehem, where he was the Executive Director of a non-profit organisation called Masar Ibrahim al-Khalil (MIAK), which translates relatively directly to 'The Path of Abraham the Friend'. The Masar Ibrahim is, in its simplest form, a hiking trail. It has existed for a decade, and the pioneers – both international and Palestinian – sought from the outset to grow community tourism, and to encourage foreign visitors to come and explore Palestine on foot, as well as building a culture of recreational hiking among Palestinians.

The trail itself runs from Jenin in the north to Hebron in the south and snakes through the West Bank, connecting communities and putting in place the building blocks for wider-scale tourism in the future. The task for MIAK is not an easy one; hiking may be growing in popularity on a global scale, but while the Camino de Santiago, the Pacific Crest Trail and their contemporaries have seen record high numbers of footfalls in 2015 and 2016, the idea of going on a leisurely hike through the West Bank is still a little too wild for most.

I first heard about the Masar Ibrahim in 2014 through a friend who used to work and hike in Jerusalem. For three years I had been tentatively planning a walking journey through the West Bank but each time I was ready to commit, I was told it probably wasn't a good idea. When Dave and I did eventually begin in December 2015, things weren't particularly calm either – a series of 'clashes' in the summer of the same year and the horrific firebombing of a young Palestinian family by Israeli settlers had left the international press wondering, often with a grim sense of satisfaction at the prediction, whether this might be a new intifada. It was not, but Jerusalem had been tense and in the week that Dave and I were there preparing for the journey there were at least four Palestinians shot dead by the IDF for allegedly attacking soldiers at checkpoints, or for ramming cars into targets near settlements.

The beauty of the Masar Ibrahim was that it removed us from that world. Our days instead were to be spent in wadis and on country tracks. When I turned on my phone to check messages from home, often whilst sat peacefully in the serene shade of a rock or tree, it would buzz and messages from friends in London would read, 'Are you OK? News from the West Bank today sounds awful – be careful.'

George Rishmawi was a bear of a man with a sizeable belly, relentless energy and a smile that started from his eyes. He greeted us at the door shouting '*Habibi, habibi*!' (My loved one, my loved one!) and wrapped us each in turn in a spine-crushing hug. He moved with great speed between tasks and talked even faster; even as he showed us into his offices he was fielding calls from two separate phones whilst answering questions from other members of staff at his side and simultaneously introducing them to us. To spend an hour with George was at once a crash course in intensive Palestinian studies and an experience akin to sitting inside a tumble dryer on full spin.

We managed to sit down for a full half-hour – being stationary seemed in itself like a minor miracle – and George talked us through a PowerPoint presentation that outlined the Palestinian loss of land since 1948. Dave and I had agreed to try and approach this journey as impartially as possible, but right from the outset we had struggled to remain entirely unaffected. The bus journey to the Bethlehem checkpoint, the mass of walls and guns and barbed wire, the immediate drop in even the most basic quality of life and infrastructure inside the Barrier, and then a visual tour-de-force lecture about the squeeze on the ordinary Palestinians – it was a sobering reminder that even the best intentions often get left at the threshold when a journey begins. I told George that his PowerPoint presentation looked very professional. He smiled. 'It's great, isn't it? I was invited to a conference with the United Nations a while ago where they showed these slides. Afterwards I took them for myself.' He paused. 'Don't tell anyone.'

George was behind schedule, unsurprisingly, so we jumped in his car to go and pick up his kids from school. When we arrived at the gates, five small children piled into the back seat beside – and on top of – Dave. 'They're not all mine,' said George. 'I don't even know who this one is!'

As he drove, he talked. And as he talked to us, he placated the hyped-up children and took more calls on his phones. His pace was exhausting. 'This trail can be a real revelation,' he said. 'For 15 years Palestinians have felt like they're drowning. There's no freedom to move, the politics is suffocating and everyone is forced to exist on top of one another in the towns. The trail gives them a way to escape that. We especially need the young people to see this because for so long we've been restricted, and a lot of young people don't know their own country.'

'Is it more important to you that locals are hiking than tourists?' I asked.

'No,' he replied. 'They work together. So far it's mostly local Palestinians but that's because it's easier for us to spread the word to them.' He stopped briefly to buy ice lollies for the kids, and then launched back onto the main road, veering past a donkey and narrowly avoiding an oncoming tractor. 'Longer-term,' he continued calmly, 'it's very important that we get large numbers of internationals. Then they can go away and tell everyone about the real Palestine.' He looked directly at me, for much longer than I was comfortable being stared at by the operator of a fast-moving car. 'Tourism is the oil of Palestine, and it is one of the only ways now that we can try and shape our own future.'

George talked a lot about travel restrictions in the West Bank. Since the 1990s it has been impossible for West Bank Palestinians to enter East Jerusalem or Israel without a permit, but during the Second Intifada the Israeli army also created an extensive series of checkpoints and physical blockades to halt free movement around the West Bank. The rationale behind this was that it would help stem the uprising and, specifically, halt the flow of suicide bombers. As of July 2012, there were 96 fixed checkpoints, 360 flying (movable) checkpoints, 358 physical obstructions (embankments, trenches, iron gates, etc.) and over 60 km of Israeli-only road (forbidden to Palestinians) in the West Bank.[27] For Palestinians, and indeed anyone, this makes it hard to get around with even a modicum of ease. It discourages even the desire to try.

As a result of the Oslo Accords, the West Bank is divided into three types of area, labelled A, B and C. They are, unsurprisingly, complex and disputed. In the simplest terms, Area A refers to land that is under the full control of the Palestinian Authority (PA). This includes the major Palestinian cities, and makes up about 18 per cent of the land. Area B is jointly controlled: Israel runs most of the security and the PA is in charge of civil affairs. This applies to hundreds of Palestinian towns and villages and some of the land around them, and accounts for about 22 per cent of the land mass. Area C, the remaining 60 per cent of the West Bank, is under almost complete Israeli control.

The Palestinian communities in Area A have large red signs at all accessible road entrances warning Israeli citizens that entry is forbidden and that an attempt 'could be dangerous to life'. Meanwhile, Area C contains all the Israeli settlements, which are mostly off-limits to Palestinians. In Jerusalem, I met an Israeli who told me that these settlements were not 'Jewish-only', but in my research I did not find any examples of Palestinians living on settlements. There are, however, many Palestinians who work as labourers on the settlements – often it is their only source of income. Someone else in Jerusalem told me that they were 'essentially building themselves out of existence'.

Other than these exceptions, there are rarely any fixed boundaries in place, so it is possible in the course of a single afternoon (or even a single hour) to walk between all three zones, especially as an international visitor. The Masar Ibrahim inevitably does this with regularity, and thus weaves an uninterrupted path from north to south, avoiding disruptions for the most part. 'It's the only way to walk in the West Bank without endless checkpoints,' said George when we finally reached his home. The kids rolled out, giggling still at the two strange foreigners, and George took us back to the office where he presented us with a Masar Ibrahim-themed coaster, two black baseball caps and four MIAK-branded T-shirts. We unfolded them slowly. 'I think we've run out of the men's,' he muttered as we noted the wide neckline and capped sleeves. 'But these are nice, I think they'll fit you.' He smiled broadly, hugged us again and then his phone rang.

Travelling on foot through the West Bank is nothing new. Before the contemporary demarcations the land was an important crossroads in trade, connecting disparate empires. Palestine was a convenient route between Egypt to the west and Anatolia and Mesopotamia to the east. Natural trails were formed then, combining the path of least resistance with suitable communities along the way to provide sustenance and supplies: the Via Maris, the King's Highway and the Rift Valley route were the major thoroughfares of the day, and there are still traces of those movements today.

The Bible tells us that Abraham and Moses walked in the Holy Land as, of course, did Jesus. Then came the fans. There are written accounts of pilgrimages from as early as 333 BC[28] and numerous adventures recounted by later seekers, in what are crucial documents of the history and geography of the wider region at their time of writing. To name but a few: John Moschos, the Byzantine monk who travelled and lived in various monasteries from about 578 onwards, and who more recently inspired the writer William Dalrymple to retrace his journey (chronicled in *From the Holy Mountain*); Bishop Arculf, who came from Gaul in AD 700 and was shipwrecked on the Scottish island of Iona upon his return; the Norwegian Sigurd the Crusader in 1107 who, having already accompanied his father into battle on the Orkney Islands, the Hebrides and in Ireland, consolidated his expertise in aggressive expeditions and became the first European to lead a crusade in the Holy Land; the Spanish rabbi Benjamin of Tudela in 1160, who gives one of the most extensive accounts of the Jewish medieval landscape; and John Mandeville of St Albans who, between 1322 and 1356, provided perhaps the most extensive descriptions of the many varied ways in which pilgrims journeyed from Europe to the Holy Land, why they went, and what they found once there.

There are wonderful stories of lions and hippos roaming through the wadis, and monks in their austere desert cells, and less wonderful accounts of the prejudices of the times and fierce, bloody battles in the streets of Jerusalem. What these accounts show collectively is that to come to this place to either further one's faith or justify it has long been a part of the fabric of this land.

Even for those not on a journey, the landscape has historically been traversed on foot. The Bedouin have roamed here for generations, and Palestine is peppered with tracks that criss-cross every geographical feature between the Mediterranean and the River Jordan. In the wadis, generations of shepherds' sandals and sheep's hooves have slowly smoothed natural ways through valley bottoms and along the sides of precipices. Desert hills may look untouched and timeless from a distance, but up close they betray a physical history of the transport of innumerable passengers and pilgrims. Then there are the paths that disappear with each shower of rain that washes clean the imprints, or with every easterly wind that blows sand over physical marks. Is a trail still a trail if it ceases to exist in a tangible manner? Palestine is full of such ways; paths that survive in memory and shared knowledge alone. Still they flourish – like the stories that they conduct, these channels can exist in many forms.

Even in the modern era, walking is not unheard of. The Masar Ibrahim is perhaps the most ambitious and well-developed trail in the region, thanks in large part to a World Bank grant of $2.3 million in 2014, but it is not the only one. There is the Nativity Trail, which runs from Nazareth (in Israel) to Bethlehem and attracts a few hardy pilgrims and hikers who have perhaps already walked more popular routes like the Camino de Santiago or the Via Francigenca. There is also a series of shorter trails in the hills around Ramallah that lead between a scattered network of Sufi shrines: the Deir Ghassaneh Trail, the Nabi Ghaith

Trail and the Nabi Anir Trail. There are weekly hiking groups, run independently or by dedicated organisations, which take Palestinians and NGO workers from Jerusalem and Ramallah to see and feel the West Bank countryside for a few hours each weekend. Beyond the wall, of course, hiking in Israel is a major part of the culture, and the land is peppered with thousands of miles of world-class trails and populated by thousands of keen hikers.

It was important that Dave and I understood all of this so that we saw our journey not as something new or exploratory. Our steps were the latest in an age-old tradition of walking through a land that is shaped by the movement of feet. We were, although we may not have realised it, pilgrims in the Holy Land, searching for experience, learning and, perhaps, enlightenment.

# Up Is Strange

To the north of Jericho, Dave and I spent a night in a small Bedouin community at the mouth of Wadi Auja as the guests of a man called Ali, whose name was given to us by George Rishmawi. Finding him had proved easy, even when we had arrived in darkness and the world around us was reduced to gloomy, imprecise shapes that floated in and out of squinted vision. A small boy had cycled up alongside us, luminous stickers on his wheels betraying a blacktop road, and I had told him who I was looking for. 'Ah, Ali. Ali is my baba!' he shouted, and we followed him back to the tent.

I had woken up to find that Dave had spent much of the night running in and out of the tent to visit the brand-new, EU-sponsored Portaloo. It was now, I wagered, fully broken in. His illness was a mystery and compounded his suffering as a virgin hiker. He had struggled with fitness and a heavy pack, and we'd both found the journey thus far mentally exhausting.

Ali's simple beige tents sat on a hillside of similar sparse encampments, some with corrugated iron and basic brick shelters alongside for goats. Scattered liberally throughout were the discoloured shells of abandoned vehicles and engine parts, lying like long-dead bodies that were waiting to decompose into the hillside. As we packed up, Ali took me outside to show me his pride and joy, which gleamed brightly amongst the detritus: a Land Rover Defender in bright yellow with black detail. He had recently purchased it from an aid worker in Ramallah and, as soon as he was finished tinkering with the engine, he'd take it south to the desert to try some off-roading. He showed me around the various parts and I tried to make the right noises of appreciation. I have no interest in cars, so it required a little bit of guesswork. Just as I was running out of steam, I heard my name ringing out across the mechanical graveyard.

'Leon, David! There you are.' A small, compact man in a cloth hat that shaded his eyes walked towards us with short, fast steps. He carried a small rucksack on his shoulders, the straps hanging loosely under his arms, and in his hand was a walking stick with a flashlight stuck to the top. 'Do you know me?' he asked.

I did, but only by reputation.

This was Anwar Dawabsheh, a Palestinian from the town of Duma, and he would accompany us for a couple of days. I had spoken to him on the phone a few times and arranged to meet at Ali's tent. Anwar had been confused by this, as I told him we planned to walk north through Wadi Auja. 'Up?' he'd asked. 'Why up? It is much better to walk down.' I'd explained that we were on a journey heading north and he finally agreed to come, but had signed off by muttering something about going up being very silly.

We set off together and Anwar brought the topic up immediately. 'Up is very strange,' he said. 'I have done this walk maybe a hundred times, but always down. It is so lovely to come downhill in this valley.' Thus began our time with Anwar, a man with more opinions than there are minutes in the day.

Anwar worked at the Ministry of Education but moonlighted as a hiking guide whenever the opportunity arose. This, he said, was his true passion. At six years old he walked to the next village alone, and now in adulthood he had covered every inch of the central West Bank. 'I've opened up at least 20 new trails around here,' he told us. 'I just come out and walk in the mornings and evenings and on my days off, and when one way is very nice, I come back and do it again some more times.'

41

Wadi Auja was one of his favourite walks. From the Auja spring that fed Ali's Bedouin community, we entered a gorge that bowed dramatically north ahead of us. It was December, but the valley shone a bright and rich emerald green, the dappled light of winter shooting piercing rays across the sky. A dirt track led us into the wadi while the walls grew around us. On the hillside, shepherds tramped along narrow and precarious-looking paths behind flocks of sure-footed sheep. Soon we joined them, climbing onto higher elevation trails that skirted the drop below. We scrambled up dry waterfalls, clambering ever higher, deeper into the heart of the opulence of the valley. Here the armed soldiers and tense streets of Jerusalem felt like a world way.

As we walked, Anwar talked. He told us about himself, about his many years as a teacher and his current job in the Ministry of Education, which he actually quite enjoyed despite bunking off to hike. He told us about his daughter working as a journalist, his son studying graphic design at university in Bethlehem and his youngest boy who, at just 11 years old, would regularly join him in the hills. Mostly though, he would tell us tangential stories that began as a description of where we were and ended as something completely different.

'The name Auja means "curve",' he said. We agreed that the valley was aptly named. 'Do you think the Bedouin here are rich?' he asked us, pointing to a shepherd on the ridgeline. 'Probably not,' I said. 'Wrong!' he replied immediately with glee. He chuckled regularly, mostly at Dave's or my expense. 'They are very rich. They can sell those lambs for maybe 120,000 Jordanian dinar [around £120,000].' This seemed ludicrous, but he was adamant. 'They have lots of money, and some of them have big houses, but they choose to be out here in the hills as much as they can because it is better.' He looked at us very solemnly. 'If you want to kill a Bedouin, put him in a palace for one week. He will not handle it.'

At the top of the wadi we could see large houses built on the higher ground. Anwar told us they were mostly empty and I asked if they belonged to the rich Bedouin. 'Of course not,' he scoffed. 'The Bedouin always live on the land.'

'But I thought you said ...'

'No, that's silly,' he cut me off. 'Those houses belong to rich Palestinians who live abroad. After the *Nakba* many Palestinians left. Everyone in the Ramallah area went to America, and people in from the Nablus countryside went to the Gulf. Before 1980 the Gulf was a great place for work, but then there were wars and changes and it became very difficult. America is now the best place. There are so many Palestinians in America. Especially in Chicago.'

'Do those people come back often?' Dave asked. 'Not very often,' said Anwar. 'Just sometimes, but they send money back and they have people look after the houses. I also heard that some of them control their houses with a computer from America. They can open the windows and doors with a button, and watch who is looking at the house from a camera. Maybe they will see us!' This tickled him.

Every half-hour or so, we'd stop for a rest. Dave was weak and unable to stomach any food, but he climbed the steep banks without complaining. The breaks were mostly at the behest of Anwar, who maintained that walking was as much about stopping as it was about moving. Most times we'd know it was time to rest because Anwar would step off the path and grab a pile of sticks that he'd stashed in previous weeks, and then he'd abruptly sit down to build a small fire over which he'd construct a small frame to hang a blackened kettle.

From his rucksack he produced a bag of tea leaves and a 1-litre sized plastic bottle full of sugar. As the water boiled over the open fire he carefully measured out the tea, then poured copious amounts of sugar on top. The mixture brewed and, ten minutes later, sweet black tea was decanted into plastic cups. It was great for energy, and it gave Anwar the chance to hold court again. 'Rest before you're tired, and move before you rest enough,' he said when I suggested that perhaps we didn't need to stop quite so often. His wisdom was often delivered in such parables. It was also questionable. When Dave sneezed, Anwar said, 'Do you know that when you sneeze, you die for a minute?' His medical advice continued soon after when he told us: 'Walking uphill too much can make you ill. It is to do with blood in the legs. I know a lot about health.'

We hit a blacktop road late in the afternoon and, before climbing the final hill into a town called Kufr Malek, Anwar took us on a detour to a small wooden shack behind some mesh fence by a field filled with colourful flowers. Abu Hamed[29] sat under a corrugated iron roof of the shack drinking tea from a battered China mug. He must have been at least 80 years old, his face lined deeply by decades of exposure to sun and hardship, and the plants behind him were his livelihood: he sold decorative flowers, herbs and vegetable seeds to the surrounding villages.

'*As Salaam alaykum,*' said Anwar. 'Peace be upon you.' '*Alaykum as-salaam,*' came the reply. 'And to you.' Anwar and he continued like this for some time – Arabic greetings often take minutes to complete, especially if they are formal. 'He is a very good man,' Anwar told us. As if to prove it, he said, 'The settlers attack him once or twice a year, but he fights them off.' Abu Hamed disappeared down an aisle of trestles covered in sweet-smelling olive-green plants, and returned with long stalks of a pale green herb. 'This is *maramia,*' said Anwar: sage. 'Squash it up a little bit and put it in hot water with some sugar. It'll be good for your stomach,' he told Dave. We would find this happened regularly whenever either of us had any complaint: there was a Palestinian remedy for every ailment, and the vast majority seemed to simply involve putting a herb into boiling water.

Our night in Kufr Malek didn't go according to plan. As soon as we arrived in the town, we heard news of a car crash on the main road to Ramallah. Four people had been injured and were on their way to hospital – one was the son of the women who had offered to host us, and now we needed to make a new plan. It was a small town, and news of the accident travelled fast. Anwar stopped to ask a shopkeeper what he knew and the whisperings were relayed. There was a truck involved. No, it was two cars. Someone was speeding. Someone was driving without a licence. The *Israelis* were to blame.

A group of five lanky teenagers in tight jeans and branded T-shirts approached us. 'You are British?' one asked Dave, who confirmed the suspicion. 'Ah, you gave away our country,' the boy nodded. Dave sighed heavily.

'Cameroon,' the boy began again, wagging his finger. Dave looked confused, perhaps wondering about the relevance of Central Africa in such a place. 'David Cameroon,' said the boy. 'Why does he not like

Muslims?' Dave laughed this off, but the boy wasn't giving up. 'What do the people in Britain think of Muslims?' he tried again.

Dave replied finally: 'Mostly, non-Muslim British people see Muslims just the same as anyone else.' There were nods all round. As we left, one of the boys told Anwar in Arabic that European people were all so beautiful. Even the men.

It was dark, and the town became a shadowy muddle of fluorescent lamps and bouncing car headlights which briefly brought to life street scenes and faces, then banished them just as quickly. The evening call to prayer from a nearby mosque sounded across the town, the guttural tones of a mullah reverberating out across the hills and bouncing back around us in stereo. Anwar told us he would like to pray, and insisted that we sit on the steps of the mosque to wait.

It was a pale fawn-coloured building with a single minaret and large dome. It was not particularly pretty: we could see in detail only the entranceway, which had some Qur'anic calligraphy above the door, and inside wooden shelves of sandals awaiting their owners' return. Ten minutes passed, during which we ate peanuts and dried fruit and complained about the cold. A few worshippers stepped out, grabbing their footwear to beat the rush, then suddenly hundreds of men were stepping past us. We were very much in the way, swallowed by the crush of bodies, our bags and hiking poles tripping people up as they pushed past. I wished we had defied Anwar and sat by the road. A grey-haired man with broad shoulders and even bigger eyebrows elbowed his way over to us. 'It is not right that you are here. Why are you here?'

Others gathered to stand and watch. For the first time, I felt a nervous energy around us. People behind the man were stretching to hear what was going on, and a spiral of Chinese whispers began. I heard snatches – one man said in Arabic, 'There's some Americans causing a problem,' and another asked, 'Are they Israeli?'

We were soon completely surrounded by men wondering what the commotion was. Some of the faces were hardened with anger. Then, a small head in a cloth hat peered through a cluster of elbows. 'Ah, you're here!' said Anwar looking at us. Then to our interrogator: 'And you, you are Yassar Salawdeh, are you not?' The tension dropped like a penny down a well, and everyone began to move on. Anwar and Yassar talked, and we moved to a coffee shop to consummate the new friendship between us all. I wondered for a long time what would have happened had Anwar not been there. After an hour, Anwar got a call to say that someone else would have us to stay, and we stumbled up a hill, exchanged some tired greetings and fell into bed in a dark, warm room.

# The Lost Ones

We awoke in a house that felt like a shrine. The living room was long but narrow and contained 12 separate portraits and photographs of the same young man. He was handsome with a strong nose, dark eyebrows and short, cropped hair. In some of the pictures, he looked down upon the room with his chin resting on his hand and a slight smile on his lips. In others, a full body shot was superimposed upon an image of the Dome of the Rock in Jerusalem. A Palestinian flag was faded in for good measure.

Abdal Aziz was the man in the pictures, although he was always referred to as a 'boy' by his mother, Ebtihaj, in whose house we had found ourselves. She was a quintessential motherly Arab, bundled up against the cold in crumpled layers of black material. She buzzed around the room checking on the levels of liquid in her guests' teacups. She smiled broadly as she laid out a display of oily scrambled eggs, thick fresh hummus, warm bread and two colours of olives.

Anwar was there too, along with two other women from the village. Some others came and went, at least two of whom were related to Ebtihaj. We learned that there was no further news from the hospital, but that the car crash was serious and four people were critically ill. There was much tutting and shaking of heads. Anwar whispered to us that it was the last thing anyone here needed. Then, Ebtihaj began to tell us about Abdal Aziz.

For most of his life, she said, Abdal Aziz had watched the IDF arrive in their village and, during the First Intifada, they were teargassed regularly. The kids had no weapons to fight back with, so throwing stones at the soldiers was the best they could do.[30] A lot of children were arrested for this, both in Kufr Malek, she said, and across the West Bank. Ebtihaj told us that one of her cousins had been in jail for 25 years for stone-throwing. One night, seven years previously, Abdal Aziz had gone out late with friends to wait for a patrol that they heard was coming. According to those friends, their group was ambushed by soldiers in a tree and Abdal Aziz was shot dead.

Dave and I listened in silence and Anwar bowed his head, translating for us in chunks. The sun was now high, golden light arcing and unravelling through the warped windows, and the cold wind that had swept through the house in the early hours was gone. We stood to leave, and Ebtihaj waved us off, smiling broadly again. I said to Anwar that it must be very hard for her to talk about Abdal Aziz. 'Yes,' he replied. 'Today especially. This would have been his birthday.'

This was the most intimate experience that I'd had so far with the family of a *shaheed*, or martyr,[31] but it was not the first time we had seen the photoshopped composite images of a dead son or brother. Every town and village we passed through had its own *shaheed*, and their pictures were often printed out and stuck to telegraph poles or shop windows. They were, one man had told us, 'the lost ones'.

Dave's food poisoning had passed and, as it was the weekend, two friends from Jerusalem drove in to walk with us for the day. Nicky, who worked for UNRWA, and Joris, a representative of the EU political affairs team, regularly came out to the West Bank on days off as a break from the stress and intensity of their jobs. The landscape here that was home for Anwar and an adventure for us was, for them, an escape. In Jerusalem and Ramallah there are thousands of foreign residents working for NGOs, or as journalists, or in diplomacy. Few of them have an easy ride – this is not a part of the world that encourages a relaxed working environment.

Many of those expats find a release in Dead Sea resorts or amongst the excesses and beaches of Tel Aviv. Some – a small minority – choose to go walking instead.

My friend Stefan Szepesi was one of the first to do this. On his days off he would set out into the Palestinian hills, exploring new tracks and trails each time until eventually he inadvertently started a movement: by 2008, a walking community of over 200 Palestinians and foreigners was joining him at various points on his journeys.[32] Nicky and Joris were diplomats cut from the same cloth: for them, this was a very different Palestine than the complex one they dealt with on weekdays. This was a Palestine of tea, stories and good, wild hiking.

We wound past the last of the village houses to a spring called Ein Sarnia, flanked by terraces of long, heavily worked olive groves, then struck north into a rugged canyon. At its entrance was a large open quarry about the size of a football pitch, with five men and two yellow diggers surrounded by huge, motor-car-sized blocks of marble and granite. 'This stuff is like white gold,' said Nicky. We took turns at guessing the value of a nearby chunk. I had no frame of reference but was still surprised when we were told it was worth $2,000.

'Quarries are very important,' said Anwar. 'They're one of the few places where Palestinians can claim ownership over their land.' He went off to talk to the owners while we wandered amongst the blocks that had been extracted. They towered about us and were dropped at regular intervals along the periphery, like exhibits in some strange modernist museum. 'This area now is worth $7 million,' said Anwar when he returned. 'This man has been very lucky.'

Anwar thrived on having an audience of four. He spent a good amount of time gently teasing Dave and I about our journey – 'You don't start in Jerusalem. You *end* in Jerusalem. Going the other way is silly' – and regaling us all with stories of his own adventures, and of other groups that he had guided. 'Once I went looking for bees,' he said. 'I wanted honey but I got stuck on a cliff and had to slide down the slope. My trousers fell off and I had to walk home with a scarf around my legs.' Then: 'The Italians are the worst. And the stupidest. They never listen.' We all laughed at the stupid Italians. During our breaks, which were as regular as ever, he handed out snacks. I ate some of the halwa with my tea and he observed, for the benefit of the group, that 'in Palestine, if someone eats their halwa with their tea, then they are a foolish person'.

We passed through a small village, Mughayir, a name that means the 'changing of the weather'. A family stopped us to talk, and Nicky inadvertently got caught in a conversation about religions. The outcome was that Islam and Christianity were good, and Judaism was fine too, in theory. As long as a person believed in a single God, then they had a chance of being saved. One of the children confided to her afterwards that 'I heard that Christians and Muslims should be friends. My dad also said though that Muslims are slightly better, because they know that Allah is the one true God. That bit might be a secret.'

In a quiet valley, Anwar taught us a rock-throwing game. The irony of a Palestinian teaching such a game was not lost on him. A small cairn was set up, and we took turns to try and knock it over from a distance. Joris was the undisputed winner. Anwar was clearly slightly disappointed to have lost and so told us a long and indecipherable story about a donkey. Then he sang a song and began walking again.

It had been a day of high spirits, so it was disconcerting to arrive into Duma – Anwar's hometown – that evening to be confronted with one of the most heartbreaking examples of the modern-era conflict. The story was one that both Dave and I already knew, and even by the grim standards of the West Bank it was tragic. On 29 July 2015, masked assailants smashed windows and threw Molotov cocktails into two homes in Duma. The first was empty, but inside the second was a family of four. An 18-month-old boy called Ali Dawabsheh died in the blaze. His father, Sa'ed, died in hospital a few days later and his mother, Riham, also passed away the following month. Ali's brother, Ahmad, who was four at the time, survived, but with third-degree burns over 60 per cent of his body.

The story caused an uproar in Palestinian and Israeli media, and soon internationally too. An embargo was put on the press to smother the details, but by the time Dave and I passed through, there were a few hard facts mixed in with the rumours. A senior IDF official had stated that it was 'unequivocally an act of Jewish terror', and three days before we arrived a number of suspects were arrested. We had heard Palestinians speculate that it was 'price-tagging' – a catch-all term for revenge attacks or vandalism carried out by fundamentalist settlers in supposed retaliation for any Israeli government actions that were deemed to hinder the settler movement. It is still unclear if this was the case. In January 2016 – a month after we left – a 21-year-old Israeli, Amiram Ben-Uriel, was charged with triple murder. At the time of writing there was yet to be a verdict, but the only other suspect, a well-known extremist called Meir Ettinger, was released in June 2016.[33]

Amiram Ben-Uriel had most recently been living on a bus in the nearby outpost[34] of Adei Ad. As Anwar walked with us into the village, he told us that they often had problems from the settlers nearby. They would beat people up and set fire to olive groves and, in general, he said, were 'very bad neighbours'. We were led to the Dawabsheh house, which had a large banner outside showing a picture of the family, smiling and happy in a studio somewhere. The outside walls of the building were still intact, but through the iron bars on the glassless window we could see a black, charred mess inside. 'We will leave it as a museum for the hate,' said Anwar.

It was clear that he saw this as a necessary pilgrimage for us to make; a fundamental part of our understanding the West Bank. Increasingly it was becoming obvious that my idealistic goal of an apolitical journey in Palestine was folly; this was a place where politics and the pain were so engrained in some parts of everyday life that they were impossible to ignore. Anwar told us that, after the firebombing, Riham Dawabsheh ran back inside, despite her injuries, to grab Ali, but when she got outside she realised she had lifted only blankets and left the child inside. He spoke quietly. I had no words for him in reply. We walked a silent lap of the house, Anwar pointed out some graffiti daubed on the wall – 'Long Live the Messiah' in Hebrew and a large, hastily sketched Star of David – and then we left. We all sat on a high wall and I looked at Dave. He stared off into space and we swung our legs in silence.

Nicky and Joris left us to head back to Jerusalem. As they got into the taxi, Joris mentioned that they had both received a text message – part of the security package in their organisations – which said there had been a clash in Mughayir, the village we had been in that afternoon. 'Clash' is a vague term, but generally refers to anything involving the IDF and local Palestinians facing off against one another. It had happened just a couple of hours after we'd left. I couldn't imagine what might have started it. There were so few houses there, and my only real memory was of 10 or 15 kids kicking a football up and down the single street in a blink-and-you'll-miss-it village.

That evening I contemplated how the evils of the world seem to seize control of my thinking so much more easily than the good. Throughout the West Bank I had met with many acts of kindness and hospitality, small and large, and I'd seen resilience and positivity at every turn. I'd laughed for hours each day, and my cheeks hurt from returning the smiles of almost everyone I saw. Later, I would remember that the tragedy at Duma and those sporadic clashes in the countryside do not define the West Bank; that there is more to Palestine than conflict.

# Making a Small Land Big Again

T he first thing I saw when I opened my eyes was the wispy vapour of a breath hovering above my face, dancing briefly in the half light of morning before dissipating into the ether. Dave and I had slept inside our winter-rated sleeping bags underneath thick blankets in Anwar's front room, and yet my feet were still numb. I assumed it was down to having gone soft from too many months of not doing things like this. Dave had developed a rasping cough, and we were both taking ibuprofen as a matter of habit. We had only been walking 20 or 25 km a day, but it was taking us eight to ten hours each time and our packs were heavier than they should have been for rookie back muscles. I felt stiff and was grateful to have had hard, flat concrete beneath my back for a night to straighten things out. It occurred to me afterwards that this probably hadn't helped with the cold.

We didn't see much of Anwar's family, not unnaturally. His wife stayed mostly out of sight, as did his daughters. Anwar's youngest son, the keen hiker, was brought in and introduced to us, but quickly bounded out of the room in search of more interesting things to do. Anwar had awoken us early with his usual chirpiness, immediately casting off the darkness of the previous evening. 'Look!' he shouted to us from another room. 'Mr Obama is on the television. He is the second face of Israel.' This phrase had cropped up more than once, expressing a belief that the American administration, both current and past, acted entirely at the behest of the Israeli government. While much of the rest of the world viewed the leadership and policies of Obama as a significant change from those of George W. Bush, I found little credence given to that idea in the West Bank. He simply continued the same injustices towards the Palestinian people, I was told by Anwar, and there would be no tears shed when his time came to leave office.

We shouldered our bags and stepped out into a fresh winter morning. I told Anwar he had a nice house and he asked me about mine. 'I don't have one,' I replied. I told him I couldn't afford a house in London, or anywhere else. 'That is amazing,' said Anwar, shaking his head. 'Here, everybody has a house. Even a big one only costs about US$40,000.'

Duma, we now saw, was tiny. The population was just over 2,000, and it took us less than five minutes to walk from one end of the village to the other. Everyone waved to Anwar and asked him who his guests were, and he smiled at the attention. We walked up through the olive groves, climbing gradually on country tracks, and by afternoon arrived in a village called Aqraba. To the east, a wide vista opened up between the trees; myriad shades of brown, green and yellow stepped their way down to a patchwork of furrowed fields in the plain, and beyond that the hills of Jordan reared up with layers of crumpled folds stretching back to the horizon until their colours faded into the sky and everything became one. We were now nearly 600 m above sea level and had been climbing continuously since Jericho.

Almonds, corn and lentils were growing in the fertile valley below, and in the summer Anwar said tomatoes and zucchinis would be planted too, but olives were always the main source of income for this area. The olive tree holds a very special place in the psyche of the West Bank: as well as a rooting in the Qur'an, the Torah and the Bible, I had often heard of it referred to as a physical symbol of the resilience of the Palestinians. Olive trees can live to be 1,000 years old or more and, in Palestine and beyond, they provide, in Anwar's words: food, furniture, heating, light, cosmetics and more. He occasionally wondered if some of the Arab farmers that we met loved their olive trees more than their wives.

Perhaps because of their symbolism as much as their practical uses, olive trees often become targets for violence. Anwar told me that, since 1967, over 1 million olive trees have been cut down or uprooted by Israelis. I have no way to verify this, but it's beyond doubt that the number is high. The perpetrators are usually either settlers or the IDF, who claim that the groves can act as protection and cover for stone-throwers or gunmen, and so destroying them is an act of self-defence. To Palestinians, the clearing of the trees destroys livelihoods and forces them to vacate land that they suspect will ultimately be incorporated into a settlement. While the burnings or clearings are often seen as ad hoc violence in tense areas, there is also a compelling argument too to say that it is in fact a systematic, organised campaign to slowly but surely intimidate and threaten Palestinian farmers. The olive harvest may constitute as much as 25 per cent of the agricultural economy in the West Bank, and so the impact is keenly felt by many thousands of people across the territory.

Anwar pointed towards some smaller olive trees growing in a small orchard by the main road through the village. 'These olive trees are different,' he said. 'They're not very good, and we don't like them.'

'What's their name?' I asked, getting out my notebook.

Anwar paused with a comedian's timing. 'We call them: *Israeli* Trees.' He smiled and laughed his trademark shotgun laugh, and walked on.

It was our last day with Anwar, and he seemed truly at peace in the hills. In his beautiful and painful memoir, the most famous Palestinian walker of all, Raja Shehadeh, writes that:

> Palestine has been one of the countries most visited by pilgrims and travellers over the ages. The accounts I have read do not describe a land familiar to me, but rather a land of these travellers' imaginations. Palestine has been constantly re-invented, with devastating consequences to its original inhabitants.[35]

I had read many of those same accounts but, as one of those very pilgrims and travellers that he disowns, I was inclined to fall into the same trap of projecting my own desires and characteristics onto the landscape. To have Anwar with me was to have a direct line into the Palestinian psyche or, at least, the psyche of one Palestinian. The views across the valley were spectacular, and he often stopped just to stare out into the distance. 'I wish I had wings, just for one day so that I could fly over all of this,' he said. On a small summit he pointed to an old canal system and said, 'This is from the Roman times.' I asked him how he knew, and he walked a few hundred metres away to a small hole in the ground, lined with smooth stones of even sizes, all cut from larger rock. 'Down here is where the Romans stored their water,' he said. 'What I don't know is – how did they get the stones up here?' The story of this land is a layered one, with each new occupying force building its empire on top of its conquered predecessor's. Throughout my walk, I would see these glimpses of the past peeking through, subtle reminders of what went before.

In the late afternoon we entered a place called Awarta and, by now, Palestinian towns and villages had a familiar feel to them. Bottle-green undulations would form natural borders and, in the folds, there would collect tightly packed two- or three-storey concrete buildings. All would be mostly symmetrical, with a couple of narrow rectangular windows looking out, and many would be unpainted. Many of the houses had some initial structures built on the roof to provide for another floor, but they were left in a state of flux. I'd heard two stories about why this was – one suggested that less tax was paid if the house seemed unfinished. More likely was the second suggestion, that the fledgling additions were left there for the next generation of the family to move into when the children of the owners got married.

Dotted throughout would be the minarets of multiple mosques and, more commonly in the south, two or three church steeples too. In the villages of this central region, the population felt overwhelmingly Islamic.[36] The minarets would reach for the sky, high above the nearby houses, and the rounded domes of the mosques were distinct from the squared-off edges all around. Most visible of all were the maverick colourful buildings peppered randomly throughout – a bright yellow house here, a neon pink office block there. It would be a stretch to describe these places as handsome, but there was a certain arresting beauty in the chaotic jumble of structures, and I never grew tired of scanning them as we'd walk into new places.

Anwar broke the news to us that we couldn't walk any further. We needed to get to Nablus, which was less than 10 km away, but the only viable route was compromised: it led along the main road to a checkpoint known as Huwarah. Since the firebomb attack in Duma, the West Bank and Jerusalem had seen a huge surge in clashes, which would often be reported as beginning with a Palestinian running towards soldiers or checkpoints with a knife. The assailant would then be shot. There had been at least two shootings like this at Huwarah in the weeks before we arrived, and Anwar was insistent that walking up to the checkpoint would be a very bad idea.

Most Palestinians we met shared his fears. Often, in idle conversations in the villages, men would say to us that it had gotten so bad that, if the IDF were close by, they couldn't even put their hands in their pockets to reach for a mobile phone in case it was mistaken for reaching for a knife. Others were even more candid and said it just simply wasn't worth being seen anywhere near checkpoints at all because it gave the IDF an opportunity to shoot them and then throw a knife down beside the body and say *He tried to stab me.* From another perspective, it is difficult to imagine the challenges of the job of a solider at a checkpoint, scanning every body and car that approaches with the fear of the previous weeks of attacks fresh in their minds.

It was hard to know where the truth lay here, but to be in either position was far from appealing. The IDF has grown and adapted since its inception in 1948 to match the particular set of security circumstances in which Israel finds itself. Surrounded by hostile states, it is generously funded – the defence budget per capita in Israel is one of the highest in the world – and the role and importance of the IDF is woven into the very fabric of society; the majority of Israelis are proud and grateful for the protection that it affords them. It is undoubtedly one of the most effective security forces in the world, but this efficiency is often seen – by the international community, though there are critics at home too – as crossing into ruthlessness and brutality. To most Palestinians, the IDF are simply oppressors who impose an occupation with little humanity or empathy.

From what I'd seen in the West Bank, the IDF seemed staffed largely by young soldiers, some barely out of their teens, who were covered in body armour and holding M-16 assault rifles with foregrips, magazines and optics protruding from the smooth steel. They often looked nervous, and it was hard to blame then. Most were on duty as part of their National Service, which in Israel is mandatory and lasts two years for women and nearly three for men. Although they were sent to the Negev Desert in the south too, and to other military bases around the country, much of their training was done in the crucible of the checkpoints inside the Occupied Territories. While it must have been even more challenging – practically and ethically – for those called up during the intifadas, the recruits in 2015 still had an enormously difficult task as a spate of stabbings escalated around them. With this undoubtedly playing on their minds, policing a people who hated and feared them in equal measure was near-impossible for the IDF soldiers. Few would engage in conversations with me, but it was clear that most were certainly not monsters – they were, quite simply, in a tough spot and befittingly afraid. Equally, the Palestinians were terrified, and this latest round of violence had eroded any belief that might previously have existed in the integrity of the IDF.

We agreed to get into a car to pass the checkpoint, but I hated the idea. I visualised my unbroken line of footprints leading back to Jerusalem, and tried to imagine the steps I had not yet taken. I knew that this gap would annoy me later. When I was younger, I took long journeys on bicycles and on foot and I was often pedantic about making sure I covered every inch. I once spent a day and a night camped at an international border post in Southeast Asia until the immigration officials allowed me to push my bike through the no-man's land instead of getting on a bus. Another time, in China, I was picked up by the police for trying to walk through a road tunnel. They offered to deposit me at the far end of the tunnel, but I insisted that

I restart walking from an equidistant point in the mountains, adding three days to my journey. It seemed like perhaps it would be for the best if we were forced into a car in Awarta; I could see if I'd matured at all in the intervening years.

Our taxi passed some soldiers who peered in through the windows; a manned watchtower on the embankment housed a bored-looking sniper, and a few cars crawled through from the other direction. On the far side we got out about 500 m from the checkpoint. That was it. Anwar stayed with the car; he planned to hike from Duma to the Jordan Valley that night to have a barbecue with friends. He was probably the only true hiker I met in Palestine; a man for whom walking is not just enjoyable, but a requisite part of a happy life. 'I hope you have enjoyed my company,' he said. 'It has been a pleasure to walk with you. It's such an important thing to do here. This is how we make a small land feel big again.'

We promised to call him from Nablus, and he fussed around us like a concerned parent before getting in the car and leaving. We walked the final few kilometres as the sun dropped below the mass of buildings ahead, and a dark blue sky settled in over the mountains. Each step gathered us further into the urbanisation of a major city until the countryside was just a memory. A group of teenagers followed us for a while and one asked me, 'Are you Hamas, or Fatah?' By the time we reached the city centre it was dark and the streets were pulsating with families crowding the sidewalk, and street vendors hawking corn and bread from the curbstones. We were swallowed by the mass, and carried along to the Old City where we found a hotel and checked in. We were halfway through our journey in the West Bank.

# The (Other) Holy
# Mountain

Nablus is the largest city in the northern West Bank. Like most other modern-day communities there, it is built upon the ruins of those that came before it. Josephus, the Roman-Jewish scholar, helps us to locate Nablus as the site of the Canaanite city of Shechem – listed in the Hebrew Bible as the first capital of Israel. The Roman city of Neapolis followed and now the modern incarnation is long and sprawling, wedged in a valley between the mountains of Ebal and Gerizim. It is famous for cake, soap and archaeological significance – rather a heady mix.

Dave and I congratulated ourselves on finding the best hotel in town. In fact, it seemed to have been the *only* hotel in town. The Yasmeen was simple but, to us, glorious. It had heating, hot water, and we were given a private room on the side farthest from the street. The hotel had been built into a fifteenth-century ruin: 10 ft through the thick 500-year-old walls of our room lay the beginning of the casbah, from where narrow, lightless alleyways wended their way outwards in all directions. In the spring of 2002, during the Israeli Army's Operation Defensive Shield, the Nablus casbah was the site of one of the fiercest battles of the Second Intifada. The operation, ostensibly to stop terror attacks in Israel, was the largest that the Israeli military had mounted since the Six Day Way and it began with incursions into the six biggest cities in the West Bank. In Nablus, the ancient labyrinth of the casbah housed Palestinian fighters who used its thick walls as protection from a siege by two Israeli battalions; when the battle was finally over, on 8 April, more than 70 fighters and eight civilians had died, along with at least one Israeli soldier.

Among the dead in the casbah were the bodies of Hamas fighters, some of whom wore a green bandana around their neck to signify their allegiance. At that point Hamas – a militant Islamist organisation with political and military wings – had been in existence for 15 years, having initially been founded as an offshoot of the Muslim Brotherhood. In governmental elections in the West Bank in 2006, Hamas defeated the ruling party, Fatah – the largest faction of the PLO, and the secular group of founder and former president Yasser Arafat. Western players in the region, however, including the US and the EU, refused to accept this result on the basis that they saw Hamas as a terrorist organisation. The following year, Hamas ousted Fatah from the Gaza Strip and they have governed the territory ever since, continuing to launch rocket attacks on Israel from the strip (often justifying them as 'retaliatory'). Politics in the West Bank descended into chaos, and it took another 10 years before another round of elections was held. Following these, in 2016 at the time of writing, there was news of a pending agreement between Hamas and Fatah to form a unity government. The outcome of the deal could well be key to the Palestinian approach to any future peace negotiations, and many in the Palestinian territories and beyond hope that somehow the alliance holds.

The Yasmeen windows still had bullet holes from this time. When I asked the concierge about them, he laughed. 'Who can afford new windows these days?' he replied. Dave and I wandered out into the casbah; it was still morning but even now preparations were underway in the covered markets for the day ahead. Soon we would be engulfed in the madness of the *souq* and so we scurried on past churches, mosques and apartments that leant out aggressively over the alleyways. The 'Battle of Nablus' – the name given to the siege during Operation Defensive Shield – destroyed a lot of the historical sites in the casbah, and still some pathways led to a dead end of rubble. What hadn't been lost was the feeling of travelling back through time and space, to another era, another world, where daylight only pierced through the fractured roof at periodic intervals, and the universe contracted into a funnelled passageway of excited, ageless energy around the stalls selling fresh fish, odorous spices, colourful sweets and nuts that were stacked in wicker baskets along the cobbles.

Leaving the casbah, the city opened out onto Martyrs' Square. The concept of martyrdom holds a special place in the Palestinian psyche, as it does in much of the Islamic world. It is intrinsically connected to the idea of *jihad* – the concept of a Holy Struggle – and the distinction is bestowed upon those who are seen to have given their life fulfilling a religious calling. The Qur'an says that the martyr, or *shaheed*, is guaranteed a place in paradise for their sacrifice. Across the West Bank I came across many posters of these *shaheed*s, and I soon learned that their stories vary hugely. Some are innocent civilians killed in crossfire by Israeli forces. Others are armed fighters who died in bloody gun battles. There are also, however, the suicide bombers, who are hailed by some militant organisations as *shaheed*s despite the abhorrence of the act and obvious clash that this implies with Islam's claim to be a peaceful religion. The term martyr has therefore become a complicated one, often misunderstood, and representing the different sentiments of different users. Nablus itself contained a microcosm of this complexity in a single place, with martyrs from all these backgrounds commemorated around the city.

Beyond the square were busy streets, awash with the manic cacophony of an Arab city during the morning rush. Most of the cars were old and dilapidated, and white taxicabs from the 1980s wreaked havoc. A bored-looking policeman stood in the middle of a roundabout waving vehicles past at random. On the footpaths, tall trees grew up through the pavement, and a variety of objects blocked the way: motorbikes, donkeys and the spilling-out of a hardware store or tea house.

We spent the day resting weary limbs and catching up on sleep. Walking was reduced to wandering, sauntering. We were overjoyed to have a small electric heater in our room. We promised the staff that we'd only turn it on for an hour in the morning and evening, but once alone inside the room we cranked it up full blast and both sat on the floor beside it, giggling at the illicit warmth.

Dave looked ill, and sounded it too. His cough had gotten worse and his face was drawn. He complained very little, which I was grateful for, but his health concerned me. Now, with time on our hands, we had a chance to talk. It had all been a lot to take in, he said, but he was enjoying the challenge. From this point onwards we would be a little more in control of our schedule, and he was looking forward to that. I had not arranged for us to walk with anyone for the next few days and the terrain ahead was mostly countryside.

Dave was most excited about the thought of reaching Jordan, where we could camp wild. Both of us were more used to that arrangement, but we had been cautioned not to camp in the West Bank. It was unusual for Palestinians to sleep outside in pop-up tents in the way that Europeans and Americans are wont to do and, had we done so, our presence might put local Palestinians ill at ease, especially in areas where there were tensions with settlers. Camping would also, on a practical level, limit our chances to see towns and villages in the evenings, so we had sent our tents ahead to Jenin in the north, and now it was appealing to think again of the freedom of camping and choosing one's own place to stop and sleep.

Towering above Nablus is Gerizim, one of the two mountains that enclose the city, and whose summit is home to perhaps the world's smallest and oldest ethno-religious group, the Samaritans. The name is familiar from the parable of the Good Samaritan and has been borrowed by the UK support charity, but the Samaritans still in existence today are unique, and really rather odd. They are the remnants of an ancient people, and can trace their roots back 127 generations through the Holy Land; in a land dominated by the monotheistic trinity of Judaism, Islam and Christianity, the Samaritans are a fourth, distinct Abrahamic faith, living out a unique and harmonious relationship with their neighbours. They claim to be descended from two of the Twelve Tribes of Israel – Menashe and Ephraim, dating them to the seventh century BC – and at one point during Roman times their members numbered well over a million. Today, the Samaritan population is registered as just 802, split between an enclave in the Israeli city of Holon and the village of Kiryat Luza atop Mount Gerizim.

Kiryat Luza is a gated community that is both physically and politically separated from the Israeli – Palestinian conflict. In a region beset with ethnic and religious divisions, the Samaritans stand alone as impartial and unaffiliated. They share many commonalities with their Jewish neighbours, in as far as celebrating the seven festivals mentioned in the Torah and following the Five Books of Moses (Genesis, Exodus, Leviticus, Deuteronomy and Numbers). Culturally, however, given their geographical location, the Samaritans in Kiryat Luza are closer to the Arabs. Many work in Palestinian offices in Nablus and beyond, they use the Palestinian school system and all speak a local dialect of Arabic. As a rule, the Samaritans categorically refuse to associate with either 'side' of the geopolitical divide. They are well liked by both communities, carry both Israeli passports and Palestinian ID cards (and occasionally Jordanian passports too) and they often have a confusing but rather wonderful cross-pollination of names: Anwar Cohen, for example.

Dave needed to rest so I went to visit the Samaritans of Kiryat Luza alone. Outside the hotel I looked for a taxi and instead found a man called Majdi lurking by the entrance. He was very short with slicked-back hair and a sideways smile. His shoulders were permanently hunched: he looked like a Hollywood casting agent's impression of a 1980s Italian mobster. Majdi said that Kiryat Luza would be closed to visitors at that time of the evening, but that he knew the Samaritans well. He could get me in, *if* there were a few dollars in it for his trouble. He called a friend who arrived in a yellow taxi, and we set off up a long winding hill, climbing high above the city until the lights of Nablus spread out beneath us like a blanket.

We parked up in the village and I followed Majdi down a wide and quiet street. A blind man walked past us, feeling his way with a white stick. While Majdi repeatedly rang a doorbell, two other Samaritans passed us; one had a severe clubfoot and was resting heavily on the other. A very skinny teenager limped past after them. I glanced at Majdi but he offered no explanation.

The door opened, and we walked up some stairs in darkness, through a glass door and into an office. There sat a priest behind a computer, tapping away furiously. He wore a grey tunic and had a thick ashen beard. His head was covered by a heavy-knit and very un-cleric-like woollen bobble hat. 'This is Mr Husney Cohen,' said Majdi. 'He's a very important Samaritan priest, and he runs the museum. He knows more about the Samaritans than anyone else.'

Mr Husney Cohen did a great job of ignoring me and complained to Majdi that he shouldn't bring people to the village, especially late at night. It took five more minutes of typing before he even looked at me. 'Don't film me here,' he said. I casually lowered my camera, which had been recording everything. 'What are you writing?' I asked.

'I'm writing a Facebook post, and it's very important. That's why I didn't want to be interrupted. I have a new theory.'

'What is it?' I asked.

'That the original woman, Eve, caused all of the problems we have in the world right now,' he said sternly. Then, with a smile, he added, 'Her and the Arabs.' He winked at Majdi and they both laughed. Until now I hadn't noticed how close the two men were, but the joke showed affection underneath Husney's grumpiness.

He tore himself away from Facebook, changed into a smart red priestly cap, and we walked down the street to a large locked wooden door. Inside we would find the Samaritan Museum. I knew this because there was a small sign that read 'Samaritan Museum' by the door – otherwise, in the fading light of evening, it looked just like anywhere else in the quiet, ghostly town.

Husney switched on the lights inside. 'Okay,' he said. 'This is the history of the Israelite Samaritans. Please listen.'

For the next hour he spoke at me, almost non-stop. It was a tour de force: performance, part history lesson, part sermon. He traced for me his own lineage back to Moses, and pointed to a chart that proved the bloodline. He held up some family trees and pictures of previous high priests. Oil paintings of Romans and men in loincloths on mountain tops were pointed to, and I was told to write everything down. The schism with Judaism, he said, came early. 'We are *not* Jews,' he reminded me more than once. Jews believe that Jerusalem was the location of God's commandment to Moses to kill his son, Isaac. The Samaritans know the real site to be Mount Gerizim. There were some artefacts and a few barbs aimed at the other religions. There were a lot of maps, and a small amount of singing. His phone rang regularly and he would answer, chastise the person at the other end, and then continue once more with his encyclopaedic lecture on Samaritan culture.

Mark Twain also met the Samaritans. 'Talk of family and old descent!' he writes. 'The Samaritans could [...] name their fathers straight back without a flaw.' It was quite something, now as then, and Husney was rather enjoying himself. I was shown a copy of the Ten Commandments of the Samaritans, which are different from the Christian and Jewish decrees in that they dictate the sanctity of Mount Gerizim, and finally I was treated to a lengthy chant in Ancient Hebrew while Husney stared trance-like at a leather-bound and very old-looking copy of the Torah which had been carefully placed on a red felt altar. I felt like I had, very briefly, entered another world.

Husney Cohen told me he had written 17 books – he has published at least another one since then. He had discovered, he said, 'the secret to why the Israelites spent 40 years in the Sinai Desert'.

'Why?' I asked.

'I can't tell you.'

'Oh.' I said. 'Can you give me a clue?'

'No. You wouldn't understand, and it's really a very big secret now. But it will be very important soon.'

'Did they just get lost?'

'No! They were much too clever for that. I cannot tell you why, but they did *not* get lost. Write that down.'

I wrote down '*Husney says the Israelites did NOT get lost. Research if this is true.*' 'Did you write it down just like I said?' he asked me. I nodded.

Husney Cohen's brother was the 133rd high priest of the Samaritans. He showed me a picture of them together and then his phone rang again. I wondered what it was like to have a brother as a high priest – perhaps it was like Ireland in the old days where there was a hierarchy of male offspring, with the eldest being the most important. I thought that being in charge of the museum might be a little frustrating for him if he was an author and a genius. When he came back, I asked: 'Is it frustrating being an author and maybe a genius, but having to run the museum while your brother is a high priest?' 'No. My book will be very important,' he said again. 'No one else has ever discovered this thing apart from me. It is entirely new.' I promised to read it when it was translated into English.

Majdi and I left, and went to the corner shop where we bought a couple of beers and drank them at a table outside. Alcohol is prohibited in Nablus, but Kiryat Luza operates with impunity, and Majdi and I raised our glasses in an unspoken toast to sneaky beers and a very bizarre encounter.

I asked about the strange cast of limping and blind men we'd seen when we first arrived, and Majdi set down his glass. 'The Samaritans are dying out,' he began. Traditionally, he said, members could only marry within the community, and over many generations the inevitable inbreeding has resulted in an extremely high number of birth defects and disabilities. The situation was becoming critical. 'But don't worry about them,' he smiled. We ordered another drink.

I learned later that the desperation has encouraged two rather remarkable forays into the modern world: genetic testing and internet brides. The latter has led a small number of foreign women – mostly from the Ukraine – to move to Mount Gerizim and convert to Samaritanism. I wished that I had more time to explore the village, although I didn't particularly like the idea of telling Husney that I wanted to ask more questions.

We drove back to the hotel. I thought about the Samaritans for a long time. I've long been fascinated by sectarianism; in Northern

Ireland, it's a part of the social fabric. In the West Bank, the Samaritans had a unique position as potential mediators; in a conflict created by religious intolerance and resulting actions, I wondered if this ancient sect trying to adapt to modern life atop a hill in the West Bank might play an important role. It would not be the strangest thing to happen here, by a long shot.

# Sky Trails

D ave and I left Nablus on a bright, warm day, walking along broad and busy streets and waving politely to the many beeping taxis that drove past. We had been told not to leave the city without sampling its two most famous exports: soap made from olive oil, and a cheesy pastry soaked in sweet syrup called *kanafe*. There's only so much excitement that can be generated by even the greatest of soaps, so we went straight for the cake. *Kanafe* is eaten across the Middle East, but Nablus is said to be its original home, and Nablusis are adamant that theirs is the best. We ordered two slices from the stall of an old Arab with a wooden stick, just outside the *souq*. He smiled a chequered grin as he served us, piling extra sugary syrup on top. Dave and I agreed that it was tasty and sickly in equal measure – the sort of food that requires a lie-down afterwards. '*Zaki, zaki*, eh?' the old man said. 'Delicious, delicious!' We replied that it was, and were rewarded with two more, even larger slices.

Nablus sprawled for miles to the north before slowly the houses thinned out and we were back in fields of wheat and barley. In the distance, olive-green mounds rolled onwards to the horizon in all directions, with the occasional telltale red roofs of the settlements atop some, and blocky Palestinian villages in the valleys below. Oleander and cypress trees grew out of the earth nearby at an angle, their branches reaching out in a frozen grasp for the sun. A road in the distance carried some cars heading north, but an easterly wind took the sound of motors away to the ears of others. The clicking of crickets and melody of unseen birdsong were our only audible company.

For all of the access problems in the West Bank, there is one group of visitors that manage to travel entirely freely: birds. Twice a year, in spring and autumn, over half a billion birds – and nearly 300 species – pass over Palestine on their annual migration between southern Africa and northern Europe. Their journey is often a hazardous one with hunters, storms and exhaustion threatening at various turns but, in stark contrast to the political situation on the ground, Palestine has always been a relatively safe and stable place en route for these particular migrants. Dave and I did not see the griffon vultures, with their 3-m wingspans and distinctive black-tipped wings, nor the highly regarded ospreys with their young, but we did see a variety of other species like kingfishers, egrets, starlings, jays, and others that I was not qualified to identify.

It was a short walk to the town of Sebastia, another modern town that stood perched on the shoulders of the past. The main road consisted of two potholed concrete strips and a few mangled street lamps, and on it we were met by a group of young Palestinian men, who walked down the centre of the road while along the edges a couple of young women in bright pink hijabs stepped nimbly over piles of garbage. In the main square we kicked a football around with some schoolboys, who cheered when Dave or I passed it to them accurately. Most wore football shirts of Real Madrid or Barcelona. Football is a wonderful ice-breaker around the world, and we had learned early on that an effective way to form a connection with the groups of children that we met was to ask them the question that plays on the mind of every little boy: 'Do you prefer Ronaldo, or Messi?'

Cups of tea were brought and we sat in the shade of the square. A young man called Zaid with an immaculately preened beard told us that the coffee shop behind us had been built in the 1920s by the British during the Mandate era, along with a school across the road. They had tried to outdo the Ottomans, who had previously built a mosque and a Qur'anic study hall. Across the road, we could see the remains of a

Crusader church which now housed an ornate and beautiful mosque, the minaret of which peeked up above the strata of constructions from other eras. 'It was built on the ruins of a Byzantine church,' said Zaid. 'In the crypt is the burial place of John the Baptist. We have all sorts of history here.'

'We have rummy too!' shouted an elderly man in a keffiyeh with a bushy moustache and deeply lined face. 'Rummy is better than history,' he mumbled. He took out some cards and other old men began to appear, as if in response to some silent summons. Soon there was a small army of them. Two large tables were requisitioned, and the game began. Teas were brought, sticks set down, and faces that began with toothless smiles and crinkled cheeks now set their jaws hard for the battle ahead.

Zaid led us through the town to the jewel in the crown of Sebastia's relics – the remains of the Roman city. 'It used to be called Augustus,' said Zaid. 'King Herod named it after the Emperor. They say that the site is 10,000 years old. It has been lived in by Canaanites, Israelites, ancient Greeks, Romans and Byzantines. Then it was run by Ottomans and British, and then Jordanians and Israelis. And now we are in charge.'

The city was originally called Samaria (this is where the Samaritans take their name from). It is referred to frequently in the Bible, and the archaeological site is now extensive. Over an area the size of many football fields were spread the ruins of a Roman stadium, a colonnaded forum and a theatre. Most impressive of all, the remains of Herod's great temple to his emperor Augustus sprawled out across the hillside towards the nearest summit, and it was not hard to see the strategic value of the location. Below, in the valleys on either side, every village was visible.

We wandered around the ancient streets and I ran my hand over the base of the columns, some of which were inscribed with now indecipherable markings. Zaid said there was much more beneath the ground: a group of international archaeologists had plans to excavate further. Someone in the town said they'd heard only 6 per cent had been uncovered so far. The sun dropped to caress the hilltops, and Dave and I ran to the summit to watch it fall. An ethereal orange light flooded the ancient city around us, saturating the green, greys and browns of Sebastia, and another day was gone.

# Coffee and Cigarettes

Our guest house was a quaint arrangement of old stone buildings constructed around a small courtyard decorated with mosaics. The room that Dave and I shared was on the third floor, accessible via an M.C. Escher-esque set of metal stairwells that wound around and behind the walls until we could see the water tanks on roofs nearby. It seemed a shame to have to go. What I really wanted was another day off.

Dave lured me out with the promise of freshly baked bread and we set off north, leaving behind the ruins of Sebastia. We passed too the remnants of Masoudiya station, a stop on the once-great Hijaz railway that, in a very different political landscape, had connected Medina, Damascus and Haifa. It ran for 1,600 km – about the same distance that I would walk to reach Mount Sinai – and was built to dramatically ease the journey to Mecca for Haj. Its potential, however, was always just out of reach and World War I, the collapse of the Ottoman Empire and the series of subsequent disasters that befell the Levant all conspired to doom the railway. Lawrence of Arabia made sure of its demise by repeatedly blowing it up so that now all that endures from the mighty project are brief reminders like that at Sebastia – modern-day fossils of unrealised ambition.

There was a chill in the winter morning despite a cobalt blue sky, and goats clustered under citrus trees for warmth in numbers. It was a long and steady climb through land that was cultivated on every possible square inch, before a final steep, rocky and rutted hillside took us to the summit of Mount Bayzeed, past two very confused looking farmers with a broken-down tractor. We stood at well over 700 m altitude, and atop the otherwise bare plateau we found a small and relatively intact rectangular *maqam*. These *maqam*s are tombs of Islamic holy men and dot many of the hilltops of the West Bank; this particular one, which Zaid had told us to look out for, was constructed during Ottoman rule, and the mountain on which it stood had been named for the ninth-century Sufi mystic Bayazid Bastami.

There are many connections between high, elevated, remote places and the act of worship, and the most obvious is the literal 'closeness' to God; an attempt to climb up as far as possible towards an elevated, omniscient deity. Both Christians and Muslims are recorded as having prayed at the *maqam*s that dot the high points of the Palestinian countryside, but when we arrived it seemed no one had been there in quite some time. Dave and I took shelter from the wind inside the crumbling walls, and I imagined ascending from Sebastia in the hope that my wishes would be granted. The walk alone would release enough endorphins to make most people feel better.

When we stood on top of the cornerstones, we could see farther than at any other time in our journey through the Holy Land. To the east was the coast, a cerulean blue ocean punctuated by the high-rise skyscrapers of Tel Aviv. Hazy blocks from the port city of Haifa were visible beyond that, and to the north the mountains of the occupied Golan Heights – the Syrian territory that has been occupied by Israel since 1967 – towered above the Palestinian landscape. It was the closest thing I'd had so far to a religious experience. That is, until Dave opened a bag of chocolate-covered cashew nuts and we nestled into the shelter once more, gorging on sugar.

We talked about walking, and how rubbish it often was. I then grumbled about our packs and Dave whinged about the lack of proper paths. That was a perfect warm-up and we moved on to complain mercilessly about everyone that we'd ever met, and how annoying all the Palestinians were. We tore into the Israelis for making everything so difficult and then, one by one, we dissected our mutual friends back home until their flaws were evident for all to see. It was fabulous.

As it stood, we were walking 25 km a day, and both of us were exhausted. My head hurt from trying to understand everything, my hand ached from scribbling furiously each time we met someone, and most of my limbs felt like they would probably fall off at some point in the next few days. Dave, by his own admission, was much worse. He had recovered fully from the food poisoning and he was getting stronger, but the rigours of repeatedly walking eight hours a day for the first time ever left him constantly fatigued. His feet in particular were in constant agony.

'I do like walking, though,' he said brightly. Our earlier complaints were now completely forgotten, and I joined in. 'It's the best way to travel,' I enthused. That is true for anywhere, but perhaps a place like the West Bank most of all. A journey here in a car would have been one of checkpoints, questions and limited access. On foot, we had the impression of total freedom. Our brains moved at 3 miles an hour in time with our feet, and we cut unimposing figures when we turned up in villages.

Our path followed a long saddle from the summit of Bayzeed to that of Mount Hureish where we rested by another *maqam* and then descended into the town of Sanur. The next morning, we walked out of town and past an outpost. It sat right at the top of the hill above Sanur, only a few metres away from the country track used by Palestinians. The outpost consisted of just three buildings, all of which were heavily bricked up to fortify its walls. There were no windows, and the roofs were reinforced with corrugated iron. Barbed wire adorned the perimeter. Everything that possibly could be was enveloped in thick, black chain-links, and a barking dog the size of a small bear heralded our passing. The most notable feature of all was a huge plastic poster of Israeli Prime Minister Benjamin Netanyahu, accompanied by some text in Hebrew. His face had been smeared with blood.

The land around us now felt bigger, just as Anwar had said it would. Below our high paths, large verdant plains opened up. This was the first sign that we were nearing the flat lands around the city of Jenin, and the end of our time in the West Bank. We met only a few shepherds on the trails, and our exchanges were brief: they would ask us where we were going, and I would lie to them. I would only tell them our next destination rather than saying we were heading to Jenin, or Jordan, or Sinai, because inevitably they would not believe that it was possible for anyone to walk that far, or insist that we were headed in the wrong direction.

Dave was not a man with thin patience, but I could tell he was beginning to get annoyed with me after I misdirected us over two summits that we had no need to climb to. On the far side I realised I was quite lost, and so began to follow a compass bearing in the rough direction of our destination that evening. This took us through a large orchard, over two fields with high fences, across a main road and almost into someone's kitchen. 'Are we lost?' asked Dave finally. 'Of course not,' I snapped. 'This is a short cut.' We didn't speak for the next hour.

The Masar Ibrahim is not a hiking trail in the sense of the great American routes like the PCT or Appalachian, or the European *Grande Randonée* routes. At least, not yet. There are no waymarkings,[37] and there is no purpose-built path for hikers. Instead, there are digital GPX points created by those who scouted the routes, and these can be imported into a GPS for hikers like Dave and me to follow. I also carried a compass and a printout of some topographical maps that the Masar Ibrahim team had created. The best general maps of the West Bank are made by the Israeli military, and they are surprisingly easy to get hold of. In Jerusalem, a friend who had lived and worked there for a decade had told us that it might be worth putting half a day into learning Hebrew so we could read these maps. He also warned us to be careful of firing zones: there were certain sections of the trail that passed through parts of Area C which, on particular weekdays, were used for shooting practice. Both parts of his advice felt very much like the casual tips that could only be given by someone who had spent 10 years in this odd world.

We briefly joined a road on which the highlight was seeing a cow asleep in the car park of a restaurant. It was not a pleasant road; cars sped past much too fast, and the unforgiving nature of the tarmac made my feet hurt. Beside the restaurant was a shipping container which had been converted into the office of an auto-shop, and a very pale-looking Palestinian called us inside. His hair was blond and his skin fairer than Dave's. His name was Haman and he made us thick, black viscous coffee and offered us a seat in the office. In the background, a bearded colleague nodded at us and said 'Shalom'. This was a greeting occasionally offered by those unsure of us – it felt like a test, feeling us out to see if we were secretly Israeli.[38]

Haman asked where we were from. 'Ah,' he said, looking at Dave. 'His lot gave our country away.' His English was superb – he said he had learned first at school and then honed it by watching HBO box sets on Netflix. We talked about the upcoming presidential elections in the US. 'I dislike all of them,' he said, 'but Donald Trump is probably the best.' Dave or I, or both, snorted involuntarily. 'But he's a bigot and a racist and [...] all sorts of other things!' said Dave. 'He's a strong man,' said Haman. 'He's like a proper Arab dictator.'

He asked us when we thought the Palestinians would get freedom. I shrugged non-committally. 'We cannot do it without international assistance,' he said. 'But it will come. We need to kick out the Jewish, and make Palestine a land for the Arabs again.' It was rare that I heard opinions like this. Many Palestinians would talk about their dislike for Israelis, but most would be careful to distinguish between *Israelis* and a general slur of all Jews. It was also relatively typical for Palestinians to clarify that they did not see Judaism as an inherently bad religion, and for them to tell us about the many Jews who had once lived in the Middle East and had been an important part of the fabric of the region before the creation of Israel. A further caveat was that often when Palestinians said *Israelis*, they really meant, rather more specifically, *settlers* (or occasionally a slightly more general *Zionists*). It is hard to generalise such things, of course, but settlers are the primary cause of Palestinian fury because it is they who are building on land inside the West Bank; that is to say, *Palestinian* land. The motivation for Israelis to move to settlements varies: some do so for cheaper housing and more space, while others do so for ideological reasons. Most Palestinians I met did not much care for such distinctions: anyone on a settlement was breaking international law.

I asked Haman whether he preferred the one- or two-state solution.[39] 'One state,' he said. 'But with us in charge, and everyone else leaving!' By now we had a small audience in the doorway. A mechanic spoke up. 'I'd live under the banner of Israel, if it meant peace.' The men either side of him exclaimed loudly in disgust. Did they not want peace? asked the mechanic. Of course, said a lanky man in greasy overalls. 'But there are [...]' He deferred to Haman for a translation. 'Non-negotiables,' he said. Haman pointed to the man in overalls. 'He says it's simple. We must have our own land. We must feel like we have freedom, which means we must be able to have hope. And we must get back our own currency.'[40] Suddenly, things had gotten quite tense. Dave looked at the man in overalls. 'So do you prefer Ronaldo, or Messi [...]?'

We arrived in the village of Arraba by early afternoon. Like Nablus and Sebastia, Arraba too had been inhabited in Roman times, and during the Ottoman era it was a hub on the trade route that connected Nablus to Mount Carmel via the great plain below. The town sat on a hill overlooking the 'Plain of Arraba', and the centre was awash with relics of the past. Smooth cobbles led us into a maze of streets past jaundiced, tumbling structures left behind by the Ottomans, and terminating at the palace of Abd al-Hadi, the seat of a clan that once ruled much of the region. The shell of their compound had been used during the First Intifada as a hide-out for gunmen and now was regenerating as the site of the local municipality. There were plans to create guest houses and a women's co-operative, and various plaques hung from the brickwork with the logos of international funding bodies that had committed to the refurbishment.

We stopped at a small shop and were greeted by Amir, whose entire day seemed brightened by our very presence. He was a big jolly fellow with a huge lustrous beard and a traditional tunic, and he was young, perhaps my age, but dressed in the conservative style of someone much

older. 'You are foreign,' he shouted to us. '*Ahlan wa sahlan*' – Come in!
We sat as he made us a lunch of lentil soup and toasted pitta bread,
cooked over a single gas burner behind the counter. The shop was small
but crowded, selling everything a villager might need, from water to
vegetables to yellow rubber gloves and bin bags.

'I am a Muslim!' he told us. We tried to look surprised. 'Islam is just
so wonderful,' he enthused. 'Once, I was a bad Muslim. I was only
interested in cars and motorbikes and women. Then, I realised that
I wasn't being true to Allah, so I changed. Allah is in my heart now.'
He left us briefly to serve a customer. I wasn't that interested in cars,
but I did think motorbikes were cool. I also liked women. Dave and
I agreed that we'd probably both make very bad Muslims by Amir's
reckoning scale. 'Being a good Muslim is about charity and kindness, and
also worship,' Amir continued. 'It is peace. This [...] Da'esh [...] they
are not Islam. They are nothing. Islam is peace.' He smiled at us with the
face of a true believer. 'I hope to see you in paradise.'

The afternoon *adhan* – the call to prayer – rang out across the
cobbles outside. *Allahu Akbar* – God is Great – sounded four times.
Then: *Ash hadu an-la ilaha illa Allah.* 'There is no god but God.' The
muezzin had a deep, gravelly voice, and spluttered into a coughing fit
through the microphone. There was a short pause, and a tape recording
was turned on to play through the loudspeaker instead. Amir smiled at
us again. 'Will you come with me to the mosque?'

It was a pretty mosque, but simple. A single minaret soared high
above the dome, which was set in amongst the palaces of the ancient
village. A small adornment from the Qur'an weaved across the top of the
entrance. We took off our shoes and stepped inside the threshold where
a strange man hugged us both three times. Amir went to perform his
ablutions; a noisy affair and a source of great pleasure to all those taking
part. It involved a line of men spitting, coughing and washing every
part of their body that could conceivably be reached without stripping
off inappropriately. Dave and I sat cross-legged in a small alcove off to
the side.

We watched from an alcove as seven or eight men lined up facing
the imam and, making sure they were orientated towards Mecca, began

their rituals – formalities that have changed little in 1,400 years. A friend in Muscat once told me that the movements are designed to combine as many beneficial elements as possible: physical work, meditation, spiritual elevation. The men in front of us recited the holy words to themselves and then prostrated themselves multiple times. It took about 15 minutes, after which Amir came over to us, his grin as wide as ever.

'There are many good men here. Some bad men too,' he said. 'But I try to teach them. Allah is so good to me.' I asked what some of the good things were that Allah had done for him. 'Last year I decided it was time for a wife,' Amir replied immediately. 'So I asked Allah, and he provided one. She has memorised the whole Qur'an and in public she wears a face veil. Only people who cannot marry her are allowed to see her face. She is quite wonderful.'

As we left, Dave was gently told off for putting his left foot into a shoe first. It was bad luck. I asked how luck worked with Islam and Amir laughed. 'Oh, Leon,' he said. There was nothing he could say to help the foolish enquiries of an unbeliever.

On top of a small rise on the outskirts of town lay a large house belonging to the Mardawi family, who had offered to host us for the night. Mustafa Mardawi greeted us. His shirt was neatly pressed and he bowed slightly as he shook our hands. 'Please mind the dogs,' he said, indicating a pit bull and a chihuahua who buzzed around our ankles.

Inside, the Mardawi house was modestly well decorated. Two plush sofas arced around a large TV and, off to the left, a big kitchen opened up behind a breakfast bar. From behind a collection of hanging pots, Mustafa's wife Ayat rushed out to meet us. 'We're so glad you could come,' she said, shaking our hands and beaming. We were handed cups of tea; this was the beginning of a consumption that would last many hours.

When dinner time arrived, the table was laden with meticulously prepared *mensef* – lamb, dried yoghurt and rice – and alongside it an array of hummus, baba ganoush, peppers, olives, goat's cheese boiled in water to soften it, pitta, tomatoes, fried potatoes, and oil pressed from the olives that grew in the trees below the house. Ayat Mardawi's olive salad was the most important item on the table, served in a special bowl and taking pride of place in the centre of the table. It was famous all across the region, I was told, and I had no reason to doubt it.

We were joined by the Mardawi offspring and some of their friends from the village. Everyone spoke wonderful English and either side of me Mahmoud and Adnan – Mustafa's teenage sons – talked about Shakespeare and HBO television series. 'I preferred *The Sopranos* to *The Wire*,' said Adnan, just as his sister was simultaneously guiding Dave through their collection of literature that sat on a shelf above the sofa.

'Are you surprised by us?' asked Adnan later. I said they were certainly a very special family. 'We've had quite a few people come to stay with us. I think many of them expect to find people fighting in the West Bank, and that the families here will be super-conservative and maybe judgemental or whatever. But there are other families like us. Not everyone, but there are others who value a variety of education and culture like we do.'

More people arrived and the evening drifted into a haze of sugar and coffee, and smoke from the cigarettes of the many mustachioed men who sat with us on the sofa. Mahmoud sat alongside me and said, 'You know, sometimes I hate it here. It's so complicated. But it's also home, and we're really proud of our country. I think it's up to all of us individually to make a difference. I read this quote once that said *"Be the change you want to see in the world."* That makes sense to me. I'd like to be an artist, I think.'

When we eventually retired to bed, Mahmoud hugged us and Adnan said, 'It's been a real joy for all of us to talk with you. We love hearing your opinion on the world.' I had not expected to spend an evening in such fine conversational company, and certainly not to hear a Palestinian teenager quote Gandhi to me. What I wanted to say to him was that families like them gave me great hope for Palestine and for the region. Instead I hiccupped loudly and tripped over a toy tractor as I backed out of the room. They were all so polite that no one laughed until they thought I was well out of earshot.

# Please Meet Jesus

More than once, the West Bank felt to me like Northern Ireland. I have developed a reputation amongst friends for comparing places that I have been to my homeland, but Palestine felt justified. On a base level both shared hills, some of which were green. The shades and sizes were different, but I'm not picky. More emphatically the West Bank, like Northern Ireland, would often feel like one big connected community. It was hard for us to walk anywhere without meeting someone that knew someone that we'd already met. In most villages we were apprehended upon arrival before we could begin to ask for our contacts. Someone would spot us and say: 'Hey, you're the foreign hikers! Are you looking for Ali?'

Family names carried weight and recognition, and we'd be asked who we knew; when we listed them, there would be nods of approval. Gossip spread like wildfire through the villages as we'd seen in Kufr Malek but, perhaps because it was such a small area, or maybe because we weren't privy to everything, it didn't seem fierce. There were no warnings to be wary of a certain family or town or region as I'd found elsewhere. Perhaps that was a part of it too: Palestinians felt like they had a common enemy and so, on a basic human level, there was little to distrust among themselves. The mess of internal Palestinian politics would indicate this to be false on that level, but it was our experience whilst walking.

After leaving the Mardawi family we walked in the company of Mohammed Atari, an archaeologist by trade who took great pleasure in talking us through thousands of years of history on the plains where we walked. Nowadays the valley floor was covered in onions, wheat, Egyptian cucumbers and, mostly, tobacco. 'We're very proud of our tobacco,' said Mohammed. 'The big companies like Marlboro never did well here. We grow it all ourselves. Arab cigarettes are only about 4 shekels[41] for 20. They're cheaper than food!' As with most Palestinian men, Mohammed was serious about his smoking, and life sometimes seemed to him to be simply the events that filled the breaks between cigarettes.

On top of Mount Barid we rested and looked out across the plains. A man on a donkey appeared, as was to be expected by this point. The view was a new type of vista to us, dominated by large, flat expanses of ruffled brown fields. Most striking of all we could once again see the Separation Barrier – the first time since Jerusalem. From the hilltop it looked simpler than I remembered. The last time I saw it, it had been 8 m high and made out of concrete blocks. In the countryside of the Jenin region it was less physically imposing. It was not, however, less effective. The Barrier here consisted of a large barbed wire fence in the middle, often electrified. On either side was a walkway of sand – to show footprints – and then a trench. Beyond that, a military road patrolled by Humvees. Finally, there was another row of barbed wire.

Mohammed remembered when it was built. His home was in a small village that became surrounded on three sides by the Barrier. 'Before the wall,' he said, 'I used to cycle to Nazareth and out to the coast. We used to see the Israelis all the time. We had to, because we lived so close. We would talk to them and buy things from them, and we got to know many of them well.' The wall changed everything, he said, but not for the reasons that were usually talked about. 'When the wall went up there were no more interactions,' he said. 'Now there are Palestinians who have no idea who is living on the other side. They don't know like I do that many of the people there are very normal. So they are scared and imagine the worst. The Israelis do the same and both governments encourage that.'

This seemed to be perhaps the most concise and damning summation of the problem that I'd heard so far. We sat in silence while Mohammed made a small fire and brewed tea, dropping stalks of thyme into the boiling water. The land stretched out before us, broken only by the unnatural barrier. On the Israeli and the Palestinian sides, the earth was the same colour and texture, but for Mohammed, the wire was a boundary to his world.

We stopped in the afternoon in the town of Burquin. The name, Mohammed told us, was derived from the Arabic word for leprosy. In the centre there was a church which claimed to be the third oldest in the world (after the Holy Sepulchre in Jerusalem and the Nativity in Bethlehem) and which was built on the site of Jesus's miraculous healing of the Ten Lepers. By now, age and eminence seemed almost irrelevant – a holy site needed to really pull out all the stops to impress us. We reserved judgement. Mohammed got in a taxi on the outskirts to head home, and we walked alone to the church to meet his friend Osama, a Christian Arab who was big and bald and looked grumpy even when he wasn't. His English was poor, and outside the church he unsmilingly beckoned to us: 'Come – please meet Jesus.'

It was a pretty church set inside old, worn walls. A heavenly light picked out the creamy beige of the facade, and metal icons glinted back at the sun. A small courtyard was decorated with a large Christmas tree. Inside, the church shimmered with gold. There were images of Jesus everywhere and, by the sanctuary, a large red velvet altar underneath a chandelier of blown glass. In the corner was a small stone shrine, set by the hole where the lepers were said to been kept in isolation until Jesus saved them.

A Greek Orthodox priest came out to meet us. He was too small for his hat, and he shook our hands solemnly. I told him he had a very lovely church and he nodded. There was a brief silence. 'Would you like biscuit?' he said. We drank tea and ate biscuits and smiled at each other and then the priest showed us a tunnel outside where the Christians had hidden from the Romans. 'Bad Romans,' said Osama. We agreed.

Beyond Burquin, the city sprawl of Jenin enveloped the countryside. It was Friday, the Islamic holy day, and the streets were packed. Tractors, donkeys and groups of giggling girls and well-groomed boys blocked our path. We were tired and pushed through the crowds until we arrived at Cinema Jenin, an old picture-house that had been refurbished with international aid money and reimagined as a hostel-cum-cinema. On a plaque outside it said: 'Thank you to Roger Waters for his kind donation.' The receptionists grinned at us. 'You know Pink Floyd?' he asked. I nodded. 'Another Brick in the Wall!' he said, to make sure. I had High Hopes for our Time there, and handed over the Money. We were shown to our room.

The only other guests were two Germans in their early 20s who had been working at a kibbutz near Haifa. 'When we finished, we decided to travel around,' said one. 'This is our first stop on our tour of Israel. Next we'll go to Nablus and then to Bethlehem.' I suggested to him that the Palestinians might not like it if he referred to those places as being in Israel. He didn't understand, so Dave and I left him and went to find a burger joint. It was our last night in the West Bank.

The last Palestinian that we spoke to in the West Bank was stood on a roadside about 500 m from the checkpoint. He was selling CDs and beach footballs from a small cart, and fat, cold raindrops hammered on the hood of my coat as I huddled under a makeshift awning to hear him. He asked Dave where we were from. 'Ah,' he said. 'You gave away our country.'

A crowd of 100 or more Palestinian men were gathered outside the checkpoint. Some had permits to work in Israel and would cross there and back each day. For others, the checkpoint was simply a business opportunity: they sold tea and plastic-wrapped snacks to workers going to and fro. Dave and I were about to wave our European passports and make a journey that they never could, into a land that they believed was theirs.

The Holy Land can be an overwhelming place – it always has been. Much of the historical writing from the litany of pilgrims and travellers begins with sycophantic proclamations before arrival but often ends with forthright, disconcerting conclusions. It was not until we were in the process of crossing the checkpoint that I could see how I might unwittingly fit into this canon myself. It was also true that the alchemy of elements at play in the West Bank had created a particularly intense experience that was unlikely to be replicated on any other parts of this journey. I had arrived with expectations very much rooted in the Christian traditions, and I had indeed found a place where faith and conviction were conspicuously central. Many – perhaps most – of the men that we met in the towns and villages talked often about their religion. Their stories would almost always circle back to faith, either as the start or end point of their thoughts: the genesis or justification of ideas.

This trend sat naturally enough on a land steeped in the history of zealots and fanatics as well as the more calmly pious and devoted, and meant that we would often hear a full spectrum of opinion returning to the same root. The implications of all this struck me only later, but they were best summed up by a Palestinian-American that I met in the *souq* in Nablus. 'Everyone is moving to the extremes of their religions,' he said. 'The Muslims are getting stricter, and the Christians are looking inwards to try and protect themselves from disappearing. The Jews on the other side become more hard-line. People do it as a reaction to everyone else doing it, and it means that society is growing apart. We are splitting at the seams.'

It was a damming prediction, but I had also seen another side: families like the Mardawis, and hikers like Mohammed Atari and Anwar Dawabsheh. The Masar Ibrahim had taken us directly through the heart of Palestine and exposed, however briefly, the strata of society for us to see in snapshot. At times it did feel like it was splitting apart – in Kufr Malek, and in Duma – but at others it was being stitched back together by those with a vision of a path forward. I left with much more hope than fear, and that felt like a sentiment in keeping with the Palestinians I had spoken to. Dave and I had met angry people, but rarely, if at all, had we met violent people. We encountered much more sadness than we did aggression, and we saw no weapons among civilians, nor did we hear of wishes to cause harm to soldiers or settlers. Most of all, we heard plans for the future: sometimes wishes for a simpler or freer life, but often, too, tangible, actionable plans for shaping the course of what would come. It is impossible to be surrounded by courage, resilience and confidence like this and to come away feeling pessimistic. In a land of such faith, one must believe that things will get better, and the very existence of the Masar Ibrahim and the ambitious, forward-thinking people that it connected gave me a platform for such optimism.

# The Forbidden Land

There are 1.5 million Arabs living in present-day Israel – over 20 per cent of the population – many of whom are based in hubs like Nazareth and Rahat. The majority are Muslims, but just under 20 per cent identify as Christian or Druze. Their position as a significant minority is a strange one: they ostensibly enjoy greater civil rights than Palestinians in the West Bank (for example, the right to vote), and villages like Sandala, which Dave and I passed through immediately beyond the checkpoint, do not feel all that different from those across the Wall (except perhaps that the roads are better and there is less litter). There are, however, many layers to the coexistence.

The Israeli parliament, the Knesset, has 120 seats, 17 of which, at the time of writing, are held by Arab members. Religious Zionism and ultra-Orthodox parties control 30 seats, and the current government coalition includes members of both a right-wing nationalist party and one committed to religious Zionism.[42] There are a number of laws that are widely thought to be discriminatory to Arab citizens of Israel;[43] ethnic separation is encouraged by the school system, and internal racism is on the rise. Despite efforts to combat the increasing atmosphere of nationalism and separationism, Israel seems to be at one of its lowest ebbs in the gulf between Jews and Arabs.[44]

We traced the route of the Separation Barrier – this time from the Israeli side – and climbed into a dense thicket of trees that would lead us to the mountains beyond. Surrounded by the thick, musty smell of pine trees, I looked up at the heavy canopy which filtered the sunlight so it fell about us in dappled bursts. This was the first forest we had seen since arriving in the Holy Land.

The trails that we followed were beautifully beaten through surrounding undergrowth, and regular blazes allowed us to completely dispense with maps. Israel has over 15,000 km of marked hiking trails in the country, all of which are maintained by a non-profit environmental organisation. This includes the 1,000 km-long Israel National Trail (INT). Israeli trails are often included in various 'World's Best Hiking Route'-type round-ups and, unlike in the West Bank, walking is a popular recreational activity with tens of thousands of hikers taking to the INT each year.

Healthy-looking walkers sporting daypacks and branded neon windcheaters occasionally passed us by. At a scenic pull-off by a road, a young couple watched their toddlers totter unsteadily along a small section of trail. Everyone we saw categorically ignored us – not through any rudeness or distrust, but simply because we were no longer anomalies. Only one, later that afternoon, smiled and offered a 'shalom'. The sudden change from our cult status in the West Bank was jarring, but not entirely unpleasant. It felt, in fact, like trails in more conservative Western countries, where I generally feel that I'm unlikely to extract much conversation from anyone I meet, but that if I broke a leg they'd probably know how to make a splint and there'd be a chopper on the way in minutes.

Between the Jordan Valley and the adjacent Jezreel Valley lies the impressive Gilboa mountain range, where King Saul is said to have fallen on his sword before the advancing Philistine army in 1010 BC. King David then cursed the mountain to avenge his slain ruler, but if there are any lasting effects of the jinx they are not obvious – it was a very beautiful mountain, with waist-high grass lining the trail even in winter. From the peak of Mount Barkan we could look out across the patchwork quilt of Palestinian tobacco fields, a pattern that led all the way back to Mount Barid where we had sat with Mohammed Atari a few days prior.

We camped for the first time since leaving Jerusalem, pitching our tents by a small picnic area while two families in American-style sport utility vehicles lit a barbecue close by. A light rain fell that night; it was glorious to be outside at nightfall and I fell asleep to the gentle sounds of raindrops on canvas and the scurries and scuttles of forest life in the undergrowth.

I awoke to find that Dave had hidden a 1-kg bag of chocolate cashew nuts at the bottom of my rucksack as a Christmas surprise; I'd been obliviously carrying it since Nablus, and my discovery, at long last, caused him much amusement. Weight on hiking trips is a constant concern, and rarely does an hour pass without a reassessment of what a pack contains and what might be sacrificed. I spent most of the morning planning revenge for being forced to carry an extra $\frac{1}{25}$ of my overall bulk, feeding my vicious thoughts with chocolate cashews and ignoring the irony.

We descended a steep switchback to the fertile Jezreel Valley, which spread out before us in a series of rich emerald green fields and deep blue fish pools and streams that reflected the early eastern sunlight back up the mountain. More exotic crops like watermelon and oranges grew alongside the standard fare of wheat and beans, and kibbutzim were dotted along the plain, seemingly at random. In the distance the bleached buildings of the city of Beit She'an were just visible at the point where sky and ground became one in the haze.

The Gilboa area is popular with Israeli tourists, especially in winter, and the nearby Gan HaShlosha National Park, famed for its hot springs that form around the Amal Stream, was named by *Time* magazine as one of the 20 best parks in the world. Thirty kilometres to the north of us lay Nazareth, the de facto capital of Israeli Arabs, with a population that is almost entirely made up of Muslims and Christians.[45] Even closer was Megiddo, a small kibbutz built on an ancient city and a place that, according to an evangelical Christian reading of the Book of Revelation, will be the site of the final battle between Jesus Christ and Satan. Its Greek name is perhaps more familiar: Armageddon.

Our ears were full of marginal chatter in Hebrew. Neither of us understood anything beyond 'shalom' but it was a pleasant language to listen to, sharing some of the guttural resonances of Arabic but also with occasional severe thuds and crashes mid-sentence. We followed the growing crowds out of the park and directly into the centre of Beit She'an. At one time it was the major city of the Decapolis[46] and shared the expansive, bloody histories of many places that we'd passed through so far, playing host to Egyptians, Canaanites, Philistines, Israelites and Assyrians, before the Greeks reconstructed it as Scythopolis. We walked alongside the ruins, which are amongst the most extensive remains anywhere in the region, and under the shade of a once-bustling Roman marketplace we ate overpriced schnitzel and cowered from the sun.

I had forgiven Dave his practical joke, mostly because he seemed in so much pain from a large white blister on his right foot that required regular lancing and dressing. We plodded on with little enjoyment of the scenery or the historical significance of our surroundings, deriving only mild pleasure from a pack of jackals that crossed the path in front of us, and camping that night on a small dry corner of a wheat field. Less than 2 km away lay the Jordanian border post; beyond that, 700 km of land mass to the south and, eventually, the Red Sea.

I had spent only two days in Gilboa, which was nowhere near long enough to get any real impression of the region – let alone the country – and my overwhelming feeling while there was that I needed to return. My West Bank experience had lasted weeks, and I was about to spend at least another three months in the Arab world. Predictably I would continue to hear frustration, justified or otherwise, aimed at the Israelis, and it seemed only fair to spend some time listening to the other side. It played on my mind.

The journey to Jordan required a short bus ride; at the border post we were told that this was how we would cross the sacred River Jordan. I briefly began to question the official and to outline our unique and heroic journey, but I was shut down so efficiently and categorically that I did not even bother to continue. The American journalist Paul Salopek, who was walking around the world in the footsteps of our first human ancestors (from Ethiopia to Patagonia), had passed through this same crossing not long before, and he too had failed to elicit a waiver. Dave and I shuffled into line behind three Italian nuns, paid our exit taxes and boarded a large air-conditioned bus that would be our passage back to the Arab world.

For five minutes the bus crawled past armed soldiers and slalomed through large concrete blockades. Two officials boarded, checked everyone's documents and disembarked. Finally we crossed a small metal bridge and below, just visible through the tinted windows, bubbled the once-mighty but now-feeble River Jordan, where Moses led the Israelites but was not allowed to cross over; where Jesus was baptised by (possibly) John the Baptist; which in 1967 was a factor in causing the Six Day War as Israel and the surrounding Arab nations quarrelled over how to share the water sources that were so crucial to their survival; and whose vastly reduced course still sits at the heart of geopolitical squabbling in the twenty-first century. Since the 1960s, both Jordan and Israel have been siphoning off water from the river and its tributaries, so that while the flow into its terminus at the Dead Sea was once 1.3 billion cubic metres per year, it is now estimated to be less than a fifth of that. At the Sheikh Hussein Bridge where we crossed, I wagered I could have leapt over it given a reasonable run-up.

The River Jordan seemed to have a history of disappointing travellers. It is perhaps to do with the great fuss that is made about it in the Bible, which is impossible to live up to. Mark Twain was terribly disheartened to discover that it was not 4,000 miles long and 35 miles wide as he had believed since childhood, and the French nobleman Francois-René de Chateaubriand said upon arrival that:

> I was desirous of seeing the river Jordan [. . .] [but] I perceived to see what appeared to be sand in motion. On drawing nearer to this singular object, I beheld a yellow current, which I could scarcely distinguish from the sand on its shores. It was deeply sunk below its banks, and its sluggish stream rolled slowly on. This was the Jordan.[47]

It was oddly comforting to know we were not alone in our disenchantment.

We followed the Holy Sisters through a queue for visas, and I went through the familiar rigmarole of having Arab officials laugh at my surname and pronounce it 'macaroon'. ('You are Mr Biscuit, no?') Only one haphazard and cursory baggage scanner remained between us and freedom, and it was watched over by three Arab women who played on their phones and nibbled pieces of *shrak* bread torn from within a black plastic bag. Upon seeing us the foremost burst out laughing, doubling over with the force of mirth and turned to the other two: 'Look,' she said in Arabic, 'these two think they are Ibn Battuta!'

Our initiation into Jordan – officially the Hashemite Kingdom of Jordan – was not a grand one. The road was poor quality and the drivers careless; the day was hot, and we plodded south quietly along a flat road in the shadow of the mountains. After a couple of hours the town of Sheikh Mohammed appeared, spread out long and thin along the highway. It was distinctly run-down: most houses looked cobbled together from leftover materials, and kids and adults alike sloped along scrubby ground in stained shirts and scuffed sandals.

A dirt trail took us through the Roman ruins of Pella, another of the Decapolis cities, where we briefly exchanged greetings with two shepherds who sat on a toppled column listening to music through their phones. We would not speak to anyone else until evening.

We gained altitude on a path along the top of a deep wadi and then descended into the Beit Idis valley, named for the town at the far end. Suddenly all was peaceful once more, and we slowed our pace. A large oak tree stood alone in the centre of the wadi, and I asked Dave to walk past it while I took a picture. He clambered up and over the roots and then stopped. 'There's something wrong with my foot,' he shouted back. 'Really wrong. As in, it's really painful to walk.'

We investigated; I furrowed my brow and poked at his pale fleshy digits, trying very hard to look both concerned and medically well informed. Dave confided that the top of his left foot had been sore for a few days. Beside the old oak tree, he said, something clicked, or popped – or worse. His ankle looked slightly puffy but was not obviously swollen, so I used my years of walking experience to diagnose him. 'I'm afraid,' I said, 'that you're just a wimp.' He hung his head and smiled. 'It's curable,' I told him. 'Take two ibuprofen and keep walking, and you'll be back to normal by tomorrow.' We set off along the valley.

By evening, however, Dave was hobbling badly, dragging his left foot behind the rest of his body. We camped in an orchard, and in the morning he was unable to put any weight on it at all. I was forced to reassess my diagnosis. 'I can't do this,' he said finally. 'I mean, I've had injuries before, and I know what it's possible to just suck up and ignore. I need to see a doctor.'

We staggered to a road and waited for traffic. 'Is there any etiquette here for how to hitch a ride? Do I just stick out my thumb like in the UK?' Dave asked. I thought, and recalled vaguely from previous journeys how most people seemed to use the 'patting the dog' method that was popular across Asia – holding out the hand face down and raising and lowering in mid-air (as if, perhaps, patting a dog's head.) Someone had also told me once that, in some parts of the Middle East, holding out a thumb was actually a particular solicitation for prostitutes. 'Nothing different,' I said to Dave. 'Your thumb will be just fine.'

We successfully hitched a ride in three separate cars to a small village, then took a bus to the nearest hospital. Four hours later we were in Amman, the capital city, and I took a seat in a whitewashed waiting room while Dave's foot was X-rayed. We stayed that night in a cheap hostel, spoke little and thought too much, joylessly shared a beer and the next day we picked up the results. 'You have a double stress fracture in your left foot,' said the doctor immediately. 'You will not be able to walk for at least a month.' Dave flew home the following morning to recover. Our plans were in tatters, and I was alone in Amman with no idea of what would happen next. It was four days until Christmas.

# PART II

## EAST OF THE JORDAN

*Why is walking so full of woe?*

(Werner Herzog)

# The Road to Damascus

The Hashemite Kingdom of Jordan is an oddly shaped country – I've often thought that on a map it looks a little like one half of a snow angel. The present-day incarnation is a combination of ancient natural boundaries to the west – the river from which it takes its name and, beyond that, the Dead Sea and Wadi Araba leading south to the Gulf of Aqaba – and the most arbitrary of lines in the sand to the east, drawn after World War I as Britain and France agreed their spheres of influence. The secretive Sykes–Picot Agreement of 1916 had rejected the claims of Arab nationalism to create an independent state and, instead, the area east of the river became the British protectorate of Transjordan.

The locations that have appealed to successive rulers since Neolithic times are the same as those that now draw tourists. They are almost without fail found in the Great Rift Valley and around the mountains that climb out of the Jordan River basin, which is the lowest in the world, dropping to around 430 m below sea level at its terminus in the Dead Sea. The route that I hoped to follow south would trace the shape of this valley, and with it the history of the Holy Land west of the River Jordan. The desert to the east, which I would not see on this journey, is by all accounts a wild and barren place – the finger that reaches out across the Hauran – especially so since it leads only to the major cities of Iraq, which since the invasion of 2003 have held much less appeal for Jordanian tourism or trade.

I passed a month in Amman, the Jordanian capital, during which I celebrated Christmas twice: first on 25 December at the Anglican Redeemer Church, and then again a couple of weeks later in January at a Syriac Orthodox Church in the east of the city. At home I would not normally go to a Christmas Service, but it felt fitting to do so given the trajectory of my journey. I also had time on my hands: Dave was in the UK, recovering, and we were both bound to a waiting game to hear when his stress fracture might recover well enough to restart our trek.

Amman is a wonderful city, the sort of place where it is frustrating to spend such a limited time – visiting, even for a month, seemed only to open the window to the possibilities. Oddly, aside from the opinion of the city's own inhabitants, who love it unconditionally, it does not seem all that well liked: Damascus, Aleppo and Beirut are more usually touted as the great cities of the Near East. It's true that it's not particularly attractive as a whole – it sprawls aggressively across the Zarqa Valley towards the Balqa Hills, rising and falling upon a whim with little order or architectural continuity – but it is undoubtedly dynamic and energetic, and I had more fun there than I could possibly have hoped for.

I moved around, sleeping in cheap guest houses, spare rooms and on sofas of friends (or friends of friends), and each week took me to a new part of the city. I soon felt relatively well orientated. My various hosts took me to gloomy coffee shops that sold soul-enriching local falafel, and to plush and modern restaurants where we drank local beers and picked at Western-style tapas. I spent time with climbers and runners, artists and linguists, academics and chancers. I walked endlessly around the winding, steep streets of downtown, and along the chaotic smoke-filled highways that criss-cross the suburbs.

I was in a house in the east of the city when Dave called with news. A doctor in London had looked at his progress, and was incredulous at the original diagnosis of a one-month layoff. It would take at least three, he said, and even after that it was far from advisable to begin walking 30 km a day with a heavy backpack. 'I think it's over,' said Dave on our call.

It was what we had both feared but not spoken about – perhaps for some strange fear of jinxing it – and there were no arguments. It was the first time I'd come across such an immovable and certain obstacle to a journey. The decision to continue alone, however, had already formed in my mind and, when I finally suggested it, Dave gave his blessing and we both said how sorry we were that it hadn't worked out. He signed off to fill two empty months in his diary,[48] and I laid out my maps for the first time in weeks.

I had always been slightly disappointed that when Dave and I originally crossed into Jordan, we didn't get to see the extreme north of the country and now, because it felt like a new start and because I wanted to begin somewhere definitive, I hired a taxi to drive me to a small town called Umm Qais, which sits high on a plateau looking down on the River Yarmouk and the Jordanian border with Syria and the Golan Heights. Within 36 hours of speaking to Dave I was back on the road once more, alone in the Middle East, with months of travel left between me and Mount Sinai.

I was driven north out of Amman on a major highway by Yasser, who was a big man with a diagonal streak of grey across his hair, wrap-around shades covering half of his face, and a penchant for eating biscuits while he talked. 'This is the road to Damascus,' he said as we left the northern suburbs. 'I used to go there all the time.'

'Could you still go now, if you wanted to?' I asked.

'Now it's not possible. I could maybe cross the border and drive to the south side of the city where the rebels are, but after that it is the front line. You want to go there instead?' He craned his neck to look at me.

'No, just curious.'

'Good. Stay in Jordan where it's safe. It's very sad. Syria is falling apart.'

We passed the city of Irbid on a ring road and turned onto smaller and smaller roads until we finally switchbacked up to a nondescript town where Yasser left me at a roundabout. Heavy droplets of cold rain began to fall. He pointed his index finger at me, the gold ring that surrounded it glinting with the fading light: 'Be safe. Jordan is whatever you want it to be,' he said, then sped off back to the capital.

The modern part of Umm Qais was a bland town, built haphazardly on a plateau and centred around the ancient city of Gadara, which dates from the third century BC. I had the contact details for the man who ran the museum, so I walked into the archaeological site and began looking for him. Like the ruins that I'd seen at Pella, Scythopolis (Beit She'an) and Philadelphia (Amman), Gadara was yet another of the Decapolis cities and it was as extensive as I had come to expect. Here, though, the familiar limestone structures were now interspersed with heavy black basalt columns. Rain continued to fall and only pinpricks of light pierced through the film of cloud; the result was a world of chiaroscuro, the rays bleaching out the beige blocks of the theatres while making basalt arches ever darker. Dotted throughout the Roman relics were ruins of an Ottoman-era village built on the same site: column drums reappropriated as entranceways and blocks and lintels given a second life as load-bearing structures.

I was conspicuously alone until I finally found Ahmad in his office, in an outhouse of an old Byzantine villa; as with much of the region, the city had changed hands many times but, having fallen largely into disrepair by the time of the Muslim conquest, it was not until the Ottoman era that it was rebuilt with something resembling the grandeur it had known in the early centuries of the first millennium. Ahmad slumped in a decrepit swivel chair, bundled in multiple jackets and an oversized black hat, and in front of him Manchester City were losing to Leicester on a TV that showed only the colour yellow. 'You have come at a good time,' he said, looking up. 'This game is terrible. Shall we drink coffee?'

Ahmad had grown up on the site of the Acropolis. The ancient city had been incorporated into a functioning agricultural village until 1987, at which point it was designated as an archaeological site. All of the residents were given a settlement payment and moved out, to the town next door. 'I would pay them back all that money twice over to live back here,' Ahmad said with a lopsided smile.

We waited until the rain had abated to a slow drizzle, then I drew my jacket around my neck and joined Ahmad outside. He led me up a winding stone staircase, around the outside of the courtyard of the old mansion, and onto the roof with a panoramic view. 'We are on top of the world!' he shouted, his words lost to the wind.

He pointed out a few of his favourite parts of the site from our omniscient perspective – a fertility goddess carved into a wall; an inverted swastika in the garden below that he claimed came from India; a stone door beyond the threshold of the museum. 'There's a tombstone down there from AD 354, carved into volcanic rock,' Ahmad shouted to me above the blowing gale. 'It says, "As you are now, I once was, and as I am now, you too will also be. So enjoy life, as a mortal." I like that a lot.'

More impressive still was the view to the north. Directly ahead of us lay the Sea of Galilee, a dull sapphire blue in the winter light and, nestled on its western shore, the Israeli town of Tiberias, established in around AD 20 and named for the Roman emperor Tiberius. 'It's the lowest freshwater lake in the world,' said Ahmad. I asked if he'd been there. 'No,' he replied. 'I can't get a visa, but someday I'd like to take tourists from here. It's only 12 km away.'

Between us and the lake lay the Yarmouk Gorge – a natural gash in the earth through which the River Yarmouk flowed, forming the border between Jordan and Israel – and just visible in the distance were snowy peaks from the Lebanon Mountains. 'I *have* been there!' said Ahmad gleefully. 'It was silly though. To get home to Gadara I had to go to Beirut and fly to Amman and then get a car to come here. Borders can be such a terrible thing.'

Just to the east of the lake, the land that we gazed out upon was the Golan Heights – Syrian territory that was seized by Israel during the Six Day War. Initially it looked like Israel might be willing to return the territory, until Syria tried and failed to recapture it during the Arab–Israeli War in 1973. Successive Israeli administrations have supported settlement building on the occupied land and, while the international community (and the UN Security Council) have denounced their actions, Israel persists. Even further to the east lay Syria itself and, no more than 60 miles away, the city of Damascus. It occurred to me that spread out in front of us in the guise of a scenic view was the story the Middle East in miniature: Hellenistic cities and Biblical landscapes, arbitrary borders and occupied lands, civil wars and an uncertain future. 'Despite everything that goes on there,' Ahmad waved to the areas to the north as he spoke, 'I love it here. And in Jordan, we just watch things happen. It is always OK and safe here. I just wish more people came to see it.'

It was the second time in just a few hours that someone had pressed upon me the peaceful nature of Jordan. It was a curious tick, as if Jordanians felt the need to justify why their country was stable while all else crumbled. I asked how many visitors came to Umm Qais.

'Today? Just you, plus one married couple this morning. This week there were maybe 12.'

'That doesn't seem like enough to pay the bills here.'

He shrugged and answered rhetorically, speaking back into the wind once more. 'Yes, but what to do?'

We stood on the roof for a long time – long enough for the rain to stop and for the wind to howl even louder. We stood there until a patch of blue was torn into the grey, and a rainbow arched over the Sea of Galilee. We stood until finally all light drained from the day, and the horizon became as black as the basalt rock beneath our feet. I turned and looked to the south. For the next three months, this would be my orientation. It was time to go.

I set off the next day down a long, sloping valley, through the worst weather I had seen since leaving Jerusalem. I hid inside the hood of my jacket, blinkered from the world around and pausing only to throw stones at packs of dogs that would descend from the hills. They would bark aggressively and snarl and, given the chance, snap at my heels, but I had enough experience of walking in places like this to know that these dogs were terrified of humans. Most likely these animals belonged to shepherds. I was thankful, though, to have my hiking poles ready for when they came at me, and most of them would retreat at the sound of an aggressive clashing of one pole on the ground.

The valley opened up in the early afternoon, and I saw for the first time what happens when intense rainfall in a mountainous area fills the many wadis that crisscross the slopes. Wadis are, by definition, dry river beds, which for much of the year lie empty. In some places the lack of water is permanent, and they are simply a reminder of less arid times, but in northern Jordan they revert back to their original function after heavy rains. By the time I reached a large reservoir called Wadi al-Arab, the canyon which I had hoped to cross had become a churning, tumultuous torrent, tossing and turning the spoils of its flood from further upstream: a football first, then a block of concrete, then part of a tree, all of which bobbed briefly above the surface before being ominously slammed underneath once more. To attempt to cross would have been madness.

I retraced my steps along a treacherous high-level path, only to find that the tarmac road in the valley had also been washed away. Four Bedouin in a pick-up were already standing by the edge of the rushing water, debating what their options were. As men tend to do in the face of a crisis, we all stared at the problem and pointed, nodding occasionally. 'Looks like it's flooded,' I said, needlessly.

'It does,' replied a Bedouin, nodding. Another pointed at where the road used to be. 'That's where the road used to be,' he said. We all nodded.

'If you try to cross [...] you maybe die!' laughed the driver.

Eventually I cut my losses and walked all the way back up the valley to Umm Qais, where I called Ahmad. He took me for dinner with his friends who were working on developing the local Yarmouk Nature Reserve, and introduced me to an ecotourism specialist who was visiting from Amman.

'This will be the most amazing place in all of the north of Jordan,' said a local guide, as a huge plate of food was brought to the table. Ahmad looked at me and said, 'Don't be concerned about your adventure. You will try again tomorrow. Tonight, enjoy food and company. Life is about taking each moment as it comes.'

I almost wished he was coming with me – his wisdom and sideways grin would have been welcome in the uncertainty ahead for, as much as I told myself that I'd done this before, I was anxious about the journey ahead.

# I Am Happier Than You Are

For nearly two days I bypassed the flooded mountains by walking along the Jordan Valley Highway, whose name was probably the most interesting thing about it. Storms blew through in tandem with patches of clear sky, and there was little to do but slip back into an internal world far from the concrete beneath my feet. I thought of my time at university, and my friends there, and how I'd been so happy just to while away days sitting in the park or playing a guitar. I marvelled at the once-carefree attitude; now I felt so highly strung, even on a lonely road many miles from home.

When I escaped the road, it was through thick, oozing soil that led up a switchbacked trail. I then followed a narrow valley upstream until I was back at an altitude where I could look across the Jordan Valley to Israel and the West Bank, from whence I came. I pitched my tent and woke to a clear sky and a distinct lack of wind. A deep jade green covered much of the landscape, scarred here and there with coffee-coloured trails. Jordan is said to be the third most water-scarce country in the world, but the northern regions are an ecosystem unto themselves.

Herds of goats swept across the hills, each chased by a lone shepherd and flanked by two or three scruffy dogs, and for a while the only sound was the tinkling bells of the flock; for millennia, this scene would have changed very little.

Already, my routine was becoming slicker than I had managed in the West Bank. The enforced minimalism of expeditions was working its magic, and the excess baggage of my life was down to the bare minimum. I lived in a pair of tough nylon hiking trousers and a merino wool base layer. In the cold I used a heavy fleece and a down jacket, and a light raincoat for the storms. When I pack for journeys, I always think of the great geographer Nicholas Crane and his account of his walk across Europe's chain of mountains. Crane is the ultimate minimalist, and his sole luxury was taking an extra sock; he had initially been advised to carry just three, operating on a rotation system of two on and one off. I also took four, but as a special extra treat, I also carried a blue collared shirt which, along with my spare underpants, I was saving for a special occasion.

My tent was light and easy to assemble, and my sleeping bag fitted nicely into a gap in the pack between the tent and a camping mat. My medical kit comprised five plasters and a small bottle of iodine, and the two blades of my Leatherman knife served as cutlery and as surgical instrument. I carried a collapsible hiking hat, a keffiyeh, and a pair of sturdy sunglasses. At the top of my pack were maps and an e-reader, and in a waterproof and padded case were the tools of my trade: a small computer, two hard drives, a bag of cables and some camera accessories. A camera slotted into a bag that I strapped to my front, and an audio recorder was placed in a hip-belt pocket. Finally, I had my passport, wallet, mobile phone and a reporter's notepad in the cargo pockets of my trousers. If this sounds like a lot, then it probably was, but as long as I didn't have to carry too much food or water I moved easily and freely and only occasionally resented the heavy electronics that weighed upon my shoulders.

It came almost as a surprise to walk back into the town of Pella, where Dave and I had paused briefly before Christmas. Although I would eventually cover a thousand miles or more, my journey involved a relatively small area of land on a map looping as it did around the Dead Sea on three sides so that, at any given point during the first half of the walk, I was usually less than 100 miles in a straight line away from my starting point in Jerusalem.

Pella was the first place where my new path had stepped into the prints of our old journey, and those prior wanderings already felt like the happenings and actions of someone else. In the shadow of the Corinthian columns of what was once the nave of a large church, I met a man called Deeb who had greeted me when we passed through before.

'Some people think this is the oldest city in the world,' he said. 'Jericho was under water when this place was flourishing.' He raised his eyebrows to me and smiled. 'I am so happy that you are here!' he said, his round face broken in an ear-to-ear grin.

'I'm happy too,' I said, trying to muster even a fraction of his enthusiasm.

'No,' he insisted. 'I am *even* happier than you are that you're here!' Deeb was, to put it mildly, eccentric. He was a historian and an archaeologist and he enjoyed giving long monologues about all the things that he knew.

As we wandered around the ruins of Pella, Deeb told me about its beginnings in the Neolithic period, and its significance as a Canaanite city in the Middle Bronze Age. 'You know also that Christians would flee here from Jerusalem during the Jewish – Roman wars in the first century?'

I said that I hadn't known that.

'Well, to be honest, yes. They did.'

Did I know whether this place was important to Jews? I shook my head again.

'Well to be honest yes, yes it was.'

Did I know if it was important to Muslims? I nodded this time, picking up on the theme. 'Yes! Good.' he said. 'By the way, have I ever told you about the cave that I discovered where Jesus took a rest on his way back from Jerusalem?'

We made tea and sat in the shade of the central nave of what had once been a large church. The afternoon lengthened the shadows of the Corinthian columns around us, bringing a dancing liveliness to the tumbled rocks as the wind picked up.

'Remember,' Deeb said, 'this was once great. The buildings would have reached to the sky and blocked out the sun. We have had all religions here. This is the history of Jordan in one place, maybe even the world. Just imagine what it would have looked like. It must have been glorious.'

The fateful valley in which Dave had injured his foot was as beautiful now as then, and in the intervening weeks the first hardy flowers of spring had begun to blossom. As I inspected them, an elderly, stooped Bedouin called Yassar beckoned me from a ridgeline to hear my catechism.

'Ah, Ireland!' he repeated when I was finished. 'You have Bobby Sands and George Best. Thank you for that.'

I nodded solemnly, accepting his kind words with grace on behalf of Irish people everywhere. These, I've found through extensive first-hand research, are the two most looked-up-to Irishmen in the Middle East: a hunger-striking member of the IRA and an alcoholic footballer.

I was on my own for hours at a time in these northern hills, yet never felt lonely. It was a much-needed antidote to the intensity of the West Bank, and the routes that I followed struck a nice balance between beauty, functionality and the level of exertion required to tackle them. I was now following the 'Jordan Trail' which, in its entirety, traces the rocky spine of the country from north to south. As with the trails that I walked in Palestine, the Jordanian endeavour was not a new one – the landscape here mirrored that on the far side of the river, and for thousands of years it too was etched with trade routes, pilgrimage roads and agricultural paths. The Book of Genesis tells of a route used by four kings to march to battle, which they call the King's Highway; it took traders – Nabateans, Moabites, Edomites, Ammonites and others – from Egypt to Damascus and passed through the same mountains that I walked in. Indeed, I would cross its trajectory many times on my way south. There is a modern-day incarnation in the form of a rather rutted and meandering main road, but it is not quite as exciting.

The Jordan Trail grew into existence alongside an emergent hiking scene amongst local Jordanians, and its route was initially based on a plan drawn up by British climber Tony Howard and his wife Di Taylor, both of whom had spent years exploring the country and writing inaugural guidebooks describing the adventurous opportunities. Together with Mark Khano, a British – Palestinian businessman who ran pilgrimage tours from Amman and Jerusalem, they began putting the theory into practice.

It was in their footsteps, as well as those of Romans, pilgrims and Bedouin, that I now followed. Mark had helped greatly in planning my journey, telling me what was feasible and what was foolish, and in the Al Ayoun region he suggested that I'd very much enjoy meeting Eisa Dweecat, who had pioneered many of the trails around his home village of Orjan. Just as the sun set above the western peaks across the valley, I arrived at the address that I'd been given and knocked on his door. Thousands of miles from home, hobbled by language and cultural barriers, it felt wonderfully natural to travel like this – with my life on my back and a small notebook filled with the names of friendly people that I could meet along the way.

Eisa was a handsome and trim man in his fifties, dressed like a 1970s TV detective with a roll-necked sweater and long brown leather jacket. In his home we reclined on cushions on the floor arranged around the edges of the wall. This was standard in most village homes that I visited, mirroring the set-up in a Bedouin tent. It allowed us to stretch out, bundling extra cushions under our elbows so we that could sit just upright enough to talk. In the centre, a stove connected to the roof by a single long pipe pumped heat out into the room, and in the far corner a TV blared out cartoons in Arabic.

Eisa's children ran in circles around us. The two eldest, Samir and Tamir, were boys of around six or seven with cute curly locks and enough energy to power a jet plane. I was initially an obstacle to avoid during their laps of the living room – the privilege of being a guest, perhaps – but soon I became the target for backflips, headbutts and bellyflops from a ramp of cushions nearby. Eisa laughed good-naturedly as his children battered me, and he continued to chain-smoke long, thin local cigarettes.

'I've been hiking for 11 years,' he told me as Tamir landed a direct hit on my stomach and Samir pinned my arms behind my back. 'I know every trail between the River Yarmouk and the Talal Dam.'

That was a large area – the dam was still four or five days to the south. Tamir climbed onto my shoulders and poked me in the eye.

'I think sometimes that I must walk 100,000 km in a year,' said Eisa, and then he laughed. 'Or maybe I mean 10,000. The point is that this is the most exciting part of Jordan. You'll see tomorrow.'

We began early, setting out on a small blacktop road just as first light flooded the valley. 'This is called Wadi Orjan,' said Eisa. 'People say it is the fruit basket of this region.' On either side of us were pomegranate and fig trees, and just out of sight below them a series of hand-cut canals irrigated the orchards, carrying a continuous water supply from springs further down the valley.

'Everybody knows their own bit of the orchard,' said Eisa, 'so we don't have any need for fences.'

He pointed to the olive trees set further back from the road, and told me that they needed less water so could grow higher up the embankment. Eisa and I looked at the same scene with different eyes – to me there was a jumble of half-recognisable trees and the low gurgle of water, but to him it was perfectly ordered agriculture, based on a series of scientific principles that all the local farmers implicitly understood.

We passed through three villages in quick succession – Orjan, Rasoun and Baoun – and stopped for tea in each with friends of Eisa's. In Rasoun we visited his brother Mohammed, and together they took me to the local bakery which, although it was barely 10 square metres in size, had attracted a queue of hungry villagers snaking out into the road. I bought two large, flat squares of thick dough fished out of a clay *taboon* oven, and which still bore the imprints of the stones upon which they were cooked.

Mohammed joined us on a short pilgrimage to the ruins of one of the oldest Byzantine churches in Jordan.

'We call it Tell Mar Elias,' said Eisa. It was hidden behind a large olive grove, and we were the only people there.

'It is said to be the birthplace of the prophet Elijah.'

I asked how they knew, and Eisa smiled. 'How do we ever know?'

Elijah was a prophet and a rather impressive miracle worker with a penchant for resurrection. His name is still invoked weekly by Jews at the end of Shabbat, and it is said that, if he ever returns, his presence will be a harbinger for the end times. He is mentioned in the Talmud and the Qur'an, as well as in the New Testament, and is one of the many religious figures that seem to bring faiths together, however temporary the connection might be.[49] Eisa noted this too. 'This is a holy site for everyone,' he said. 'I think it is wrong for just one faith to claim any place. There are many similarities. We must share these things.'

'Look,' said Mohammed, pointing to a cross-shaped rosette etched into the rock. 'This is very old,' he said.

'Are there Christians still here?' I asked them.

'Not in Rasoun,' said Eisa, 'but there is a small Christian village near to Orjan, and south there are a lot more. Christians are a big part of this landscape.'

He started off down the hill. 'Come, look at this,' he said, leading us back down to open ground, pointing to voids in the crumbling rock high above the valley.

'Do you see those caves?' he asked, and I nodded. 'Those are where the ancient Christian monks lived. Just like the places you walked through in Palestine. There were many here.'

'I will show you one more thing,' Eisa said, 'because otherwise your brain will become tired from too many new ideas.' Mohammed left, and we walked alongside 500-year-old walnut trees, each gnarled into impossibly contorted shapes so that as I passed by, they briefly resembled first the face of an old man, then a sail boat, then an elephant. Ancient olive trees – possibly planted by the Romans – grew too in timeless groves, some 4 or 5 in girth, like works of art on display in this most remote of galleries.

On the far side of an orchard, Eisa pointed at a large slab of rock balancing on long, vertical rocks below. 'This is a dolmen,' he said. 'It's from maybe 5,000 years ago, and it's a kind of burial chamber. I don't know much more than that.'

'Maybe there's something nice about having some mystery left here,' I suggested. 'We have no choice,' Eisa replied. 'There will always be things we cannot know. It is not useful to try and guess.'

We circled the dolmen a few times and finally sat under the shade of an olive tree to look across the valley which stretched out to the east, sloping ever downwards and eventually, out of sight, feeding into the Jordan Valley beyond. I wondered how many before us had done just this.

'My point is that there are so many layers here,' said Eisa, nibbling on the bread from Rasoun. 'If you scrape away, you find reminders of all of it. We have to tread lightly here, to remember what was before and do our best to leave it as it is.'

# Water, Water, Everywhere

The following day we left the valley and scrambled up a steep-sided hill flecked with blue irises. In a thicket near the start of the climb, a family of three worked together to gather figs and chop down trees for firewood. A teenage son did the grunt work with the freshly cut logs while his mother, wearing a colourful abaya dashed with bright purple, helped load them onto his shoulders. She then carried the smaller chunks, cradling them like a child in her arms. Eisa introduced me to her husband, Abu Ahmed, and we made tea while his wife and son shuttled back and forth up the rise with their loads.

Eisa was easy to talk to, and it was obvious that people liked him. For 30 minutes he and Abu Ahmed talked at length about the price of figs. At its best, I learned, the market supported a price of about £2.50 per kilo. I raised my eyebrows at this, hoping that was the correct response, and Abu Ahmed nodded. He asked Eisa if I farmed figs too. When the tea was drunk we all lay down flat for a few moments – to aid digestion or simply to rest I wasn't sure, but it was very pleasant indeed. Later a tall, dark herder called Feras stopped us for yet more tea, and told

**1** The view east towards St George's Monastery in Wadi Qelt between Jerusalem and Jericho – this is said to be the 'Valley of the Shadow of Death' from Psalm 23:4.

**2** Looking out east to the mountains of Jordan from an olive grove in the West Bank, just north of Jericho.

3    Anwar making tea over a fire and resting in the shade in Wadi Auja, West Bank.

4    Um Fares and members of the women's co-operative in Aqbat Jabr refugee camp near Jericho in the West Bank.

5    The elders of the Samaritan community on Mount Gerizim, above Nablus city.

**6** Eisa stopping for one of many tea breaks in the rolling green hills near Ajloun, Jordan.

**7** Suleiman, the desert philosopher, watching the sunset in Feynan, Jordan.

**8** Author sleeping in a cave near Burbeita, Jordan.

9    Author and Sean Conway walking through the mountains between Petra and Rum.

10    The mouth of Wadi Feid, Jordan.

**11**   The Monastery at Petra, Jordan.

**12**   Austin climbing Jebel Milehis, with the view back across the peninsula to the east. In the distance are the mountains of Saudi Arabia, across the Red Sea.

**13**   Shepherds south of Kerak, Jordan, making tea and camping out while they look after the newly born kids.

**14**   Musallem and Suleiman sharing stories and cigarettes around a fire in the Sinai Desert.

**15**   Suleiman and Harboush the camel walking in highlands close to the town of St Catherine.

**16**   Suleiman and Musallem smoking cigarettes and loading a reluctant Harboush for the day.

**17** The final day: (from left) Author, Suleiman, Harboush, Musallem, Austin, Nasr.

**18** Musallem and Austin walking through the wadis in the coastal range near Nuweiba, Sinai.

me that he had met an American once with a beard like mine. He pointed to parts of the hillside that he liked, and when I told him they all looked the same to me he said he felt the same about cities. 'I don't like to live among the people,' he said. 'The hills are beautiful and quiet.'

Once Eisa and I had breached the highest summit in the vicinity, we immediately descended again. I could not remember that last significant stretch of flat ground that I'd seen. I was also discovering that Eisa's style of navigation was extremely laissez-faire. The previous day we had walked nearly 30 km on circuitous trails, yet managed less than an hour's walk in the right direction. In these hills – *his* hills – he seemed to know which way he would *normally* use, but was unable to rein in his curiosity to take the path already trodden. Thus we found ourselves sliding down steep precipices on our behinds, giggling and sweating, and pushing through thick, dense overgrowth on rocky outcrops. When we finally found a road in the next valley, Eisa agreed to follow it until we were at altitude again, and this time we arrived in the shadow of a great castle. 'This is the *Qasr* of Ajloun,' Eisa told me, as if it had been part of his plan all along. 'It's one of the greatest Islamic castles anywhere.'

The view over the valley was astonishing – it was certainly the most commanding outlook I'd seen since Umm Qais. Below us the modern-day town of Ajloun lolled across the slopes, and beyond it were three distinctly visible valleys bending around the mountain. The castle had been built on the site of a monastery in 1184 by a nephew of Salah ad-Din al-Ayyubi (Saladin),[50] in part to monitor the region below and, crucially, as defence from the onrushing Crusaders. Eisa told me that a Bedouin tribe in one of the valleys had allied with the Christian forces of the time, and the castle was part of a communications network that could take news of such treachery back to headquarters in Damascus. Under the Mamluks, who expanded the original building, messages could pass from Cairo to Damascus using this chain of castles, pigeon post, heliograph and fire beacons in just 12 hours.[51]

Eisa sat on a rock to admire the view and to smoke, and I went inside to explore. It was a warren of beige brick passageways and large, open rooms and hallways, with long, narrow slits looking out over the land beyond.

113

'The Crusaders never took this place,' a young volunteer told me. 'They tried, but they were not strong enough. On the other side of the Jordan Valley they had their own castle, called Belvoir. I sometimes imagine the people there and here looking at each other wondering what to do.'

He led me out to the battlements and said, 'You'll like this. These are the murder holes. The soldiers would pour boiling oil out from here to burn people! *Mumtaz*,[52] eh?'

He looked at my pack and asked where I was travelling to. 'You're in good company,' he said. 'Ibn Battuta was here too. He wrote that our city was very beautiful.'

'Are there many other Arab travellers who've left writings about their journeys in Jordan?' I asked.

'So many!' he said. 'A lot of accounts are only in Arabic though. Here we had Ibn Shaddad in the thirteenth century. He was from Mosul in Iraq and also wrote about how impressive the castle was. Later he made a biography of Saladin, so he was a very clever man.'

'Why was he here?'

'The same reason as most Muslim travellers of that time,' he said. 'He was either going to Hajj in Mecca, or coming back. Your journey is happening on holy roads. You should remember that.'

It was an interesting parallel – while it was pilgrimage to places like Jerusalem that first brought Christian tourists to the Holy Land, it was often the same desire (or obligation) to worship at sacred places that led early Muslims from other parts of the Islamic world to travel, in this case following the direction to which they had prayed five times a day for most of their lives, to the city of Mecca. I was now on one of the major Islamic pilgrimage routes that brought worshippers from Syria and beyond and, for once, I was heading in the right direction.

Mankind has a history of perpetual movement, of course, and religion can be seen as just another reason, or excuse, in the canon of catalytic events that provide the soft push to go. My motive on this journey was less pious, and entirely self-directed out of a comfortable and pleasant existence, but it had felt impossible to ignore, and there was an odd comfort to knowing so many before me, like Ibn Battuta and Ibn Shaddad, had felt the same pull.

Eisa left me in the town of Anjara, which has perhaps 10,000 Christians, and is probably the second largest such community in Jordan. Church bells rang as I walked through the town, and a small crowd accompanied me asking if the Christian God in England was the same as in Jordan. I told them it was, and an argument ensued.

'I told you so!' said a young man in an Adidas sweatshirt to his friend.

'It's still not right,' came the reply. 'I don't believe it. Why do we believe the foreigner?'

'Because foreigners are clever,' said an old lady from a doorway.

'How much did your rucksack cost?' asked Adidas.

'About 150 dinars,' I said. He whistled through his teeth.

'And how much does someone in your country earn in a year?'

'Maybe 20,000 dinars a year,' I said. 'But things cost a lot more in the UK.'

The last part did not register and the young boys clucked in excitement.

'Bill Gates!' they shouted. 'You're Bill Gates!'

I walked past a ruined village called Sarabees, whose existence had been based on a plentiful spring that still ran just beyond its boundary. Now there was just a tumble of rocks, and for half a day I saw little else to distract me from my thoughts. In a village called Burma I bought falafel wraps, and the police chief was called to come and keep me company while I waited.

'Do you like gold?' he asked, out of the blue.

'Gold? Sure,' I replied.

'We have it here!' he said, excitedly. Then his shoulders slumped. 'But it's under the hills.'

'There's always a catch,' I told him and began the rigmarole of trying to convince the café owner to accept payment for my sandwiches.

A road out of town took me along a finger of a plateau where, at the end, I was rewarded with a stunning view of the King Talal Dam.

The dam is built on the second largest tributary of the Jordan, the River Zarqa, and was designed to improve the efficiency of year-round irrigation in the northern regions. In Jordan, the dry season runs from April to October; even the seemingly verdant north through which I'd been walking would experience only relatively minimal rainfall each year during that time. The south would often get none at all.

Water is at the heart of much of the discontent and political wrangling in the Holy Land. To the west of the River Jordan, Israeli citizens have unlimited running water all year round, while Palestinians often experience shortages in the summer months. They lack basic infrastructure, while the Israeli system is renowned for its high-tech operation. A major problem for the Palestinians is that much of the rainwater that falls over the West Bank eventually resurfaces in springs inside Israel: Ramallah, for example, has more annual rainfall than London, but 80 per cent of the water is taken by Israel.[53] The Palestinian Authority needs permission from Israel to drill wells that exploit the aquifers underneath the West Bank, but almost all such requests are refused. This forces West Bank Palestinians to buy water instead, and their only option is to purchase it from Israel's national water company, Mekorot.

The situation is made worse by the use of water from the aquifers under the West Bank to irrigate and supply the Israeli settlements. In 2014, 400,000 Israeli settlers used the same volume of water as 1.25 million Palestinians – half the entire Arab population of the territory. The Israeli settlements augment their reserves with water from Mekorot, which they buy at a subsidised price (this is not the case for the Palestinian Authority).

Jordan too is facing a water crisis. The water supply per capita is said to be the lowest in the world, and is predicted to drop by half again by 2025.[54] Three-quarters of the population live in cities without a natural supply – Amman, for example – and so are reliant on water piped in from elsewhere. More than half of the country's resources come from groundwater, 90 per cent of which evaporates before it can be processed. Ageing infrastructure allows a lot of the potable water to become polluted and, in desperation, the historically low aquifers are over-pumped to compensate for a burgeoning population. Dams like King Talal provide water for irrigation and power generation, but do little to protect the ecosystem or the watershed of the River Zarqa.

I crossed the dam on a footbridge and watched as a huge, sloping concrete wall carried trickles of water out of the sluice gates to the valley beyond, perhaps 100 m below. From a distance, the reservoir had glimmered in the sunlight and reached out effortlessly across a chasm in the earth, but from the footbridge I could see that behind the dam wall was collected the plastic refuse of much of the northern countryside: hundreds of thousands of bleached white bottles and containers, piled up and stretching back 40 or 50 m.

I was now walking much faster and more efficiently that at any point since I had left Jerusalem. Mostly I would rise at 6 a.m. and stop 12 hours later, and if it was a day where I met few other people then I would find that 40 km had easily passed me by before I sought a spot to pitch my tent.

A track followed the mountains along a spine that took me between the city of Al-Salt to the west and Amman to the east. In reality, the two conurbations are now more or less connected by the sprawl of urbanisation, and in a small rural town called Rmemeen I stopped to listen to the imam broadcast Friday prayers through the loudspeaker of the main mosque, his words drifting across the streets. A sea of worshippers surrounded the doorway, while outside the market too was so crowded that, to make any progress forwards, I had to stand sideways and move like a crab.

A large, fat man with a toothless smile found me wedged up against his vegetable stall, and by way of conversation I asked if he would go to mosque soon. 'Not if the sky fell down to the earth!' he laughed. He was a Christian, and pointed to the Orthodox church that was built directly alongside the mosque so that, framed against a clear blue sky, the cross atop the steeple almost overlapped with the crescent of the minaret.

'They are close together so that we remember to be friends,' he said, conspiratorially. 'Do you know what the secret to religion is?' he asked.

I said no, and he handed me a carrot. There was a pause.

'Is it something to do with vegetables?' I asked.

'It is never to judge,' he said. 'When you do not judge, you can be clear with your God.' He looked at me quizzically. 'The carrot is just a gift.'

The man's name was Hassan, and by the look of his girth he ate more than just the vegetables that he sold. As church bells began to ring out, clashing with the cries from the mosque megaphone, he suggested that we go and eat shawarmas together in a little place he knew which made 'real-sized portions'.

'Do you want to know a secret?' he asked me as we sat down on plastic chairs. I said that I did.

'I am not Jordanian.'

He smiled as he told me. It was not a particularly juicy piece of gossip – of Jordan's population of roughly 9.5 million, only a minority could claim to be native Jordanian. Technically speaking, native Jordanians are those whose ancestors lived east of the River Jordan before 1948. Between 1948 and 1967, Jordan offered citizenship to Palestinian citizens fleeing the conflict across the river (it was the only Arab country to do so), and as much as 70 per cent of Jordan's current population could be made up of these naturalised Palestinians. Queen Rania is of Palestinian origin, and her marriage to the Hashemitek king Abdullah II helps to smooth over some of the cracks in a society with so many ethnic lines. The Bedouin are sometimes considered to be the most authentic of all Jordanians – certainly amongst themselves, if my experience was anything of a litmus test.

Jordan may be defined as a place that provides refuge to those in need. Whilst much of the rest of the region has been volatile, somehow Jordan has remained an island of stability. Its steadfastness has allowed it to take in vast numbers of desperate people, even as other countries with more resources begin to shut their borders.

Two million Palestinians still live in registered refugee camps. Since the start of the Syrian civil war, over 600,000 refugees have registered in Jordan, but the 2015 census showed the actual total of Syrians in the country to be at least 1.25 million. There are just under 55,000 registered Iraqi refugees, but again the true number is much higher – probably somewhere in the region of 200,000. It is not always an easy mixture of peoples and cultures, especially in a country with such sparse resources.

My new friend, Hassan, was originally from Homs in Syria. He left, he said, at the last possible moment, when he became convinced that there was no life for him there anymore. Many others had fled before him, and even more since then. Some of those refugees were still in camps, like the city-sized Zaatari in the north, but with the blessings of God, he said, not all had had to suffer that fate, and there were many others like him living in the towns and villages. Others were working illegally in the Jordan Valley picking vegetables for $11 a day.

I asked if he liked Jordan, and he said I should answer the same question first. 'Yes,' I said. 'I like it a lot, actually.'

'Now,' he said, 'imagine that you had to live here, probably forever. You cannot go back home, or to any other place far away. Maybe you can't work, except to spend all day picking vegetables in the sunshine. How do you feel now?'

I asked him what he missed from Syria.

'Everything!' said Hassan. 'Jordan is actually a great country. If you ask me the question again I say "yes": I like this place. But it is not home. I miss Homs, and Damascus, and the markets there. I miss the music and all the conversation. And, my God in Heaven, I miss the food!'

With that, we fell quiet; a refugee and I observing a reverent silence for the lost cuisine of his broken homeland.

# Golden Hills

In a small town called Iraq al-Amir, built around a second-century Hellenistic castle, I made a beeline for the Women's Co-operative where I hoped to find a place to stay. Ostensibly it was a handicraft operation, making and selling pottery, carpets and fabrics, but Aliyah, who greeted me at the gate, said they also did much more. 'We run this town,' she said matter-of-factly. 'Anything important that needs doing is done by us.'

'How many of you are there?'

'Thousands!' she said.

Thousands was an exaggeration, but I did spend the evening at a dinner table with 15 matriarchal (and maternal) Jordanian women, all of whom fussed over me and forced more chicken onto my place. 'Listen to me,' said Aliyah. 'I'm in charge, and I say eat more chicken. What would your mother say if she knew we didn't feed you?'

I was approaching a transition point in the journey. So far in Jordan and the West Bank I had passed through small towns and villages with regularity, and, even when it felt like I was in the wilds, I was probably no more than an hour's walk from some sort of community. After the fertile Wadi as-Seer and the town of Iraq al-Amir, however, where the women made up a bed for me on the floor of the newly built computer centre, everything would change. The villages would become increasingly sparse all the way to my final destination in Sinai.

The following day, as greenery drained from the land, there was no shade to be found and suddenly that air felt stiflingly hot. In reality the temperature was not much above 30°C, but just a couple of days prior it had been 10°C. The difference was palpable, especially when I tried to rest under the fierce glare of the desert sun, and I reeled into this new monochrome landscape like a drunkard, winding my way circuitously along the path. A small herd of camels watched me, motionless, as I staggered past.

I was thirsty, sweating out much more liquid than I could feasibly replenish. Only one car passed me on a service road, and the two well-dressed Arabs inside stopped to pass on some helpful information.

'I had a friend who died in the next valley,' the driver told me solemnly. 'He ran out of water.'

'Thanks,' I said.

Perhaps sensing my discomfiture, he then asked brightly, 'Did you know that King Hussein used to come here to race his rally car?' But it was too late. I was thinking about his dead friend.

'There's gold in these hills!' said the driver, making another attempt at changing the conversation. 'Roman and Byzantine coins everywhere. Next time, you should bring a metal detector. Then we could both be rich! If I was rich, I'd buy a big house and sleep in the afternoons.'

There's something enjoyable about sinking into complete misery once in a while – really wallowing in unhappiness. I cursed the weight of my pack and the undulations in the road. I swore at the cloudless sky and, when a pack of dogs hurled themselves at me from a ridgeline, I yelled with pent-up frustration and crashed my hiking poles together. The dogs scattered and one of the carbon-fibre poles split in two. I folded the remains together and tied them to the back of my pack, then lamented the extra weight on my back and the lack of support for my knees.

It was in this poor disposition that I found myself back, briefly, on a small road and passing a dainty mosque that sat adjacent to a large mound of earth. Outside it was parked a large, white tour bus, and crowded around a table were a cluster of pale faces and the unmistakable hum of American accents.

'Hi!' I shouted enthusiastically, shuffling towards them as fast as my exhausted legs would carry me. Two of the women glanced up. 'Hello yourself,' said one. She returned her gaze to the table.

'What are you doing here?' I asked, now looming over them and eyeing up the water cooler that sat by their chairs.

'Sorting pottery,' said another, matter-of-factly.

Nothing further was offered and no one else looked up, or asked why a pale sweaty man with a huge rucksack and a questionable odour had turned up at their pottery table. Eventually a man strode over from the bus. His name was Bill, he said. He was American in that way that movie stars are: perfect white teeth, straight posture and a baby blue polo shirt tucked into chinos, finished off with white sneakers. He shook my hand and I told him my story.

'Oh boy,' he said. 'Well, that's a long old way, ain't it?' I agreed. It *was* a long old way.

'You must be strong,' he laughed. I nodded again. I *was* strong. And thirsty, I thought.

'Say,' said Bill, reading the signs, 'Can we get you some water?'

We sat and I downed a full litre in one go. Bill smiled good-naturedly, occasionally muttering 'Oh boy.'

'What is this place?' I asked.

'Well, it's called Tell al-Hammam,' he said. 'But you might know it by a different name. Ever heard of the city of Sodom? I'll show you what we've got so far.'

We walked behind the mosque, away from the road, and up a steep track onto the mound, where I could hear the faint hum of voices and a generator. We crested the final rise, and in front of us was a team of close to 20 people, each dressed just like Bill. Some were loading tools onto the back of a truck while others sat crouched around sheets of paper, brows furrowed and pens in hand. In the middle, sunk 3 m into the ground, was a large square hole about 10 m wide. A man in a wide-brimmed hat stood inside, brushing dust off the wall in front of him. 'Here we are,' said Bill. 'Meet Dr Collins.'

To say that Dr Collins was something of an Indiana Jones-type character would be an understatement. His hat perfectly fitted him for the role, as did his dusty shirt and wry smile, and he leapt gracefully out of the hole to shake my hand. 'How d'you do?' he said, in a low voice, tilting his head to avoid the evening sun. 'How can I help?'

'Where am I?' I asked.

Dr Collins, it transpired, was visiting Tell al-Hammam for the 11th year of archaeological exploration. 'We're looking at a Bronze Age city here, and it was huge,' he said. The site that he was uncovering had flourished when many of the other large cities of the Holy Land were in decline. That sort of thing, I could tell, was very exciting to archaeologists. There are many such sites in Jordan, he said, but nothing on this scale and they had good reason to believe that the site was the biblical city of Sodom.

Bill and I walked back down the hill. 'The city is just monstrous,' he said. 'It would have stretched for miles. We'll be here for years, you know.' The prospect looked thrilling to him, and he grinned broadly.

'What do you do on the site, Bill?'

'Oh!' he laughed, tickled at the thought that I might be interested. 'I'm a specialist in, let's say, large impacts. This city, Sodom or otherwise, was thriving. Just thriving. Then, all of a sudden it comes to an end. So, what happened?'

'Fire and brimstone?' I asked. He laughed again.

'Maybe. Or maybe it was something else. I'm interested in another theory, which is that a meteorite might have landed in the valley. The Dead Sea is the obvious impact site, and the soil here shows a lot of similarities. So I'll be looking at that.'

'So you don't believe the Bible story?'

'I wouldn't say that,' he said. 'You must know this land a little bit by now. You can feel the history and the stories here. Some of the ancient texts are allegorical, but a lot of them have a real basis too. So it could be that there's a middle ground. Everyone reads into things in different ways, right?'

I walked a long detour around a large limestone quarry. It had been cut from the hills where I had hoped to walk – a very different type of excavation, and a much more common one – and so I found myself farther east than I had planned to be as the sun fell. When I climbed out of my tent in the morning, I saw that I had pitched up beside a spectacular view across the Jordan Valley. Directly opposite was the city of Jericho where, two months previously, I had stood and looked longingly at these very mountains. I also, for the first time, got a clear view of the lowest point on earth, the Dead Sea, which reached out across the valley, the salt in the water adding a density to the reflection of the morning sun. Or so I liked to think; I was on my own, so once I thought such things, they became true.

The Dead Sea is dying, as people like to say. Its fame is widespread, both as the lowest point on earth and because it is so salty – around nine times more so than the ocean – that it's impossible to sink in it. As a holidaymaker, you can happily float around on the surface with no effort, reading the local paper or simply soaking in the sun. ('It was a funny bath. We could not sink,' wrote Mark Twain.) The potential to do this in the future, however, may be limited. The surface of the Dead Sea is dropping at a startling rate of roughly 3 m each year, and with that the shoreline recedes too; places that 20 years ago were prime real estate on the water's edge, for example, can now be stranded nearly two miles inland. One of the more unnerving results of this change is that, on both sides of the sea, huge sinkholes have opened up where the water has retreated. There are perhaps 5,000 or more of these sinkholes – some up to 100 m deep – and they have swallowed buildings, roads and anything else that might have happened to be nearby at the time.

From my vantage point in the Jordanian mountains I could see these craters, scattered around the oozing shoreline like footprints in fresh concrete. I would often hear Jordanians talk about how important the Dead Sea was, and how they liked to go there to relax, and there was a fear that it was indeed going to disappear. Specialists say this isn't true: as the water evaporates, the density of the salt in what is left increases, and so eventually it will reach a balancing point where it cannot get any lower. The fact that it will never disappear completely, however, is not the point. The state of the Dead Sea reflects the attitude towards exploitation of natural resources by both the Jordanians and the Israelis. It is now at a stage where its future is dependent on bilateral agreement and action which, given the current political climate, seems unlikely.

For days I walked with the sea below me, just beyond the precipice of rock at the edge of the trails. I was entering the most mountainous section of the journey, and would pass through a landscape where great, chasm-like valleys carved their way mercilessly through the earth from east to west, each heading for the Jordan Valley where they would empty their payload. As I moved south I would have to cross these gorges, one by one.

With such a clear view I could also see that this was a lopsided landscape. On the far side of the valley, the hills of the West Bank and Israel were less than half the size of the Jordanian mountains; some of the mountains around me were nearly 1,000 m high. Occasionally clouds would gather above me, pulled in by the cooler air around the rugged peaks, while across the river the sky was clear all the way to the western horizon.

Fortunately, Beyond the slopes that enclosed me in the other direction, to the east, were two sites that I would very much like to have visited. The first was Mount Nebo, which Moses is said to have climbed and then died gazing across to the Holy Land. And to the south of Nebo is the city of Madaba, which has a sizeable Christian population. On the floor of the city's Greek Orthodox Church of St George are 2 million pieces of coloured stone arranged to create hills, valleys and communities – a map of the Holy Land that dates back to the sixth century.

Sadly I would see neither, as I chose to stay in the hills that lay to the west. There I had the Jordan Trail to guide me, but I would not follow it religiously: at times I would wander off-piste for a day or more, investigating nearby towns, or I would simply make my own way through the mountains, with the wonderful safety net of knowing that my GPS and the dotted red line were always there should I get stuck.

In fact, this was the first time I had ever followed a trail for such a long way. On previous journeys I had made up the route as I went along, using whatever track or trail was available to connect places that I thought might be interesting. The results were varied. Often I would be restricted to travelling on roads, on foot or by bicycle, fending off traffic and looking mournfully at the hills. On other occasions I would set out to follow some valley, or make my way through a forest, only to get stuck and be forced to turn back.

Fortunately, I am comfortable with the notion of being lost. In fact, I rarely know where I am going, which strictly speaking makes it hard to be lost. I found little pleasure to be had in following both the GPS and the trail map too closely. I preferred to trust my feet and take whichever path of beaten ground looked most appealing. It was liberating: as long as the Dead Sea was on my right and the sun moving in an arc across the sky in front of me, then I couldn't go wrong.

The Jordan Trail gave me the illusion of total freedom, but helped guide me to communities and through remnants of the past that helped me to understand and immerse myself in the country. I do not think I could have created such an experience without it.

I descended into a gorge called Wadi Hiri, where I found a sliver of water coming out of the spring and managed to fill a 2-litre bottle. This gave me a slight boost, but I still had to reach Wadi Zarqa Ma'in by nightfall that day or I'd end up in trouble. After endless hours of a heavy pack and mountainous hiking, each step was a concertina effect of pain – first to yell were the soles of my feet, then ankles and knees, followed by the red-raw skin on my hips and my back and battered shoulders. Finally, my head throbbed from the beginnings of dehydration. I moved fast, stopping only to readjust the pack or to pee. The ground was uneven, and sharp rocks and spiked vegetation created obstacles along the way. I was not the first to notice this – many other travellers have complained of the inhospitable terrain and flora. My favourite – and one of the most forlorn – is Crown Prince Rudolph of Austria who in the late 1800s travelled to Jordan to hunt, and wrote:

Everything [...] is prickly. The tall grass in spring has long thorns, with barbs which fix themselves in the flesh of man and beast; every tree is beset with prickles. It may be imagined how skin and clothes fare, and the really cruel sufferings which the sport-loving traveller in those regions must endure with resignation.[55]

Despite resting little, at around 5 p.m. the sun seemed to make a sudden dive for the horizon. Perhaps I had been too casual in the morning; it was now apparent that this was rather serious. I would not die, of course – *insha'allah* – but I could become extremely dehydrated overnight if I didn't reach the spring, which would impact my onward journey.

The route felt interminable, climbing up endless rough embankments and steep, crumbling slopes. Then I'd descend again, the weight of the pack hammering through my knees. I lost count of the minor wadis that I crossed, but I made sure to curse each one equally. At around 6 p.m. I lost the sun and checked the GPS – I was still an hour from the top of Zarqa Ma'in.

The light had gone completely when I finally reached the lip of the canyon. But, afraid of getting my footing wrong and hurtling 400 m towards the water I was so keen to find, I dumped my bag at the top and carefully descended the side of the cliff with a head-torch, and six water-bottles hanging from my waist. The riverbed below sounded like a jungle – a cacophony of crickets, frogs and birds. I eventually found a strand of the braided river, in which I plunged first my head and then my torso. I filled up with 2 litres of the cold, crisp mountain water and drank deeply, not bothering to filter it. It was the most wonderful taste I'd ever experienced. I'd made it, but only just, and as I drank I wondered how many others had been caught over the centuries in these dry mountains. These canyons were not hard to find, but were difficult to reach from the mountains. As the paths in the region evolved, so too must have done the knowledge of where to resupply. I was sure that I could not be the first weary traveller to collapse gratefully into the coolness of the wadi.

# A Different Type of Walker

In the morning, my body ached from the rigours of the previous days. I sat for a long time on the edge of the canyon, relishing the cool early hours. It took three cups of coffee before I was ready to pack away my tent and, loading the pack onto my shoulders once more, I stepped gingerly back down into the wadi.

On the far side of the gorge, once I had hauled myself up another 400-m climb, I descended once more down a well-worn dirt track into a picturesque valley lined with symmetrical rows of juniper trees. At the bottom I crossed the stream of Wadi Hidan to a chorus of ribbiting frogs, then climbed the steepest and longest single ascent of my journey so far. Halfway up, my eyes burning with sweat, I turned to look back over the Hidan Valley. The few clouds in the sky created a dappled effect with light, and the walls of the valley fell down to the river in rugged undulations. Light speckles of bottle green vegetation littered the gradients, and it all did a good job of putting me at peace again.

I spent a night on a small finger of a plateau, looking out towards the Dead Sea where the great canyons of Hidan and Mujib meet. I'd heard

Wadi Mujib called the 'Grand Canyon of Jordan', and it's true that it shares that strange effect of being so vast that it's nearly impossible to gain any perspective. The Mujib gorge tore through the landscape on one side of me, Hidan doing the same of the other, and they met to create the most remarkable, craggy drop that led, eventually, to the Dead Sea beyond. I pitched my tent behind a small building run by Jordan's Royal Society for the Conservation of Nature (RSCN) where, occasionally, a ranger would be stationed to help manage the protected landscape. This night, however, it was empty, and I had the great valleys to myself; the sun set directly over the patch of visible water to the west, then rose again behind a lone tree on the plateau. It was the most magical night of my journey thus far.

It so happened that there was a rather odd and beguiling group of people with whom I could share a few hours of trail the next day. Mark Khano, who was in large part responsible for the creation of the Jordan Trail and who had been advising me remotely on my route, had called to say that he was coming to Wadi Mujib to hike for a day. 'I'll have some other people with me,' he said.

'Who?' I asked.

'Just some colleagues, a guide, a couple of friends. Oh, and the US Ambassador to Jordan.'

They arrived at 7 a.m., and I put on my least pungent shirt for the occasion. Mark, tall and lean, gave me a strong handshake and a big smile as he got out of the first car. Behind him, a beaming Ambassador Alice Wells, small and fit, with blonde hair, stepped out. I introduced myself and told her that I'd heard all about her, and how very popular she was. This was true – Ahmad in Umm Qais and Eisa in Orjan had both expressed their admiration for her. 'Oh, Mark's just been telling me about you too,' she said. 'Your journey sounds awesome.'

With that, we were off. Her posting was a crucial one – a friend in the diplomatic corps had told me that he thought Amman was probably the fourth most important embassy in the world for the Americans (after, he supposed, Russia, China and Germany). Jordan was the safe haven in the heart of the Middle East; despite only being the same size as the state of Indiana, it was the hub for NGOs and diplomats, and a great deal of American and European aid money for the region was funnelled through it.

Ambassador Wells had been in the job for 18 months and it was clear that she was very fond of Jordan. She pointed out various rock features and landscapes that she was enjoying, and told me that this was her third hike in the country. I said it must be hard to find time, but for her this was no excuse: 'I have to make the time for the important things like this.'

Shadowing her at all times were three Jordanian bodyguards, each carrying a pistol on his hip. They took their job extremely seriously – the paperwork to let an ambassador go hiking in the Jordanian wilderness must be a nightmare – and one would dash ahead, peering down cracks in the rock for assailants. Another would flank her and a third would bring up the rear watching and listening attentively for any danger or sudden movements.

Before long, though, one of the bodyguards fell in a river, rather ruining the facade of impenetrable protection.

Ambassador Wells returned to the theme of it being important for her to see the country, especially on foot. 'It really helps to understand it,' she said, and in particular she had loved Umm Qais. I wondered if she'd drunk coffee in Ahmad's little office overlooking the Golan Heights. I remarked on how big Wadi Mujib felt, and she said that it always struck her, 'how small the region feels, despite places like this'. Like me, she regularly met people who would talk about the good old days of travelling to Lebanon and Syria and west of the Jordan.

Despite growing up on the West Coast of the USA, walking was a recent discovery for her. 'Before this I was busy being a mom,' she said, 'taking my kids to soccer practice, driving places and so on. So I guess this is my mid-life crisis.' Mid-life crisis or not, she was a formidable hiker. I had hoped to have much more time to talk to her, but she moved at such pace that we all struggled to keep up, descending nearly a vertical kilometre in just over an hour, and then exploding up the other side like our lives depended on it.

A black car was waiting for her at the nearest road access and, with a quick round of goodbyes, she was gone. 'Why such a rush?' I asked Mark. 'She's got John Kerry coming in tomorrow, so I guess she's got work to do,' he replied.

The rest of the group left shortly afterwards and I reached the plateau of the Mujib gorge alone, save for a stocky shepherd who joined me to admire the view. He stood silently beside me as I caught my breath, then introduced himself as Mohammed, from Syria.

'Whereabouts in Syria?' I asked.

'The hills,' he replied, simply. We looked out across the canyon together, revelling in the silence and the cool wind that blew over us.

'How long have you been here?'

'Three years. I ran away from the government after I got arrested.'

'How is life here?'

'Jordan has been good to me. I don't think I'll ever be able to go back to Syria again, although I would wish that. This place looks like my home did, but this is safe. Now I know these hills instead.'

I spent that night in the home of a man called Mahmoud, who had seen me hobbling along the road after dark. 'Come here,' he commanded, and we introduced ourselves.

'You must be very tired,' he said. 'I wonder if you would permit my sons and I to wash your feet?'

I was used to the innate hospitality of the Arabs by now – perhaps even taking it slightly for granted – but the sheer scale of this gesture caught me off guard and I nearly burst into tears at his kindness. Nevertheless, I tried to dissuade him on account of the fact that the smell of my feet could be fatal, but he insisted and his two boys, eight and nine years old, fetched a jug to pour over my bruised and shredded toes.

'You'll sleep here tonight,' said Mahmoud, arranging a bed out of the cushions on the floor. I had so little energy that I all I could manage was a thank you and a handshake and I was left alone, the cool water still glistening on my feet and bringing calm all the way through my body.

It was clear that I was well overdue a break. I was walking on autopilot, had lost weight – around 4 or 5 kg since Umm Qais, over the course of perhaps 150 miles – and my clothes were now falling off me. Beyond Mahmoud's house, large blocks of black basalt lined my trail, marking it as an old Roman Road – the Via Nova Traiana, to be exact. I was approaching the halfway point on my journey to the Red Sea. To the side of the path lay an untidy ruin of what was once a Roman temple, where columns had been placed upright in a crude approximation of where they might have stood. Once, this had been Areopolis, a trading post of importance along the road to Damascus, and before that it was Rabbath Moab of the Old Testament. Now, it was my shortest way to a proper night's sleep and a kebab, and I walked on with only cursory inspection.

As I tried to leave the modern town of Rabba I was stopped by a police car, and two officers, one young and aloof and the other old and astute, refused to believe that I was simply walking for the fun of it. After a brief argument, I gave up, got in the back of the car and was driven to the nearby town of Qaser, where the police chief wanted to see me. I sat in a large room with a fake mahogany desk at one end; the walls were covered in portraits of stern-looking military men with moustaches, and the Jordanian flag hung everywhere. Young police and army men wandered in and out, smoking and pointing at me. The chief reclined behind his desk observing it all.

'Can I help you?' he said finally.

'I'd like to go back to where I was before and keep walking.'

'That's not possible,' he said.

'Why?'

'Because it is too dangerous.'

'Why?'

'There are too many cars on the road.'

'I won't be on the road.'

'Then you won't know where to go.'

'I have a map and a GPS, and there's a route called the Jordan Trail that goes all the way to Kerak.'

'I don't think so, no. It will be too hard for you to find the way. You should walk on the road.'

'OK, I'll walk on the road.'

'You cannot walk on the road. There are too many cars.'

Our conversation went like on like this for a few hours. When I was finally given back my passport and told to wait until they called the office in Kerak, I got up and walked out. Four men ran after me, ordering me to come back. I kept walking, which convinced them that I meant business but worried me a little; I was reaching a limit of sorts, and I no longer cared what happened. Before I reached the edge of town, another car pulled up and the police chief leaned out of the window. I kept moving.

'How is your hiking?' he said, calmly.

'Lovely,' I lied.

'You must register with the police office in Kerak when you get there. OK?'

'OK,' I lied again.

'Good,' he said, then with a wry smile added, 'Welcome to Jordan.'

A couple of hours later I arrived in Kerak, home to one of the country's finest Crusader castles. I avoided both this and the police station, and made straight for a small guest house on the far side of town. As I took a shortcut through a narrow alleyway, I was hit on the head by something hard. I looked up and saw two boys with a box of rotten fruit. One threw an aubergine at me, then ran round the corner. I walked on until, at the end of the alleyway where another passage joined, two stones hit my pack. Then a plank of wood. I jogged out into a clearing, where five or six teenagers stood with various things to throw.

'*Laesh?*' I shouted at them – *Why?* Whatever strand of composure that remained after my encounter with the police had now snapped. It is never a good idea to shout at anyone in a foreign country, especially when they've already taken a dislike to you. I was turning into a blustering, righteous tourist, but I couldn't help it.

'I'm a guest in your country. Everyone else has been very nice, and I've had a very lovely time. Now you're ruining it. Why are you ruining it?'

It was a very British speech, delivered straight from a bygone era. The boys laughed and one of them launched another plank of wood which landed at my feet.

Up above us, five or six women leant on their windowsills and watched this play out. I appealed to them: 'Do you know these boys? Can you tell them to stop? Are these your sons?'

They looked blankly at me, then one whispered something to her friend and they both sniggered.

I charged at the boys, my pack wobbling ludicrously behind me. The sudden movement surprised them and they scarpered, briefly clearing the path. I jogged down the steps beyond and onto a main road. Just as I reached it, another rotten vegetable hit me on the head. I chose now to ignore it and walked on through the town, ashamed of my actions and furious with the boys and the women. When I got to the guest house I paid for three nights in advance, and for the next 36 hours I did not leave my room.

# You Ski, Bro?

Apart from the dead lizard in the shower, the guest house was a little patch of heaven. Finally, in an effort to break the lethargy, I left the sanctuary of my room and walked to the Crusader castle, which was built on a fine strategic point overlooking the wadis that led to the Dead Sea to the west. By the time the Crusaders left the Holy Land in 1291, they had built dozens of such fortresses, many of which still remain in Syria, Jordan, Lebanon, Israel, Cyprus and Turkey. Kerak is one of the finest still standing. The architecture was striking, mixing original Western European design with later Byzantine and Arab features. Inside, long vaulted hallways and banquet rooms led to dark towers with only narrow arrow-slits letting in the light from beyond. As usual, I was the sole Western tourist, although a couple of Jordanians from Amman joined me to read an information board about Saladin's heroic capture of the castle in 1189. We smiled at each other and they asked for a selfie. 'This is great!' enthused one of the men before asking the now-universal question: 'Can we be friends on Facebook?'

When my muscles had stopped aching and I'd begun to get restless, I began walking onwards once more, setting off through a dense fog that cloaked the land. Visibility was almost zero, so I stuck to the King's Highway until late afternoon, seeing little and speaking to no one.

I spent a damp night in a ditch, and the next morning plodded through thick mud and heavy rain. For hours I skidded along treacherous slopes, the rain turning paths into mini-landslides, and twice I fell, rolling 5 or 10 m down the hillside before I caught onto a rock to halt my descent. Somewhere behind the veil of fog was the great chasm-like Wadi Hasa, a natural boundary that formed the ancient border between Moab and Edom and, to me, a landmark which represented the last of the vast Dead Sea canyons that I would have to cross before I hit the south. Limestone changed to granite beneath my feet and, I suspected, the view beyond would be altered too. The map topography confirmed this, but of course it was all academic; I couldn't see a bloody thing.

I walked along in a mood that reflected the weather around me: grey, heavy and all-encompassing. Long journeys always force one into deep internal self-analysis. I had been through it before, but it had been some years since I'd travelled alone for such a long time, and I was not sure I could recall being so unenthused. Subconsciously I had made a habit of travelling with others to avoid the intense solitude of my own company, but now circumstances had conspired to force me into a lone journey which it was clear I had not prepared for.

What I had noticed from past experiences was that mood management was key. When I walked across China I had found that if I woke up in a good mood I would finish the day as high as a kite, relishing every inch of trail and brushing off difficulties like beads of water back to the ocean. If I awoke grumpy, however, I would spiral terribly, regardless of what the day brought, so that by evening I might be hopelessly depressed.

Ironically, of course, the cause and solution for my woes were one and the same. I needed to walk.

There is a convincing case for Rebecca Solnit's contention that 'the brain works at three miles an hour'. Since the times of the roving philosophers of ancient Greece, there has been no shortage or writers and thinkers who have both walked habitually and seen fit to record their feelings on the subject. Jean-Jacques Rousseau claimed to be completely unable to *think* without taking to his feet; Frederick Nietzche unable to *write* unless rambling up a mountain. William Wordsworth is famously said to have walked 180,000 ponderous miles during his lifetime, and Arthur Rimbaud walked himself into a fury before penning poetry. Henry David Thoreau isolated himself from the outside world so that he might march relentlessly in a quest for clarity. Virginia Woolf split her time between the streets of London for inspiration and the lanes of Dorset for reflection, and Søren Kierkegaard would rampage around the streets of Copenhagen alone before retiring to the attic in his parents' house to scribble down his revelations.

We walk too, perhaps, because it is in our DNA. Since *Homo erectus*, nearly 2 million years ago, there have been various waves of human migration. During the Stone Age, *Homo sapiens* wandered farther than ever before: initially out of the East Africa rift into other parts of the continent and then, 60,000 years ago, onwards, pushing the frontiers. The best guess is that humans started this movement to outrun a major climatic shift in the home they knew. They crossed through Sinai, or perhaps via the Bab al-Mandab Strait between modern-day Djibouti and Yemen, and moved into Eurasia. Perhaps the toughest leap of all was through the East Asian Arctic, where intrepid hunters traversed a land bridge to the Americas; 50,000 years (and 20,000 miles) later they arrived in Patagonia with no land mass left to explore, completing human dispersion. Why did they keep going all that way? Partly for survival, of course. For food and shelter, and in the hope of a more plentiful and easier existence. I like to think too, though, that it was out of curiosity. They strode out to see what was beyond the next ridgeline, across the far horizon. If this is the case, stasis is something that is relatively new to our species.

I had spent a large part of the previous few months acting out these various types of walking: walking to understand; walking as exploration; walking as human nature; walking towards something. Yet I had also, inadvertently, been walking as a means of escape – walking away from something. Long-distance journeys are a great way to avoid real life. They give a welcome break from a city-based existence of deadlines, money, rent payments and complicated relationships. For the best part of a decade I had regularly put on my boots or grabbed a bicycle and disappeared to another continent.

The fog began to lift and, with a little persuasion, my mood slowly did so too. Ahead, the trail stretched out impassively, at once

137

intimidating and appealing. There were many miles still to walk, so I picked up the pace and opened my eyes, settling into the natural loping measure of the road – the rhythm of the oldest movement we know, and the one that would carry me wherever I wanted to go.

On the descent to the bottom of Wadi Hasa I passed shapes that were once houses, created around natural caves in the granite. Modern brickwork had been used to make doorways and windows leading into the cavernous voids beyond, but the arrangement was no longer desirable for human usage; sheep scat and some old stalks of straw suggested that shepherds still kept their flocks inside during poor weather. By the waters of the river that ran through the valley, I spotted another sign of more-recent habitation, this time a white UNHCR tent on a small rise above the bulrushes. When I moved closer it was clear that the permanent residents were not refugees (these tents were sold by the UN to refugees to provide temporary shelter, and were a relatively common part of the landscape) but rather a large number of goats, and four Bedouin men lounging outside on a plastic tarpaulin soaking up the heat of the newly arrived sunshine, and watching me with much bemusement.

I sat to drink tea with them and watched as one of the Bedouin used an old hosepipe to create a splint for a goat with a broken leg. He tore a rag from his keffiyeh to hold it in place, and sent the hobbling animal back to his mother. Another of the men held on to one of the animals and stroked it as one might a much-loved housecat, while a third – the youngest of the group – was ordered by the rest to go and refill the water troughs, and to make sure the flock didn't go too far.

The men had ruddy cheeks, wore tattered clothes and laughed with ease. 'We've been out here for three nights now,' said one.

'It's more fun than going home to my wife,' said another. There were more laughs, before the youngest came over and produced a small bottle of whiskey from his pocket. 'Hey, you'll like this, Mr Ireland,' he said. 'The Irish drink this every day, eh?'

The whiskey, despite being rough and cheap, warmed my soul in a way that tea never could. They all stood to wave me off, and to giggle at my pack and hiking poles.

'What are these for?' I was asked. Then, after my rather lame explanation: 'Do you ski, bro?'

They fell about laughing and I crossed the river into a new kingdom, and a new phase of the journey, with heightened spirits and a whiskey-induced swagger in my step.

# (More) Most Ancient of Lands

Ispent the night under an overhanging rock near the summit of a
mountain near the town of Burbeita and watched angry clouds roll
across the sky. In the morning an easterly wind blew them clear of the
mountains and the sun was my sole companion along a high and lonely
shepherds' trail. The rhythm of the day seemed set until, by a small road
junction, I found Abu Samer: a large, well-built Bedouin in a flowing
white *thobe* and battered sandals. He'd been expecting me, and he led us
along a verdant spring from the town of Ein Beyda, pointing out this
house and that. We descended for a mile or more until we stood on the
lip of a gorge overlooking the ruins of an old stone village. The houses
were arranged on a sloping, terraced outcrop above the drop to the valley
below. 'This is Al Ma'tan,' he said.

'I was born here, and I lived in one of these houses until 1985,'
he said.

'Why did you move?'

'It was not possible for us to be there anymore. Life was too difficult,
so the government moved everybody out. Now this is just history.'

Across the gorge lay the remains of another ruined village. Abu Samer said that these crumbling foundations, along with Al Ma'tan, were among the last remnants of a traditional Bedouin way of life that no longer existed. In that tumbled stone, Abu Samer saw the decline of, first, the semi-nomadism of his father's generation and now too the death of his own way of life, reliant on agriculture and the land. This loss, and the lament for it, was all too familiar; I saw it all across the region.

In the valley below, there was evidence too of previous incarnations of life here; a Babylonian king had traversed the canyon on his way along an ancient trading route, and had left markings on the walls of the rock.

'Everything passes by eventually,' said Abu Samer, wistfully.

'What will happen now to Al Ma'tan?' I asked.

'I have got some funding to make this into an ecovillage. We will have foreigners come here to learn the history. They will come and listen and read, and also do yoga and things like that. I read that foreigners love to do yoga.' I nodded, sagely.

'We must make something,' he said, 'even if there is no one here yet to see it. Otherwise in the future people will say, "Why did they not take better care of their history?"'

I left Abu Samer on his hilltop perch, and began making my way into the wadi below. The descent into the gorge was steep and the soil unsteady, so I edged down slowly, occasionally sliding on my bottom when the gradient was too much to stay upright. At times there would be sheer drops of 10 m or more and I had to resort to following GPS closely.

On one of these steep drops I heard an odd sound – a little like a bird, but less lyrical and slightly higher pitched. I looked around and heard it again. I traced the tweets to their source: on a rock a few metres above me was a figure swaddled in black.

I assumed it to be a Bedouin woman, but as I walked towards her I realised she was a Westerner.

'Hi,' said the woman in a clipped English accent.

'Hi,' I said, unable to think of anything else to say.

'I think I'm stuck,' she said. 'Can you help me get down?'

The woman on the rock was called Hadija, but she said I could also call her Sue. She looked to be about 60 years old and was English, but had grown up in Africa and now lived mostly in Maui, Hawaii. At some point she'd converted to Islam and taken the new name, Hajida, first wife of the Prophet Muhammad. Quite why she was stuck on a ledge below Al Ma'tan was more difficult to figure out.

Hadija passed me her bags and we slid them down the rock face; the first was a small black backpack with a yellow Pokémon on the front, and the second a hardy-looking thing on wheels that looked like a cross between a bicycle trailer and a business suitcase. Hadija clambered down after them.

'I'm very glad you arrived,' she said. 'I was starting to wonder what I'd do.'

'What *are* you doing?' I asked finally.

'Well I'm trying to walk the Jordan Trail!' she said with an exasperated sigh.

On a visit to Wadi Rum some years previously, her daughter had met a Bedouin and fallen in love. Hadija's daughter got married and she began to visit them, getting to know Jordan much better than she might ever have expected. On one visit she heard about the fledgling Jordan Trail, and she had an idea that perhaps she could walk the whole thing to use the opportunity to raise money for a charity that she supported.

The problem was that the Trail was still very much in a trial phase. I was serving as something of a guinea pig, hiking large chunks of the trail and seeing how accurate the GPS data was for an outsider. Hadija did not have a GPS. Instead she had printed out the walking notes from the website, which said things like, 'Continue straight to the fence, then take a right at the top of the mound, and turn left at the juniper tree.'

Hadija had also assumed that the Trail was more of, well, a *trail*. It was a fair assumption on some levels; the more popular hiking trails around the world – like the Camino de Santiago – are mostly well-packed gravel paths, interspersed with a few scrambles here and there. The Jordan Trail was nothing like that. Hadija had hoped that, to save her back from aching, she could use a pack with an all-terrain wheel and drag it behind her along country tracks. If they got rough, what the hell?

She'd go slowly and dig deep. What she hadn't counted on was, for example, having to descend 400 m down a sheer cliff face.

I had come from Tafileh to the Ma'tan gorge in about half a day. It had taken Hadija three; she had got stuck first in a rainstorm in the boggy mountains, then escaped that only to find this impenetrable valley ahead of her. I helped her shuttle her bags down to the valley bottom and then back up the other side. The whole process took about two hours, and at the far side we stopped for a breather.

I called Abu Samer, who agreed to take her bags to the next town while she would walk with supplies for the rest of the day to meet him. I asked her if she would continue.

'Oh of course,' she said without a pause. 'This won't stop me. I'm absolutely determined to walk the whole way.'

'Why did you decide to do something this big?' I said.

'It seemed exciting,' she replied. 'I've always wanted to do something like this. My father was quite a famous Antarctic explorer, so I suppose I've always wanted to do something to live up to the family name.'

I arranged to meet her in the next town and we separated at the lip of the gorge. She no longer seemed weak or scared, and I hoped after Hadija's baptism of fire, things would get easier. I tried to imagine how I would have reacted to such an unforgiving initiation, and I doubted I would have been so resolute.

# Arabian Auditorium

Wadi Dana, near the fifteenth-century Ottoman village of Dana, is part of a protected nature reserve, under the watch of the RSCN. It is unique as both the biggest reserve in Jordan and the only one that includes all four of the country's biogeographical zones – Mediterranean, Irano-Turanian, Saharo-Arabian and Sudanian. It is home to hundreds of species of plants and birds that are not seen anywhere else in the kingdom, and endangered mammals like the Nubian ibex roam the hilltops freely.

The red-rock sandstone cliffs around the town were nearly 1,700 m high, but they quickly melted away into smaller granite and limestone features as the valley moved east; at the terminus, the pancake-flat Wadi Araba sat 50 m below sea level. In the belly of the canyon all was still and calm, save for an occasional buzz or slither or scuttle of something in my periphery. Then, as if in a dream, I heard the tinkle of a wind instrument; soft at first from somewhere unseen, then loud and in surround sound. I scanned the hills. The tune rose in a crescendo, swirling like a wave around a rock. Finally I spotted the source: a lone Bedouin musician sat side-saddle on a donkey. A flock of sheep heralded his arrival in the valley, moving as one in time with his jaunty melody.

When he reached me, he hopped off the donkey in one simple movement and took a flute from his lips. Immediately the walls of his theatre rang silent, save for a few echoes of the final note. We shook hands.

'That was beautiful,' I said. 'What is the name of this instrument?'

'*Shababa*,' said the shepherd. 'It's my best friend.'

It was a simple steel pipe, with six finger-holes bored out of the metal and a makeshift mouthpiece fashioned at the top. He lived in the biosphere, he said, and slept in the hills. Occasionally he'd see tourists but he never got a chance to meet them. I wondered if this also meant that they never got to hear him play. I gave him a couple of boiled eggs that I'd taken from the guest house and he hopped back on his donkey and headed back into the hills, playing a mournful, haunting tune that expanded once more to fill the canyon.

I was walking towards a place called Feynan, which had once been the heart of a copper-mining operation from the early Neolithic period. It was not far but I moved slower than usual, stopping often to take pictures and jot down notes.

Under the shaded canopy of one of the many desert acacia trees that lined the edges of the trail, two Bedouin girls sat across from each other tending a small fire in the middle. They were both around 16 or 17 years old and wore ragged, loose shawls. Grubby keffiyehs just about covered their hair, and as the girls prodded the fire they sang to each other, taking a verse each in a simple, cheerful song. It was a welcome surprise to be surrounded by so much music.

When they saw me they jumped up; I greeted them formally and made a show of continuing to walk past. As yet, I had not been able to talk to any Bedouin women, and it seemed especially unlikely that these younger girls would deem it appropriate to speak with me. I was, it turned out, mistaken.

'Hey you,' said one. 'Why aren't you stopping?'

'Hi,' I replied, feebly.

'Come and drink with us,' demanded the other.

The tea was as syrupy as I'd come to expect from the Bedouin, and the girls unwrapped some fresh *lebne* from a cloth – thick, fresh bread,

145

baked right there in the ashes of the fire. They smiled broadly and chattered to each other in an incomprehensible Bedouin dialect of Arabic. Their teeth, I noticed, were already stained black from the sweet tea despite their young age.

'Where are you from?' I was asked.

'Ireland,' I said. 'Do you know Ireland?'

'No you're not,' said the first girl. 'You look to me like [...] an Israeli!'

I replied quickly. 'No, *Ireland*. Not Israel. They're very different. *Ireland* is close to England.'

'No,' she said again defiantly. 'You're definitely an Israeli.'

They both grinned and I saw, too late, that this was fun at my expense. I'd shown my weakness with an earnest response, and now I was to be the butt of more jokes.

'So, Mr Israeli, how is Israel? And how is your walk? What is in your bag? Lots of money, I think. Israeli money, no?'

They were enjoying themselves hugely. I smiled. There was no malice intended.

'Here's a song,' one said. 'It's about you being an Israeli.'

If that was indeed the topic it was a surprisingly jolly song. I nodded along as the girls sang their separate parts and then finished with an operatic screech. I cheered and clapped.

'Now, you sing a song!' said one.

I protested, but I was on the back foot. I'd eaten their bread and drunk their tea and already shown myself to have no sense of humour, and they pressed and pressed.

'Okay,' I said, resigned. 'This one is from Ireland.' They waited eagerly.

'Oh, Danny boy,' my voice cracked with the strain. 'The pipes, the pipes are calling [...] From glen to glen, and down the mountainside [...]'

I made it through one verse and a chorus, and finished to a thunderous round of applause and a healthy amount of laughter. Once upon a time I was a decent musician, but I was never a singer. That much was obvious to us all.

As I left, I asked if I could take a photo of the girls. It was rather a remarkable encounter. Never in the countryside had I been allowed to speak with young or unmarried women; it was simply not acceptable for me to do so as an unrelated male stranger. This was my only opportunity to see how young Bedouin girls acted. Unsurprisingly, of course, they seemed the same as teenage girls the world over. They were clever and spirited and wanted to have fun.

They also enjoyed breaking the rules. However, I could not take their photo, they said, because their father would not be happy. What would he say? I asked. The smiles dropped, and one girl drew her finger across her throat. I was no longer sure if this was a joke.

'He would kill you, or me?' I asked.

'All of us!' she said and they burst out laughing again. I left to the sound of them telling me that their father was coming back at any moment, so I'd better be quick. He had a car, they said, and he'd be very, very angry. He *especially* didn't like Israelis.

At the end of a long descent, I edged around some the russet hillocks of the lower valley and there, in a clearing surrounded by more acacia trees, was a modern building called the Feynan Ecolodge. It looked at once to be both part of and separate from the landscape around it, which is very much the point of its design. The Ecolodge was a successful attempt at the type of sustainable tourism that Jordan would like much more of; it is billed as an off-grid wilderness retreat, and its client base is towards the very top end of the market. The cost of a room in the lodge for one night was probably equivalent to a week of my walking budget, but I had an invite for a complementary stay, courtesy of the owner. Briefly, it seemed, I had moved in the right circles in Amman.

I took a wander in the afternoon to the Bedouin camps beyond the lodge. They were topped with corrugated iron roofs and black goat-hair coverings. Five or six boys with bare feet played football on the hard, sharp gravel outside the tents. I joined in and for an hour I was run ragged by little Jordanian Messis and Ronaldos and, finally, sweating and hoping that I hadn't pulled a hamstring or caused myself a hernia, I left the pitch to climb a hill for sunset. At the top, by chance, I came across a small group of tourists from the lodge. There were three Spaniards and a retired couple from the UK, and making tea for them was a young Bedouin called Suleiman.

'I saw you playing football,' he said. 'You were very good.'

'Thanks,' I said, 'but you're being too generous. I was terrible.'

'Oh yes,' he replied. 'You're terrible at football. But it was good of you to play with the boys. They normally never get to talk to tourists.'

The sun set over Wadi Araba and, as it had done in Dana, its descent made the valley explode in light. The couple from Telford, in the Midlands, bade me goodnight and the Spaniards followed. I stayed with Suleiman and asked how long he'd been working at the lodge.

'A couple of years,' he said. 'My brother worked there first, then I got a job. It was built to create employment for the Bedouin here. Did you know that?'

He said that the ground upon which we sat was once one of the three main hubs for copper mining worldwide. For three or four thousand years its reserves were exploited tirelessly. In the third and fourth centuries AD, the Romans brought Christian slaves to Feynan from other parts of the Empire – they are thought to have been the first Christian martyrs, sentenced to the punishment of *metella*: quite literally, death by working in the mines.

'There are some ruins of a later Byzantine church further along the valley too,' said Suleiman. 'You'll see it tomorrow. But there's been life here since the Neolithic times. Probably since 10,000 BC. It's one of the oldest places in the world. There was one archaeologist here once that said humans could actually have been here for nearly half a million years.'

'Is there still copper here?' I asked.

'Nothing that they can use,' he replied. 'Which is good for us. For 30 years the government had a post here testing the ground, but all they found was the remains of the Neolithic settlement. Now we just have all this slag as a reminder' – he pointed to the black gravel that littered the hillside – 'and all the stories. You have to remember, this would once have been covered in trees before they cut them down for the mines.

And there would have been great industry with shops and crowds and all sorts of things happening.'

Back at the lodge, Suleiman showed me the design of the building again. 'It's based on the original caravanserais,' he said. These caravanserais were stopping points on the old caravan trading routes, and they mostly adhered to a similar style: a rectangular walled courtyard, through which the traveller and their animals would pass to an inn inside. 'We want to rebuild all of the features of that time,' said Suleiman. 'But not just the physical ones. We want this to be a place where foreigners pass through and stay and share ideas with Bedouin, and where the different worlds mix for a little while. We want to share our messages with new people, and to hear theirs.'

'What messages have you shared recently?'

'Yesterday I was showing some people from Nicaragua a video, on my phone, of the floods here in the wadi. There were some camps washed away and one family lost 150 sheep, so we all helped them to buy some more. I told the Nicaragua people: this is part of Islam, to help. We have a saying among the Bedouin. "Give without remembering, take without forgetting." I think they liked that.'

I spent much of the next day thinking of Suleiman – he was an intriguing mixture of old and new: Bedouin traditions and modern-day ambitions. Feynan too was curious, a place that had seen the best and worst of humanity over an incomprehensibly long time span. It was a frontier, then a backwater; a crucible for progress and the very essence of pure hell all at once. I walked past an amphitheatre from the 10,000-year-old settlement, then on to a standing arch of what was once the Byzantine church, built as a pilgrimage destination to remember the martyred miners. Then I left it all behind, and strode back out across the slag into the flat, arid desert beyond.

Before I left the Lodge, I asked Suleiman if he had any advice for the next leg of my journey. 'Be open to people,' he said. 'Look up at the stars. There are so many stories there, and they make you feel small in a good way. Trust your hands, and do things that require manual effort to help your brain to work too. Listen to what Bedouin say, especially the old people. Life is all about memories and connections. When all of these things are working together, we are doing it right. I think you'll be fine. Your journey is an authentic one.'

It was one of the best pieces of advice, and the nicest compliments, I've ever received.

# Accidental Empire

In an increasingly hostile landscape, I climbed high above Wadi Feid and looked back from the face of the mountain across Wadi Araba. It was easier now to imagine this as part of the Great Rift Valley; an immense chasm in the earth that begins in Lebanon and stretches all the way to Mozambique. Near the top, well over 1,100 m above the expanse below, I sat to watch a minuscule jeep in the distance traversing the vast plain. Coming towards it, even smaller and without the dust trail, was a small herd of ten or so camels. The two parties crept towards each other, with probably no one else on earth watching but me, and the jeep slowed down alongside. Then, the driver's curiosity satisfied, they passed one another by, and began to crawl away again across the plain.

Signs of agriculture began to grow around me, and it was clear that I was entering a more fertile region. In a narrow valley, walled in by sandstone rock, I pushed through a heavy patch of blooming flowers and found a gap between the boulders. It was wide enough to walk through with my pack, although it narrowed halfway. Everything around me disappeared and I was left with just the rock on either side and a narrow strip of blue sky above. Protected from the desert sun, the air was cool.

151

Just as it seemed I would get stuck, there was a gap to my left and a 20-m high stone staircase appeared in the gloom. Some of the steps were carved out of existing sandstone, while other blocks had been shaped first elsewhere then placed on top. Each was worn smooth with the passing of many millions of feet before mine. I climbed and climbed until, when it seemed I would reach the sky itself, I stepped off into a natural corridor between two huge boulders. At the far end, a small and crooked doorway was hewn out of the rock. A small, bespectacled face in a keffiyeh peered out. '*Merhaba*,' said the face. 'Welcome to Siq al-Barid.'

In Arabic, this name means 'The Cold Canyon', and I'd already benefited from the natural shade of the gorge. It had another name too, albeit one designed mostly for international visitors. Just a few hours' walk to the south was the ancient capital city of the Nabateans, and Siq al-Barid, sharing many similar features, is often called 'Little Petra'.

I wandered past the Bedouin, through the gorge and into a small opening where, all around me, staircases carved into the stone led to caves peppering the rock face. At ground level the openings were gnarled and twisted, their geometric angles worn smooth by centuries of wind, floods and the caresses of many thousands of hands. Inside, the caves too were rather shapeless, but once they had been homes and banquet halls; one even dropped down to reveal a large, square cistern.

Across the path, a stooped Bedouin woman herded a small flock of goats through the canyon, and behind her stood three ornate triclinia: formal Roman-styled dining rooms, built ostensibly for purposes of entertainment. Their facades were spectacular: razor sharp lines were etched perfectly into sandstone and the heads of the columns still sported the fine, detailed handiwork of masters long since dead. Due to their superior height they had avoided much of the damage that befell those below, and it was within this architecture that one could really begin to imagine this as what it once was: a fragment of a great, sprawling city, built by perhaps the greatest traders of their era.

The Nabateans were early Arabs who controlled much of the trade in frankincense and spices in the final three centuries BC. There is still a deal of mystery about the beginnings of their empire, but by the time of the first recorded king, in 168 BC, their state was well formed across much of northern Arabia and the southern Levant. They were nomads, reliant entirely on the seasonal movement of goods between Damascus and the Red Sea and from the Arabian desert to the Sinai – frankincense, myrrh, spices and even bitumen, which was used for embalming and was hugely valuable in Egypt. To consolidate their kingdom and facilitate smooth trade they established a great and elaborate capital across a plain that descended from the slopes of Jebel al-Madhbah, flanking Wadi Araba to the east: they called the showpiece city Raqmu. Now we call it Petra, which in Greek means, fittingly, 'rock'.

Petra, one of the seven modern wonders of the world, ranks among the most famous and recognisable places anywhere on the planet, and any description of it inevitably tends towards hyperbole. It is a unique, vast city, hewn from red sandstone rock, and during the first century BC it was at its most glorious: a great crossroads between empires, flashy and grand and majestic, with ornate palaces and theatres and towers and avenues. The Nabateans are something of an enigma: while they had the craft and guile to build such a grand capital, complete with ingenious water conduit systems that turned an arid desert environment into a thriving city, there is much that we don't know about them. Despite evidence that they were an intelligent people, they left no libraries and just a few scraps of writings. Their grandiose hub at Petra was somewhat hidden, and built over the course of just a few short years, so we can only guess as to their motivations and desires. What is clear, however, is that their trade networks – controlled via a series of oases throughout the deserts – were indispensable to the empires around them. In the years that followed their zenith in the first century, the Nabateans were then forced into an unenviable alliance with Rome, and trade on the Red Sea began to move to ports in Egypt. The realm was eventually swallowed by the Roman Empire and, although it survived through to the Byzantine era, a seventh-century earthquake finally brought it to its knees, never to recover the glory of times past.

If Petra was the capital, the settlement at 'Little Petra' was something of a suburb. It's unclear exactly who stayed there, but it would certainly have housed traders on their way along the Silk Road, and with this in mind the site begins to come to life for the visitor. Its greatest feature is a biclinium – another type of formal Romanesque dining room – inside one of the caves, known as the 'Painted House'. This was not hard to find. I climbed the ancient stairs and squeezed past tall columns to a cool, dark recess beyond. Protected by modern iron bars, the back wall revealed lavish and elaborate paintings stretching all the way across the vaulted ceiling. As my eyes adjusted to the gloom, the colours grew brighter: a vivid Palestinian sunbird was on one side, a winged cherub-like child playing a flute on another; vines, grapes and other ornamentations surrounding all. The detail was meticulous.

Mahmoud B'doul, a stocky and fast-walking Bedouin who liked smoking cigarettes and talking about football, had agreed to walk with me into Petra. He was, perhaps along with Anwar from Duma and Eisa in Orjan, one of the most naturally enthusiastic hikers that I came across anywhere in the Holy Land.

'Petra is home,' he answered unequivocally when I'd first asked him what it meant to him to work there.

'Really it is,' he said. 'I was born in Petra in the caves in 1983. I lived there for two years and then we moved out to a village on the north side. After that I was working in Petra, selling postcards to tourists on holidays and weekends and things like that. I studied all the way through and earned money to pay for it from Petra, and then I came back here as a guide.'

His tribe, the B'doul, claim to be descended directly from the Nabateans and have always been the guardians of Petra. For 170 years they lived in the caves, but in 1985 UNESCO designated the city as a World Heritage Site and, to allay fears that permanent residents would do damage, the B'doul were moved out. Now the majority of them, like Mahmoud, live in a nearby purpose-built village called Umm Sayhoun. It has not been an easy transition for many Bedouin, who were used to a semi-nomadic lifestyle. With few alternatives, most of the B'doul tribe still returned to Petra on a daily basis but now they worked as tour guides, taking visitors on donkey rides or selling trinkets, or simply adding some authenticity to the scene by crouching quietly in the recesses of the cool caves.

Mahmoud and I approached Petra from the north, which is an unusual way to see it for the first time; most visitors arrive from the city of Wadi Musa to the south and travel along the *siq*, or canyon, to the centrepiece of the city, the Treasury building, where Steven Spielberg filmed Harrison Ford as Indiana Jones, wheeling his horse around by the entrance in *Indiana Jones and the Last Crusade*. The route from the north, however, would have been a more traditional entry point 2,000 years ago, especially for traders coming from Rome, Greece and Damascus. We followed this ancient route, towered over by sandstone skyscrapers, then edged along a narrow ledge towards a hidden plateau with the great gorge of Wadi Siyyagh below. It was spectacular, but the beauty was a harsh one and nothing nearby looked like it was designed to support the habitation of living creatures. I mentioned this to Mahmoud.

'This is the great achievement of the Nabateans,' he said. 'Many people had great empires, and the buildings are very impressive, but it is the control of water that made them so powerful.'

The Nabateans developed a complex and unique system of collecting and storing rainwater, which was initially gathered by utilising dams in the rainy season and constructing terraces so that groundwater would not run off and be wasted. Cisterns like the one I'd seen in Little Petra were found all over the ancient site, and along the side of the canyons were carved water channels to move the precious cargo around the city. Ceramic pipes, now long gone, would have taken the water to its very final destinations in the homes and theatres and banquet halls of the great and the good.

'You must remember that this is from 2,300 years ago,' Mahmoud said, wagging his finger to emphasise the point. 'Also, it was not just here. They had water storages all along the trading routes so their caravans never went thirsty.'

As we climbed up and around a small, rugged rock face that briefly protected us from the piercing sun, Mahmoud pointed to something up ahead that did not quite share the jagged uncertainty of the rest of the sandstone cliffs. Another step revealed more, then more until finally, on a small plateau, it was revealed in all its glory: the great Monastery of Petra or, in Arabic, *al-Deir*. Its central doorway alone was several storeys high; the very highest point was maybe 50 m above the ground. It was built into a triangular rock, so that its straight lines and rectangular shape sat naturally and pleasingly against the backdrop. A flat plaza in front, also carved out of the rock, led to the central portal which was flanked by four great columns on either side; above, paired pilasters sat astride a tholos with the vast urn on the summit.

Mahmoud smiled like a little boy. 'Do you still enjoy coming here?' I asked. 'Every time!' he said. 'It is like asking, *do you enjoy eating delicious food, or seeing pretty girls?* Except this is better. Who could ever get tired of this?'

'Why is it called the Monastery?' I asked.

'It's mostly because it's out here in the wilderness, and also because there are some crosses inside from Christians later on. We think, though, that it was really a Nabatean temple. When I was a kid, I used to climb up to the urn at the top. Can you imagine that? It was really high, and we used to try and jump from it to other things along the top.'

The site of Petra was even more vast and sprawling than I might have expected. By the day's end I had walked nearly 20 miles in a looping, meandering fashion.

'Most tourists never get to the Monastery,' mused Mahmoud as we walked down a steep donkey track. 'It's just too far from the entrance for them.'

Slowly other visitors did begin to appear, the number increasing exponentially as we hit the heart of the city, but, perhaps because it was so big, it was never a crowded or busy experience. I remarked on this and Mahmoud sighed.

'It's nice for you to visit like this I suppose, but it's very bad for us. There used to be 5,000 people a day. All of the Bedouin had work. Now there are maybe a few hundred tourists, and that's only in the good season. So it makes it hard, and the Bedouin don't have much to do.'

He was right: dotting the landscape were Bedouin men sat in small groups on the lip of a cave, or crouched behind makeshift and quiet souvenir stands. Most seemed bored, passing time by staring out across the city of their ancestors. Some would come to see us when they spotted Mahmoud, and they'd greet each other by saying, '*Kefoo!*' in a funny, lyrical voice.

'It's a little joke thing that we have,' Mahmoud explained. 'It means, like, "How are you?" but we say it in a funny way.'[56]

Many of the Bedouin were undoubtedly handsome, and it was easy to see why European women had fallen for some of them here and in Wadi Rum to the south. They were tall and lithe, with dark features and flowing, curly hair. It was popular too to dress up and I noticed that, for all of their rugged charm, the B'doul men were rather comfortable with a level of preening that most Westerners would deem overkill. Many would wear eyeliner – or guyliner – and I spotted a number checking their reflections in small mirrors or on camera phones as they walked around. The latest fad was to style oneself as Captain Jack Sparrow, Johnny Depp's swashbuckling character from *Pirates of the Caribbean*. At first it was odd to see Bedouin wearing bandanas, waistcoats and baggy seafaring trousers but soon it became a regular sight – over the course of the day I saw at least 20 very good attempts at a Johnny Depp impression. I'm sure the effort didn't go unnoticed by female visitors either.

As we walked, Mahmoud pointed out bits and pieces of an impossibly rich history. At the end of a long, colonnaded street we ambled through the ruins of the Qasr al-Bint al-Faroun – the Castle of the Daughter of the Pharaoh – a free-standing first-century, two-storeyed temple that sat in the shadow of a rock face peppered with caves. Beyond it stood the remains of a Byzantine church with detailed mosaic floors, marble screens and a room in which had been found 152 scrolls of burnt papyri that detailed the administration of sixth-century life. Mahmoud skipped around between each, nodding to other Bedouin and stopping once in a while just to take in the view.

We climbed high above Qasr al-Bint to the ruins of another Nabatean building – Mahmoud did not think it was worth spending much time explaining – and from our vantage point we could look out of the great city to Wadi Araba beyond and, in the distance, the land west of the River Jordan. 'My grandfather used to go over there on foot,' said Mahmoud. 'It was simple back then. He'd pack some small bits of food and then walk across to get fresh tomatoes.'

I'd heard this before from others, harking back to a time when their fathers or grandfathers crossed the Jordan on a whim. Abu Samer in Al Ma'tan had even done it himself. Now, Israel and Palestine were much too complex to attempt to visit for Mahmoud, so he made do with looking out at them from his princely spot.

Petra is an overwhelming place. It takes days, if not weeks, to gain even the most modest grasp of how the city would have once worked and looked, and to learn any more than that could consume a lifetime. It is also, however, somewhere that does not disappoint, regardless of how much time one might spend there. Rarely have I been anywhere that has been spoken of so highly, and found it to match up to the hype entirely.

We walked past what Mahmoud called the 'Royal Tombs': a series of impressive facades built across a large rock face, ranging in size and colour and style but coming together to form perhaps the most striking visual snapshot of the ingenuity of Petra's creators. By the columns of one tomb, which inside was almost unfeasibly large and cool, Mahmoud called over his friend Gsaib who looked, unsurprisingly, like Jack Sparrow.

'Gsaib has also walked all of Jordan,' said Mahmoud and, sat in the cavity of a Nabatean tomb, we shared stories of blisters and warm water and long days of hiking. Gsaib has walked with an American and two Israelis, and they had been recording archaeological sites along the way. He wanted to do it again, but along a different route. Mahmoud said they were planning it for the following year if he could save up enough money.

Evening was nearly upon us, so we quickened our pace past the swirling, multicoloured marbled rocks around us, through cave entrances that had been worn away until they looked like melted candle wax. The best way to see the Treasury, Mahmoud said – our final stop – was to arrive through the *siq* to the south, so he made me close my eyes and guided me across the face of the temple. The British traveller Gertrude Bell, who was not given to offering undeserved praise, wrote of this same experience in 1900: 'We went on in ecstasies until suddenly between the narrow opening of the rocks, we saw the most beautiful sight I have ever seen.'[57]

Once in the canyon I opened my eyes too and walked back the same steps as she had, hemmed in by steep, vertical walls of deep red. A horse-drawn carriage thundered past and, when the *siq* ended abruptly, in front of me stood the 40-m high centrepiece of the city of Petra.

Like the Monastery it was carved directly into the face of the mountain, but here the architect had chosen to make the building taller rather than wider, and the result was that it loomed over the watching eyes. Six columns guarded a gaping entrance and on the second storey, above a classical roofline, a recessed portico was topped by a huge urn, riddled with bullet holes. Bedouin, and indeed early travellers, believed there to be treasure inside – hence the name – and shot at it to try and dislodge the fortune.

None was forthcoming, because the Treasury was most likely a funerary monument. Like the rest of the city it had remained hidden from the Western world until 1812, when the ruins were rediscovered by the Swiss traveller John Lewis Burckhardt. Since then it has become one of the most popular tourist destinations in the world, although Mahmoud said that visitor numbers in Jordan as a whole were down at least 80 per cent from 2010. Perhaps 20 other tourists wandered around the plaza in front of the facade, but still they were outnumbered by Bedouin. All of us, though, were transfixed by the evening light that showered and highlighted the brilliant sharp, geometric lines of the Nabateans.

Mahmoud and I grinned at each other all the way along the *siq*, sharing in the experience of something totally unique. He pointed out water channels and the recesses for the gods, or djinn blocks; Nabatean gods were mostly represented as abstract shapes, void of human features, showing the reverence that the Nabateans had for pure geometry. Finally we exited into the bustle of Wadi Musa, which exists almost entirely to service the tourists of Petra, and Mahmoud headed for home.

I stumbled past the restaurants to find my guest house, and thought about cuboid gods and urns filled with treasure. I played back the images in my mind of Bedouin dressed as Johnny Depp and the vast, towering city of caves that loomed over them. I remembered Mahmoud telling me when we passed an amphitheatre cut out of sandstone that the Nabateans used to take ideas from the Greeks and Romans who passed through, then turn their architectural styles into sandstone versions. Finally, just as I reached my bed for the night, I thought of John William Burgon's famous lines on Petra:

> The hues of youth upon a brow of woe,
> which Man deemed old two thousand years ago,
> Match me such marvel save in Eastern clime,
> a rose-red city half as old as time.[58]

Burgon had never seen Petra when he penned those words in 1845. That seemed such a terrible shame. I was grateful that I had.

# Strength in Numbers

A mass of Jordanian women squeezed off the morning bus from Amman. There was a short pause, and then a short, lithe figure with a fire-red beard and oversized backpack stepped off.

'Sean!' I shouted, and he grinned.

'Bit bloody hot out here, isn't it?'

After so many stretches of walking alone, I was about to enter a new and unprecedented phase of my walk. For the first few days heading south I would have no fewer than six fellow hikers with whom to share the trail.

Sean Conway was one of these people – a friend from the UK who, like Dave Cornthwaite and me, made a living from adventure. Unlike us though, he did things ruthlessly fast. An endurance athlete of the highest standing ('Britain's wildest adventurer', according to the *Guardian* newspaper), as well as racing around the world on a bicycle, he had also swum and run the length of Great Britain. He would walk with me to Wadi Rum and then, shortly after returning home, begin the world's longest triathlon; a 4,000-mile swim, run and cycle around the coastline of the United Kingdom.

For the first time since Dave had been injured, I was travelling with someone who already knew me; there was no need to fill in the back story. We could reminisce about good times that we'd had in the past, and dream of great journeys to make in the future. Best of all, Sean had brought a large bottle of Irish whiskey in his bag. I also noticed that, while I had attracted plenty of attention on my journey thus far, I was now a mere distraction from the real star of the show: Sean's beard. Tourists and Bedouin alike wanted just to be near him, to stroke the magical beard and, for the braver ones, to get close enough to take a selfie.

At Mahmoud B'doul's house we gathered the rest of our expedition team. The next to find us was Mark Khano, whom I'd last seen with the American Ambassador in Wadi Mujib, and with him was his friend Nasser from Amman. Finally, we were joined by Tony Howard and Di Taylor, who had mapped out much of the original route for the trail. They were legendary in these parts, both for the guidebooks that they'd produced detailing the outdoor activities in Jordan, and especially because of Tony's great climbing prowess and passion for the mountains in Wadi Rum.

As we left Wadi Musa, Sean stopped briefly to buy a wooden camel which he strapped to the back of his pack, then soon paused again to pick up two large animal bones that he hung off the straps. The previous night, he'd convinced the owner of a local restaurant to sell him a bottle of Jordanian whisky, which he now carried alongside the Irish stuff. For an accomplished athlete, he didn't really look the part. He wore a nylon T-shirt with a straw hat, and instead of hiking trousers he sported what can only be described as skinny jeans. When I questioned him on this he said simply, 'I only had one pair of trousers, so I just wore these.'

Everyone else was kitted out in the finest hiking clothes, and we moved at speed. I had worried that having spent so long alone I might struggle with group dynamics, but we gelled well. Mahmoud led us along rugged wadis, through sparse and bleached desert and past more Nabatean and Roman ruins. The company and variation in conversation was luxurious, but even that was no match for the greatest treat of all: at the end of the day, a jolly Bedouin called Suleiman met us at an agreed point that was accessible by truck, where he laid out plastic mats and used a large gas burner to make industrial-strength pots of tea.

It was this type of tourism that Mark hoped would begin to attract hikers to the Jordan Trail – a supported journey with a guide and a guaranteed meal, but with the opportunity for real adventure and total wilderness too.

'I wanted to do something like this in Palestine,' he said, 'but it was difficult. Tony and Di and I created a route called the Nativity Trail, which a lot of the Masar Ibrahim al-Khalil now follows, but it's just much easier to try and do this sort of thing in Jordan.'

By 'easier' he meant the lack of political barriers, because it was still an enormous undertaking to build a hiking trail anywhere in the Middle East. I asked him why he felt paths like this were important.

'Trails are about much more than hiking,' he said. 'They open up the beauty of the landscape, of course, but they also initiate all sorts of other opportunities and connections. They create jobs – for example, when we train guides – and they bring money to small communities that can host travellers.'

With a small team, Mark had worked tirelessly with a minute budget to bring the trail to a point where an outsider like me could feasibly hike long sections independently.

For the first time since leaving Umm Qais I was insulated from much of what surrounded me. It was beautiful, I appreciated, but my attention was elsewhere. As much as I was glad of the company, I was grateful too to have travelled for so long alone; there was so much I might have missed had I been surrounded by friends.

At night we ate well, Suleiman cooking up a storm with fresh vegetables and tinned meat on the gas burner from his truck. Mahmoud and Sean finished an entire bottle of whiskey on the first night, and the second too was nearly gone shortly afterwards. On our third morning together, Sean and I left early and alone – the rest of the team would take eight days to get to Rum, and we hoped to do it in six. We filled our packs with food and water for the next leg, and crept out into the still and silence of the morning desert. By the time the sun breached the walls of the canyon, we were many miles from a cooked breakfast.

Even Sean struggled in the deep sand, and for three days we trudged slowly through long, winding canyons. Sand can be an awful surface for trekking; each footfall means sinking exhaustingly deep into the ground, slipping backwards with every attempt to move forwards. But it also creates beautiful landscapes, and the colours changed hourly – at first deep red, then black, then grey, then a marbled effect of all three. Some of the wadis were no wider than my wingspan and we walked with necks craned upwards, looking at a vertical rise of perhaps 100 m to the sky above.

Sean's enthusiasm for a new landscape and country was infectious, and I began to see everything through his eyes. A herd of camels, met to mutual surprise in a narrow passageway, was not an inconvenience; instead it was our good fortune to see 20 of the beasts up close, their single humps wobbling comically as they cantered past. When the wadi floor became filled with deep pools of water that gathered from a rare patch of rain it was not an annoyance – it was a chance to cool our bruised feet and wade thigh-deep in cold, energising water. Even the sandstone peaks that looked like melting wax were exciting once more, no longer just an imitation of what I'd seen before.

Our encounters in the wildernesses south of Petra were mostly limited to camels and lizards; we saw just two humans, both in the distance on ridgelines, and neither of whom acknowledged our presence. It was not until we climbed out of the gorges and onto a plateau near the town of Humayma, once the settlement of Nabatean Hiwar, that we spoke with anyone. For days we had not been able to see beyond the next bend in the wadi; now we could look out for miles along an arrow-straight dirt track which led to a road in the distance and, beyond that, an all-encompassing expanse of desert.

It was on this track that an old Toyota Hilux truck crunched its way over to idle beside us, and two young Bedouin with loose chequered keffiyehs around their heads reached out to shake our hands.

'You must be careful here,' said the driver. Then, by way of explanation: 'It is because of Da'esh.'

'Da'esh?' I asked, surprised and suddenly a bit concerned. There had been very little talk of Da'esh – or ISIS – anywhere in Jordan, except occasionally when someone I met mentioned their absence in the country as an example of the safety here.

'There is a military camp nearby, and they will be worried about Da'esh maybe,' the driver continued.

'Why would they be worried?'

'Because your friend,' said the driver, pointing at Sean, 'he looks like Da'esh!'

We laughed, but the driver was being at least as earnest as he was humorous. He mentioned a Georgian Chechen ISIS commander called 'Omar the Red'; I looked him up online later and, aside from the obvious difference that he was a militant jihadist fighting in the Syrian civil war, I had to admit that he and Sean did share the same epic, red-bearded appearance. Quite what Omar the Red would have been doing in skinny jeans and orange sunglasses in the Jordanian desert is a mystery, but it was enough to warrant a warning from our new friends.

We followed the Hilux to a small Bedouin camp that lay a mile or so along the trail, and inside a long communal tent we ate a thick, oily gruel out of a steel bowl with the younger male members of the family. As the last light of another day faded, the patriarch arrived and tea was brewed. Perhaps in honour of his presence – or ours – fresh goat's milk was brought from outside and stirred in with the sugar. The old man, Abu Sabah, produced a battered tin box in which he kept photos from the last two decades of the twentieth century. Since then, he said, he had not had a camera, until very recently when his sons began snapping everything again on their mobile phones. He didn't care much for this, however, because he could not hold the results in his hand or store them in a tin box.

His collection was a wonderful document of Bedouin life or, at least, of segments of it; there were still no women in any of the photographs and only the photos in which he looked striking seemed to have been kept. In the first batch, Abu Sabah posed heroically against a series of backdrops, his wide moustache bristling in the wind and gleaming in sunlight. A second selection of pictures showed various foreign visitors to the tent over the years: Americans with flowing mullets and oversized shirts and prim, upright Germans.

Finally, there was a whole album dedicated to camels, and Sean and I were given a potted history of the family trees of Abu Sabah's favourite dromedaries. Right on cue, as we were learning about his top beast of 1998, a truck arrived from Wadi Musa with three new camels that he'd recently purchased. We all levered ourselves off the ground to watch the poor animals being hauled off the back of a lorry by an odd- and terrifying-looking system of chains and cranes. The camels bellowed for all they were worth and then, once on the ground and released from the shackles, they calmly wandered off into the night.

We returned to the tent and the tin box was carefully put away; in its place, a wooden instrument that had been hanging off a supporting beam was passed down with great care. More young boys piled expectantly into the room.

'This is called a *rababah*,' Abu Sabah told us. 'It is one of our most traditional instruments. It is made with eight pieces of wood, and over the top is stretched animal skin. Maybe sheep or goat, or sometimes wolf, if you can catch it.'

It looked a little like a violin and was about the same size, but Abu Sabah played it like a cello, resting the bottom of the instrument on the ground between his crossed legs and holding the top of the long neck in his left hand. One long, spindly string stretched down across the belly of the *rababah* to a bridge balanced on the goatskin, and Abu Sabah began to draw a wooden bow back and forth across it. A scratchy, high-pitched sound was soon replaced by long, smooth legato notes. With the forefinger of his left hand, Abu Sabah pressed lightly on the string, moving up and down almost imperceptibly to alter the pitch.

He sang too, in Arabic, with a deep, guttural voice filled with emotion and cigarette smoke. The melody of both the *rababah* and his vocals were the same, and it reminded me of the old blues music of Lightnin' Hopkins, like 'Baby Please Don't Go', or the way Jimi Hendrix mimics his guitar in the verse of 'Voodoo Child'. After he finished, I asked: 'What was the song about?'

'It is about a man who loses his camel. He is very sad, and so he begins to remember all the favourite things about his camel. He talks about its eyelashes and temperament. Then his wife becomes angry because he spends too much time thinking about the camel. He talks about the things that he does not like about his wife after that.'

'Does it have a happy ending?'

'No. He never finds the camel, and he never loses his wife. Many songs are like this.'

We walked the next day under a ceaseless sun that bored into our very skulls. I'd lost my hat somewhere near Kerak, and spent the following weeks tying a keffiyeh around my head. It was the source of much amusement – and a little pride – to Jordanians that I emulated them, albeit poorly, but now Sean had brought me a leather, wide-brimmed cowboy hat from London to replace the scarf. It helped a little, shading my eyes from the blinding light, but sweat still seeped down onto my nose and neck. There were few places to retreat to when it became unbearable so we continued our march, matching each other for pace and discussing the finer points of life at home: pubs and friends and long, lazy days with little to do. As we walked, the prints from our boots were swept away by a swirling wind, marking the transience of our passing.

Small lizards skipped away from our feet in the taupe sand and, beyond, vast lumps of sandstone and granite grew out of the yellow sea below; we were now entering the great desert of Wadi Rum, or to use another name, the Valley of the Moon. It is a land drenched in history and mysticism, and has played host to nomads since prehistoric times; more permanent habitation has always been impossible because of the sheer scale and violent aridity of the sands. It has a sharp and fierce beauty to it; as soon as we left the Desert Highway in Humayma, it was clear that we must treat the valley with the same respect as it has been afforded by the hunters, pastoralists, traders and Bedouin; it was a landscape that rewarded thoughtful travel, but it could punish carelessness with immediate and uncompromising wrath.

Out of a mountain called Jebel Kharazeh there grew a great, natural sandstone arch and, in the shade of the bowed rock, a father and son sat beside their two camels and a large jerrycan of water. The camels were for racing, they said, but the season had not yet begun so they came to the arch hoping that some tourists might appear. I apologised that we did not want to ride a camel around the rock. The father smiled.

'It's good to walk,' he said. 'The Bedouin know this. I am glad some foreigners do too.' He filled our water bottles and encouraged us to rest there in the shade for a while. I've always found that at the margins of inhospitable terrain lie some of the kindest people, and Wadi Rum was no exception. I often think at times like these of the story I heard of Abraham, or Ibrahim, whose presence is felt throughout these lands. The legend has it that his tent in the desert was open at all four corners, so travellers from every direction knew they were welcome to come and stay.

We slept that night in the middle of the valley; the nearest granite rocks that reared out from the yellow abyss were at least a few miles away to the east. Or so it seemed – distance was almost impossible to judge. Sean disappeared to gather wood and I boiled water on a gas stove for our evening fare: instant noodles with a tin of peas and chunks of unidentifiable meat. The darkness of night brought a cool wind and a chill in the air, and Sean lit the fire. The gnarled, dry sticks cracked and spat as they submitted to the inferno, and we basked in their warmth. Above us the Milky Way shimmered into life. All was quiet. We sat in silence, watching as a chalk moon climbed above the monstrous mountains, throwing pale shadows across the sands. There were no other signs of life, and we might have been the only humans on earth. When the day's exertion overcame us, we simply lay back from our seated positions. I pulled my sleeping bag over my body like a duvet; sleep came easily, taking me from one new world to another.

# Godlike Echoes

The natural gateway of Wadi Rum is probably best known to a Western audience for one of its relatively recent visitors and temporary residents. In 1917, a young British military officer called T.E. Lawrence chose it as his base and, in time, wrote *The Seven Pillars of Wisdom*, a book that is best read as a love letter to the Bedouin and harsh, ascetic desert life.

Lawrence's role in the Arab Revolt has come under scrutiny in recent years, and it seems likely that he exaggerated his influence and involvement. His book, however, remains compelling as a tale of adventure, and what is clear is his love for and appreciation of Arab culture. Lawrence's name still carries weight in Rum. Partly, it is leveraged to draw tourists; the spring where he is said to have washed, a landmark named after his book and even a carving of his head in a canyon are all offered on itineraries to those that arrive in the desert. I found too, though, that he seemed to be remembered fondly by Bedouin, irrespective of the dollar value of his brand. The father and son by the rock arch said the people of Rum loved Lawrence because he loved them. Later, as Sean and I crossed the mudflats towards a settlement called Shaqriya, a group of three young men in a battered old BMW convertible stopped us to talk about Britain's most famous desert aficionado.

'He was a Bedouin,' said one, balancing on the rear door of the old car.

'Have you read his book?' I asked.

'Of course,' they all answered. 'We read it in Arabic.'

'Do you think he was telling the truth?'

'I think he cared about Arabia and Arabs,' said the man in the passenger seat, his eyes burning into mine as I spoke. 'The details are not as important as his feelings. Since Lawrence, the British have fucked over Arabs every time.'

With this damning, but not inaccurate, indictment of British interventionism ringing in my ears, Sean and I crossed the tracks of a single-gauge railway, which once would have carried the trains of the original Hijaz Railway, which stretched from Damascus to Medina. Lawrence was connected to this part of the history too – he became adept during the Arab Revolt at helping to ambush Ottoman trains on these very tracks. The men in the BMW told me that there was a 1950s Japanese-built steamer which still ploughed up and down the line on occasion, but they hadn't seen it in a while. One joked that perhaps the ghost of Lawrence had returned to blow it up.

We arrived in Rum village just as the sun dipped below the vast granite peaks of Jebel Rum, the highest point in the valley at 1,734 m, and the second highest summit in all of Jordan. The village is just about the closest thing that there will ever be to a permanent settlement in Rum; spreading across the valley floor and comprising just a small grid-work of dirt trails, it is home to a few hundred houses and a couple of concrete grocery stores. A tarmac road runs into the village from the north, but not out; to the south lies simply desert.

Sean and I pitched our tents behind the Rum Rest House which, amongst other things, had garnered a reputation as the only place for many hundreds of miles where one could find beer. It was aimed at the tourists, of course, and for four times the normal rate we bought two litre-bottles of ice-cold lager and sat in the shade, sipping our glorious reward and looking out upon the magnificent walls of the valley. In my notebook, before leaving home, I had written down a short description of Wadi Rum by T.E. Lawrence, and now I looked at it again where it had been underlined and circled. It said that the valley was, simply, 'vast, echoing and Godlike'.

First thing the next morning Sean left for Amman. I spent the day under the shade of a slatted wooden roof by the guest house, watching the occasional passing of jeeps carrying small groups of tourists. In the middle of the day, four well-dressed Jordanians sat down to have a hushed discussion at the table next to me and, once I noticed that they all carried 9 mm pistols on their hips, I decided to take a walk.

There was another visitor who gained notoriety in these sands too, and her story is perhaps even more remarkable than that of her contemporary, Lawrence. Gertrude Bell was a writer, explorer, archaeologist and spy who also worked for the British government in Cairo during World War I. By that point, however, she had already been travelling in the Middle East for over 20 years, writing in depth about her experiences in Iran, Palestine and Syria. She worked directly with Lawrence and the Arab tribes, forging alliances and eventually, after the war was over, she was a central figure in putting King Faisal I on the throne as king of Iraq. Much of the current border between Iraq and Jordan can be traced to ideas of hers and, although she is not as famous in Rum as Lawrence, her name is still remembered by many of the Bedouin.

From Rum it was only a short hop now to the Red Sea, but the route through the Aqaba Mountains passed close to the porous border with Saudi Arabia, and the area had a reputation for harbouring narcotics smugglers.

To minimise the risk, I was going to travel with company. Matt Harms, who had walked out of Jerusalem with me on the very first day, was arriving on a bus from the Israeli border to the south, and we agreed to hire the services of a local Bedouin guide called Suleiman who we hoped would smooth over any problems that might arise. We were also joined by Pip Stewart, a friend and adventure journalist from the UK. The only time that her availability matched up with an accessible point of my route was in Rum, so I'd told her to come to the village on the same day as Matt. I had, however, neglected to tell her about the drug smuggling and the potential dangers of the empty mountains. I hoped she wouldn't hold this against me.

# The Smugglers' Route

Suleiman arrived the next morning and, somewhat surprisingly, refused to join us on foot. He was the first hiking guide I'd ever met with such a distaste for walking. His friend Ali, taller and much more reserved, drove Suleiman's battered pick-up and, as soon as they had loaded in some food and water, they sped off into the desert, promising to meet us that evening. Matt, Pip and I did what we came to do, and what I'd been doing almost as regularly as breathing since I left Umm Qais. We walked – first through the village, where early preparations were being put in place for a wedding that would last three days – and then out into the great canyon beyond.

We passed by the spring where Lawrence had apparently washed, and, on the base of sandstone rock nearby, spied Thamudic petroglyphs carved into the stone. These symbols are proto-graffiti; they tell the story of 12,000 years of nomadism in the valley. There are 25,000 petroglyphs in Rum – and some 20,000 inscriptions – and to walk along the lower reaches of any of the great granite mountains is to trace various narratives of the pastoralists who have called this place home. There was writing in Thamudic script – the Thamuds lived in the valley in around 800 BC, and in the Qur'an are said to have been annihilated by Allah – but also Nabatean, early Islamic and Arabic, and carvings showed human figures holding bows and arrows, and ibexes, camels, and horses, suggesting that the valley must have been much less arid 10,000 years ago.

In the late afternoon, shortly before we hoped to meet Suleiman at the agreed rendezvous point, the telltale dust train of a pick-up truck careered across empty desert towards us. The driver and his wife were from Saudi Arabia, which was now only 6 miles away as the crow flies. I wondered what the demarcation was like – in the Empty Quarter desert, I had gotten very close to the Saudi border from the Omani side; there was simply a large trench, but I was told later that there were all sorts of electronic eyes on the vast line in the sand, and infiltrators would soon be rounded up.

The Saudi family stopped, and produced two small children from amongst the blankets in the back of their truck. Tea was brewed, and I enjoyed seeing Pip experience this hospitality for the first time. The woman took pictures on her iPhone, and her husband told us about life in Saudi. It was *different*, he said, choosing his words carefully. It was much more conservative, and they came to Jordan five days each month as a kind of holiday. Large chunks of the valley here had been traded in a land swap, he said – Jordan was given a channel of land that stretched down to the coast, and Saudi took some desert inland. The result was that residents who had belonged to one nation suddenly became those of another, but the border was flexible. This family needed no stamp to move between the two countries, and while they lived in Saudi for work, they also had a house in the Jordanian village of Titen to the south.

Where did he feel he belonged? I asked.

'In the desert,' he laughed. The arbitrary nature of borders is especially apparent to those who must negotiate them daily, I thought, though here at least – unlike in the West Bank – the lines seemed to work to some people's advantage.

By the end of the first day we had covered over 20 miles, and Suleiman had our camp set up by the time we arrived. He jumped around fetching coffee pots and cooking utensils, only pausing occasionally to hold improbable yoga positions on the bonnet of the car.

Ali sat quietly, stirring the coffee and smiling at Suleiman's jokes, and I warmed to them both much more than before.

Pip was an inquisitive traveller, and Suleiman enjoyed her questions and attention. He taught her about the role of the left hand in Islam (for *unclean* activities, he said, and not to be used for eating or offering to strangers) and he showed her the etiquette for Arabic coffee – when the small ceramic cup is passed, you drink and it will be refilled; when you are finished, you shake the empty cup from side to side and pass it back. He giggled as he delivered these lessons, occasionally breaking out into song. 'The English woman is strong, strong, strong,' he sang, and Ali clapped along in rhythm. After a particularly lengthy workshop on how to bake *libne* bread in the fire, Suleiman and Ali both began a prodigious rendition of a song about a camel, featuring a virtuoso solo dromedary impression from Suleiman complete with snuffling, throat noises and hand gestures.

The following day we left Suleiman and Ali sleeping by the truck and continued into the mountains. Suleiman met us in a wide valley in the afternoon and, with headphones plugged into his phone, and trousers rolled up to his knees, he stripped down to a white vest and skipped off ahead of us down the trail. He was walking, at last, but seemed incapable of travelling in a straight line. He would hop, jump and vault along the trail. It was not too different from taking a young child on a walk, except that I was paying this one to protect me from smugglers.

That particular threat seemed distant now, but I knew that Suleiman had only consented to finally join us on foot as a precaution for this final stretch. Ali was a few miles away, driving along a dirt track around the mountains, and we walked quietly through rugged granite rocks towards a high pass that was the gateway to the Red Sea. In the next canyon lay a burned-out car, its shell charred black, and not far beyond that were the remains of a small camp. Suleiman licked his finger and touched the embers of a fire, then sniffed the air. I could not tell how much of it was an affectation, but he concluded that someone had been there less than an hour before.

Ali joined us in the next gorge, and we began an uneasy night between the walls of the canyon, which in the darkness formed grotesque, looming shadows above our sleeping bags. About an hour after we had eaten and fallen asleep, a pair of blinding headlights bounced into the valley and the truck halted beside us. The headlights remained on and Pip, Matt and I lay still while Suleiman went to meet the driver. 'If he comes over, make sure you do not say anything in Arabic to him,' Suleiman hissed to us as he stood up.

We could hear their conversation. The driver said that he was a local Bedouin, and for a long time it was clear that he and Suleiman did not trust each other entirely. Their greetings were as formal as any I'd ever heard, and they politely welcomed and complemented one another repeatedly. Indicating our apparently sleeping bodies, the Bedouin asked 'Are they army?' Suleiman assured him that we weren't – we were just tourists, and he was leading us to the Red Sea.

Eventually Suleiman was invited to come and visit the next day and the Bedouin gave Suleiman a small wrapped package. I wondered if it was hashish. If gifts were being handed over, I thought, we are probably OK. Family ties were discussed, and advice was offered – avoid the family farther down the valley, don't walk on that particular trail, and so on. The network of Bedouin tribes is quite incredible. It is a system that works on favours and connections and respect. Suleiman knew the right people and so, by association, we three were acceptable too.

In the morning a precarious barrier of jagged peaks lay between us and the sea. We tottered along the track and Suleiman bounded to the top.

'Ali seemed grumpy this morning,' I began, when I caught up with him. 'Did you two have an argument?'

'My licence has expired on the truck,' said Suleiman. 'I only just told him. I said if he sees any police, he is to turn around and come back into the desert and drive fast through the mountains. He did not like this.' I could see why.

'What will happen if they catch him?'

'They will think he is a smuggler. And then I don't know!' He laughed. 'Poor Ali.'

'Do you really think there are smugglers in these mountains?'

'Of course,' he said. 'The cars come from Saudi and they unload the goods onto donkeys to cross the mountains here, where we are right now. Then on the far side Jordanian jeeps pick them up and drive them through the valley.'

It was a disconcerting thought; not least because there were spent shotgun shells scattered along the trails. Suleiman skipped ahead.

'Don't worry,' he said. 'You are with Suleiman, king of the mountains!'

'You seem much happier up here,' I said.

'Of course! To walk on the flat is boring. I don't like it. But up here is amazing. A tourist once asked me what made me happy. I told her: "I like to be able to take a shit where there is a good view or a sunrise."'

We made our way down an unpleasantly steep drop of crumbling granite and there, ahead of us in the haze, lay the Red Sea. It was not the epic view that I had hoped for; instead, the water of the Gulf blended with the grey sky to create a dull monochrome, sealing us in. We were leaving the Aqaba Mountains and, had visibility been better, we could have seen Egypt, Israel and Saudi Arabia. It didn't matter. I had seen plenty of nice views, and now I was just desperate to reach this next landmark. Within an hour we hit a blacktop road, then shortly afterwards the outskirts of a seaside town. A few houses sprang up, and a concrete building with a mural of a scuba diver on the outside. The city of Aqaba was five miles north along the shore, and this suburb was an old fishing village that had been developed into a low-key tourist stop-off. There didn't seem to be many other visitors, but a few tanned Jordanians stood by the roadside and waved to us. Suleiman saluted them proudly and said things like, 'We can't stop, we are on a mission!'

At the end of the road we stepped straight onto the beach. The sand was fine, and I took off my boots to feel it between my toes. There were a few sad-looking sunloungers and, in the distance, two foreigners in scuba gear. A lifeguard's raised platform stood empty, and the dull water stretched out to the west where it faded into the haze. Suleiman grinned and lay down on the sand. Matt, Pip and I dropped our packs and, with a quick glance at each other, ran into the waves. It had been a long time since I'd felt salt water, or been anywhere deep enough to swim. After six weeks and 500 miles, I had arrived at a point where I couldn't take a single step farther, the terminus of my Jordanian walk.

Pip and Matt left to go back home and I stayed in Aqaba for three days, wandering along busy streets, whiling away afternoon hours in coffee shops with my books and journals and dealing with lackadaisical immigration officers in order to pay a fine on my visa, which had run out three weeks before.

I thought about my time in Jordan, and how it related to my earlier walks in the West Bank. They were two parts of the same puzzle, certainly, but they did not sit as naturally together as I might have predicted. In Palestine I had felt like I was witnessing a monumental struggle for existence, by a people who had no choice but to engage with the powers and politics that surrounded them. Jordan, by contrast, felt like a place of refuge. For many, from Palestine, Syria and Iraq, it was an escape from conflict elsewhere. So many people that I met identified with my notion of walking, because they too were on their way somewhere or, as they saw it, were in the midst of a displacement that was only temporary.

Before I left the UK, I had read a lot about the Irish connection to Israel and Palestine. I had expected to feel a connection or affinity there, but I did not. Not really. I had not known trouble or hardship or conflict like anyone in that land, and even in the years before my birth, when Northern Ireland was deemed a war zone and bombings were commonplace, the level of violence was never as severe. The suffering of Palestinians was simply something I could not comprehend. In Jordan too, there was anguish on a level that I'm certain I will never have to know. Within the moving masses of refugees from other nations in Jordan, however, I did notice self-reflexive questioning that was familiar, on some level, to me as an Irish/Northern Irish/British/European person: Where am I from? What is home? How do I identify? It was a strange level to connect on, though my reflections came from the privileged place of curiosity rather than desperation. To have everything you know destroyed and be forced out into the wilderness to fend for yourself and find a new home was incomprehensible. The resilience of those that I met was all the more astounding in this context.

The trails that I walked had steered me clear of big conurbations in Jordan and, for the most part my journey was skewed towards the emotions of the countryside. There were big shifts happening in the cities; globalisation had arrived, transposing American culture onto the streets of the capital and beyond. A fierce battle between heritage and independence was raging amongst the younger generations, and that disparity was reflected in the fluctuating political landscape. In the year of my walk, the Muslim Brotherhood – a hard-line and conservative Islamist movement – would field candidates in Egyptian parliamentary elections for the first time since 2003, while at the other end of the political spectrum were secular parties who proposed a separation of state and religion. There was a very clear widening of the gulf in the desires of the Jordanian populace and, as seen in other parts of the world too, a hardening of stances and a retreat into ideological silos.

This, however, was not necessarily the focus of my walk. Instead of exploring the sentiments of the urbanites – which would also be a fascinating journey – I had instead spent time with the Bedouin and those in the margins of the cities. I was constantly reminded that the land on which I walked – that we all walked – looked the same on both sides of the Jordan Valley, and that the tribes that roamed the hills and plains were connected by a shared history of thousands of years. For me, a foreign traveller, there was ubiquitous hospitality, in keeping with the traditional Islamic approach of help first, ask questions later. The Bedouin seemed uninterested, for the most part, in what lay beyond the invisible boundaries of the land that they used. Only 38 per cent of Jordan's population voted in the last elections, and almost all of those people came from the cities. For the Bedouin, the political landscape was a much inferior one to the one underneath their feet. Things could always be better, one man said, but they could be a lot worse too. To be left alone was the greatest privilege he could hope for.

During my final days in Jordan, I heard that police had unearthed a terror cell in the northern city of Irbid. It was said to be affiliated with

ISIS, but the news seemed to be quashed quickly. Jordan did not need word of such events making it out into the wider world.[59] Infiltration of such elements, however, was still of concern to some people that I'd met. 'How long can you hold a defensive line against madness coming in from all sides?' one person had asked me rhetorically. Added to that, there were worries over the burgeoning population, and the impending water shortages. Looked at from a certain perspective, it was a disquieting future.

I found it hard to view the country through that particular lens. Walking engenders optimism – after a long journey on foot, it is almost impossible to arrive at one's destination without a hopeful view of the world. Beneath my boots I felt how ancient trade routes had become pilgrimage thoroughfares and shepherds' ways, and now were morphing once more, this time into hiking trails and refugee paths. Mark Khano had been adamant that these recreational trails were about so much more than simply tourism. They were arteries that connected the disparate parts of a country built on nomadism and movement. They would create jobs, perhaps, and attract visitors, but more than that these lines on the land were linkages – between past and present, between city and countryside and between the various faiths and ethnicities that populated Jordan.

I packed up my bag once more and posted my GPS, audio recorder and wireless camera microphones to Amman; all were ostensibly banned in Sinai and I did not want to take the risk of getting arrested upon entry. A taxi took me to the port on a sticky, humid night, and I queued with 300 Egyptians for a ferry that arrived six hours late. My pack was put in a large metal storage box that smelt of fish, and I was herded onto the back of the boat between an elderly woman who glowered at me and a little girl in front who gave me the thumbs up. On board, an official took my passport and disappeared into a small wooden office. I curled up outside his door and fell asleep. Five hours later, I was accidentally kicked in the head by an unruly crowd of ship staff preparing to disembark. The first light of day was fighting to break the surface of the horizon. I sat up and rubbed my eyes. The trail to Mount Sinai was waiting.

# PART III

# THE PATH TO THE SACRED SUMMIT

*Slow Down, Find Humanity.*

(Paul Salopek)

# The Great Crossroads

I stepped off the boat in darkness and walked through a ferry terminal that had seen better days. In fact, it was nothing short of apocalyptic; the many waiting rooms and halls lay in tatters, with fresh air in place of windows and tiled floors ripped up through to concrete. It was impossible to tell whether the construction had never been finished, or if it was in the midst of being torn down. Either way it was only just holding on to its existence, and it was not a place that encouraged loitering.

I bought a visa off a man who sat quietly on a single chair in the midst of the destruction. His moustache drooped low beneath sad eyes, and the thick stubble of his chin was superimposed over an arrow-shaped scar. For $25 he pasted the paper sticker into my passport. There were no checks or scans, and only a few cursory questions from this guardian of the terminal, who rose briefly from his throne and looked down at my pack with little interest. We both wrinkled our noses at the smell of fish which the bag had collected en route.

'Why you come Sinai?' he asked, with a long sigh in his voice.

'For a holiday,' I said, trying to sound breezy. I wasn't sure exactly how to do that, so I just grinned wildly when I finished speaking.

'What you do here?'

'I'll stay at the beach, go swimming, that sort of thing.' I grinned again, and the man narrowed his eyes.

'You go to Cairo?'

'Not this time.' There was a pause.

'Too bad. Cairo very nice. Lots of parties.' His voice dropped to a whisper. 'Lots of *girls*.' This time it was his turn to grin, and the edges of his moustache rose slightly to reveal yellowing teeth. I thanked him for the advice and hurried past.

The port area was small, and within five minutes I had cleared the austere streets of the town and reached a patch of empty desert. In the moonlight I could see mountains beyond, obstructing the way to the interior. I walked for a few hundred metres towards the skyline of jagged teeth, into a gaping void of sand, until the lights of the port were far enough away that I was sure no one would find me. Then I rolled out my sleeping bag on the rutted ground and slept until sunrise, which came all too early.

The Sinai Peninsula is the great land bridge that connects the continents of Asia and Africa, and it is the most ancient of crossroads where, following the migration of our ancestors, the early civilisations of the world met, traded and fought; it has been crossed by the likes of Alexander the Great, Ramses II and Saladin and, of course, the great armies that they brought with them. Even Napoleon Bonaparte saw fit to visit, as part of his campaign to weaken the British passage to India and strengthen the French trade route. The granite mountains of Sinai are perhaps 800 million years old, and it has witnessed the passage of humankind across the towering massif and through vast swathes of desert for 100,000 years. Being a landscape that does not easily lend itself to supporting life, it is inhabited sparsely. The few hardy survivors that do call it home, however, have been there since the Bronze Age, when rich surface deposits of copper and turquoise attracted miners who by 3500 BC were moving around the peninsula with livestock and crops. Within a few centuries the pharaohs of the Nile Valley began making inroads, taking over the operation of the mines, and the Nabateans moved in 2,000 years later as their trade routes grew across the Dead Sea.

Moses led the Israelites through Sinai on their way to the Promised Land in around 1140 BC, and the story of God laying down Ten Commandments to him has inspired many thousands of pilgrims to make the journey to Mount Sinai in the intervening centuries – and they make it still.

Unlike the rest of Egypt, which fell under Roman control in 30 BC, Sinai was annexed from the Nabateans much later by the Emperor Trajan when it became part of Arabia Petraea, an area that also included the southern Levant, the northern portion of the Arabian Peninsula and much of Jordan. Christian anchorites – reclusive religious figures who withdrew from society to live a pious life in isolation – arrived as early as the third century, and a couple of hundred years later, when Egypt became part of the Christian Byzantine Empire, pilgrimage to Sinai increased, and the monastic tradition flourished in the desert. The most enduring feature from this time, in the fifth century, was the building of the Monastery of St Catherine near to where I would finish my journey. Today it is the oldest working monastery in the world.

Egypt held out against the spread of Islam, but eventually succumbed to the Muslim conquest led by the military commander Amr Ibn al Aas in AD 639. It is even said that the young Prophet Muhammad visited Mount Sinai whilst travelling with a caravan across the peninsula. Whilst Egypt fell under the rule of a series of Islamic governments, Sinai became something of a political vacuum in the decades that followed, leading to the rise of the Bedouin, who arrived from Yemen and the Hijaz. Now, it is the descendants of those tribes who are the de facto chiefs of Sinai, answerable, as I was once told, only to God and nature.[60]

Nuweiba, where I had arrived, faces east onto the Gulf of Aqaba, looking across to the mountains of the Hijaz in Saudi Arabia. To the south is Sharm el-Sheikh – South Sinai's tourist hub – and the more relaxed diving town of Dahab. Nuweiba had once been a quiet fishing village but, as tourism from Western Europe and Russia grew, the sprawl of resorts and hotels from Sharm el-Sheikh and Dahab stretched northwards, until finally it was swallowed and reborn in the new image of commercialism.

In the wake of 9/11, tourism across the Middle East took a hit, and Sinai's current nadir began in the wake of bombings in Taba (2004), Sharm el-Sheikh (2005) and Dahab (2006). The motives for the attacks appeared to differ. The Taba bombing was at the Hilton Hotel, where the majority of guests were Israelis, while the latter two bombings were said to have been motivated by Bedouin militants who opposed the often hostile policies of the Mubarak government, but the result was the same – tourism ground to a halt. In retaliation for the Dahab attack, thousands of Sinai Bedouin were arrested, and resentment still remains about the brutality and perceived discrimination that occurred during this time. The relationship between the wandering nomads of the desert and the central authority in Cairo never worked well at the best of times – the Bedouin feel they have been marginalised and subjected to repression and economic exclusion – and here reached a new low.

The Arab Spring of 2011 brought further mayhem to Egypt and to the region. In the first year following the turmoil, tourist revenue fell by $135 million. It has continued to plummet. At the time of writing, tourist numbers to the country were down by 95 per cent on 2010, and Sinai was hit as hard as anywhere.

Sinai is a much more diverse landscape than it might first appear. Running across the peninsula from east to west is the Tih Divide, a clear demarcation line between the northern plateau and the mountain massif to the south. Northern Sinai, already one of Egypt's poorest governorates, suffered from a political void after the revolution of 2011 and became a hub for Islamic militants. The Arab Gas Pipeline that runs from El-'Arish to Israel and Jordan was repeatedly bombed, weapons were smuggled in from Libya and armed groups began to take control, pushing an extreme jihadist ideology. Splintered factions of Bedouin in the north had found a common enemy in the Egyptian forces, and this, coupled with a loose affiliation to Al Qaeda, tied them together. In 2014 an outfit who are now called 'Sinai Province' aligned themselves with Da'esh and, over the 18 months that followed the rebranding, launched an unprecedented number of attacks on Egyptian military targets in the northern towns of Sheikh Zuweid and El-'Arish.

After the bombings in Dahab in 2006, South Sinai had remained largely unaffected by the unrest in the north, except perhaps through associations made in the minds of nervous visitors. On 31 October 2015, however, that all changed. Less than an hour after Metrojet Flight 9268 had taken off from Sharm el-Sheikh airport, an improvised explosive was detonated on board, causing the plane to disintegrate in mid-air over the deserts of northern Sinai. The flight was destined for St Petersburg, Russia, and was mostly filled with homeward-bound tourists. All 224 passengers on board were killed. A few days later, the Sinai affiliate of Da'esh claimed the attack and Russia responded by stopping all direct flights to the peninsula. British airlines did the same and, almost overnight, the little tourism that had continued to trickle into the resorts of southern Sinai stopped. Tourism is perhaps more resilient to terror than we are generally led to believe but, for now, the Red Sea resorts are at a low ebb.

In the morning light and from the vantage point of my sleeping spot in the desert, I could see that the port area of Nuweiba was a crumbling reminder of better times. Around the terminal was a ramshackle, dusty collection of run-down buildings, while a single tarmac road struck out to the north, flanked by mountains on one side and a series of skeletal, ruined resorts by the water. Many of these were abandoned, and the crenulations of the faux-*qasr* towers and blocky white apartment blocks were covered in a layer of sand as the desert sought to reclaim the land.

I walked back into the town in the afternoon and bought a kebab in a small shack by the ferry terminal. Huddled under a small strip of roadside shade were two large families, the men gaunt and dressed in battered suits, and the women in brightly coloured abayas that had faded in the sun. There were perhaps ten of them in total, sat in a circle around a pile of suitcases and boxes tied with strings.

One of the men told me that his family was Syrian, the other from Iraq. They had met on the boat from Jordan, having fled overland from their home towns as Da'esh approached. Now they would travel across Egypt to Libya, where they hoped to pay a smuggler to take them to Europe. He did not want to go into any details of this. As I left, he called

187

back to me, 'Maybe I'll see you in London next time!' His daughter smiled. I smiled back, but I felt a fraud; I knew how difficult it would be for them.

Their route was an unusual one, but not completely untrodden. Many of the refugees from the east (primarily, though not exclusively, those fleeing come from Syria, Iraq, Iran and Afghanistan) who wanted to reach Europe would go first to Turkey and then into the Balkans by land or, more commonly, across the water to Greece. From there they would take their chances trying to cross the European land mass on a journey of increasing peril as many countries began shutting the borders and, as in Macedonia, Slovenia and Hungary, constructing seemingly impenetrable walls to redirect the refugees onto another path.

It was these walls, perhaps, that led families like those that I met to move away from the eastern Mediterranean and western Balkan paths, and to seek another route. The men, women and children that I met in Nuweiba would join refugees from across the African continent – particularly Eritrea, Somalia and Nigeria – in taking on the hazardous journey across the central Mediterranean from Libya towards Italy or the western Greek islands. Their only solace might be that they didn't have to deal with what many African refugees refer to as 'the two seas': first, crossing the Sahara – a sea of sand – and then the Mediterranean, often in small and overcrowded dinghies.

When I left the UK in late 2015, it was in the shadow of rising anti-immigration sentiment, and an apparent hardening of resolve along similar lines across much of Europe.[61] That is why I had little hope that the families in Nuweiba would reach the UK. In total, including through normal asylum channels, the UK took 20,000 refugees in 2015. Over a million refugees made the journey to Europe that year;[62] roughly 370,000 arrived in 2016. Between January and September 2016, the UK accepted only 580 Syrian refugees, in addition to 487 refugee children from places like Iraq and Sudan.[63] Simply put: the chances for this family, with no obvious prior connections to the country, did not look good.

This mass migration and movement of people is perhaps the biggest crisis of our time, and might well be a portent of things to come, as climate change refugees begin to move alongside those displaced by conflict-ravaged and failing states. The paths that carried many of these refugees, often on foot, across countries and continents were being once more reinvented – from their original purpose as ancient migration trails, to trade routes, to pilgrimage paths, and now full circle back to the mass movement of people. The tracks are predominantly the same; it is our actions and motivations that change.

I would not be alone on my walk across Sinai. The rigours of documenting my journey had been difficult to balance with the pure act of walking, so I had asked friends back in London if any filmmakers were keen to join me. One was: a man called Austin Vince, an ex-maths teacher with a personality as big as his adventuring CV. Austin had motorcycled around the world twice, and ran the Adventure Travel Film Festival in the UK. He had years of experience making films – though perhaps not as many years of experience walking long distances – and arrived in a taxi from Sharm el-Sheikh airport dressed in his trademark retro white 1970s overalls. Momentarily, it was déjà vu: as when Sean arrived and his beard stole the show, so too did Austin's gleaming white overalls. Confused men walked over to inspect the 'Honda' badges, or to feel the red, hand-sewn stripes that ran down the arms.

'Are you working for an oil company?' one man asked. Another came up alongside to hear the answer. Behind them, by Chinese whispers, the conversation passed down a line of bystanders. I imagined word spreading that two Westerners had arrived prospecting for oil. The woes of Sinai would be over – they'd all be rich! We quickly put them right, and there were a few groans. Someone else asked a more prescient question: 'Do you want a beer?'

We drank two cans of warm lager in the sunshine, directly outside the front room of a small house which had been converted into a makeshift off-licence. Crates of room-temperature Egyptian beer, stacked neatly in front of a broken fridge, filled the interior. Austin regaled the bemused owner with an enthusiastic story about falling off a motorbike, before realising that none of the locals spoke English. Unperturbed, he repeated the story by acting it out, finishing by dramatically flinging himself to the ground as if being thrown from a bike. The men liked this.

The Egyptian dialect, though the most widely spoken of all Arabic dialects, was a mystery to me because I was more familiar with Gulf Arabic, and what I'd picked up in Palestine and Jordan, and so the party was cut short when Austin ran out of gesticulations. A taxi driver pulled up and this time we were prepared to do a deal. One hour – and a hair-raising ride along the coastline of broken dreams – later we arrived at a small desert camp called 'Sahara Beach'. This unpretentious collection of beach huts and palm-tree shaded sunloungers was to be the start of our grand desert adventure, and the beginning of the end of my walk through the Holy Land.

The Bedouin of Sinai live by strict tribal codes, with firm demarcations delineating the territory of each. There are perhaps 23 tribes in Sinai, and in the south a regional alliance called the *Towarah* – People of the Mountain – comprises seven or eight of them.[64] Sahara Beach was owned by a man called Musallem Al-Faraj, who was also going to join us on the way to Mount Sinai or, as the Bedouin called it, *Jebel Musa*. Musallem was a member of the Tarabine tribe, who controlled an oblong area of land stretching from the eastern coastline around Nuweiba into the heart of the desert. In total we would pass through three separate tribal regions on our journey: Tarabine, Muzeina and Jebeleya. It was important that I travelled with someone who knew the practicalities of crossing the deserts and mountains, but it was also essential to walk in the company of someone who would vouch for me in each area and smooth the transitions.

Austin and I spent a wretched night in a mosquito-infested beach hut, sharing a bed and engaging in hours of pillow talk to while away the painful, itchy hours. In the morning, a crimson sun rose across the Gulf, and all misery was forgotten as the sands around us came to life in the golden light.

We found Musallem sitting cross-legged on a cushion, nursing a cup of tea in one hand. He was wiry and lithe, with a salt-and-pepper beard that grew around a huge, gap-toothed smile, reaching all the way to his eyes. As soon as he saw us he jumped to his feet to shake our hands.

'The adventurers!' he said. He smiled so widely that the skin on his cheeks looked stretched to breaking point.

'Are you ready for this journey?' he asked.

'Absolutely!' said Austin, grinning almost as broadly as Musallem.

'This will be wonderful,' he replied. 'We have some weeks ahead of us in the wilderness, and we can leave all of our problems behind. I always think that the mountains are paradise, and hell is in the cities.'

We followed him to the courtyard, where a younger Bedouin in a crisp white *thobe* stood alongside a crouching camel. 'This is Suleiman,' said Musallem. 'He is from the Jebeleya tribe who live in the Monastery of St Catherine and around Jebel Musa. He's going to walk with us, back to his home.'

'And who is this?' I asked, pointing to the camel.

Suleiman spoke up. 'Harboush!' he said, speaking with a flourish.

'Harboush!' laughed Musallem, mimicking Suleiman's grand delivery. 'He will be our best friend, carrying all of our food and water and clothes. We must always be nice to everyone in life, but especially to Harboush the camel for the next weeks.'

Harboush was, Musallem told me, a very handsome camel. I approached tentatively. I had had minor dealings with camels before, but I had never yet travelled with one. It seemed wise to try and create a bond in the way that one might do with a horse, and so I patted his flanks and told him that he was a good camel. The muscles along his back seemed to relax. When I came to stand in front of him, I saw what Musallem was alluding to – camels have angular, striking faces and, although I hadn't given it much thought until now, exceedingly long eyelashes and big, emotive eyes. This is why, I was told, so many Bedouin compare their camels to their women. It did not seem like a comparison that would please their wives. I don't know how the camels felt about it either.

A pair of cloth sacks hung across Harboush's back, acting as rudimentary pannier bags. As with all camels in the Middle East he was a dromedary, with one hump instead of the two sported by his Bactrian cousins in the steppes of Central Asia. Into the bags were placed water for a week, food for two weeks, and all of our separate travelling bags.

Each new item was forced in on top of the other, then the girth tightened around Harboush's belly. He wailed, then uttered a deep, throaty cry.

'Don't worry. It doesn't hurt him,' said Musallem, noting my expression. 'But he doesn't like it either because he knows it means the resting time is over.'

We stepped back, and Harboush rose to his feet in that gravity-defying way that camels do. From his crouched position, his legs folded almost completely flat underneath, he first threw his weight to the front, his neck stretching out. He rose to his knees on the front legs, and the hind legs, spindly as they were, levered his rear end into a standing position. Finally, one by one, those knobbly knees pushed his chest into an upright position. None of the actions looked probable yet it was clear that there were many thousands of years of evolution at work to make this efficient, if not exactly graceful.

At full height, his withers (the ridge between the shoulder blades, where most four-legged animals are measured from) were in line with my head while his powerful, curved neck added another metre to his reach. He weighed close to 500 kg, Suleiman said, and he pointed out the powerful hind legs and deep chest that made him such a good pack animal.

'If you buy your own camel someday,' said Musallem, speaking like a father imparting advice to his children on their first purchase of a car or house, 'you should look for one with these things [that Suleiman had pointed out]. If they have a small nose and big eyes, this is also good, and the neck should not be too short. You must check the toes,[65] and make sure of the age. Camels should not carry a load until after they are five or six. The ideal age for a journey is maybe eight or nine.'

The girth was re-tightened, accompanied by another wail, and the relative size of the loads on the left and right checked for equilibrium. Suleiman moved in close to Harboush and spoke to him gently, whispering just an inch from his nose. He stroked him on the forehead, and Musallem confirmed the packing was a success. '*Yalla!*' he said – 'Let's go!'

# Two Bedouin, a Camel and an Irishman

From Sahara Beach we crossed a tarmac road, left behind an area called Ras Shetan, or 'Devil's Head', a small collection of buildings, and soon the mountains were upon us. Musallem turned to us and, with a smile so infectious it sounded like he was promising a treat, stated, 'We may not see any people for some days now. Remember what this looks like now. Soon it will just be the wilderness.'

The ground underfoot was fractured with sharp rock, heavily packed by constant usage. Harboush picked his way through, guided by Suleiman. Looming overhead were dark, towering granite cliffs that banished the sun from the sky. Musallem led Austin and I towards one wadi entrance, while Harboush and Suleiman peeled off to another. 'They will go a different way, just for today. I want to show you some things that Harboush cannot reach.'

The canyon walls grew as we walked west, narrowing into sheer cliff at one point as two minor wadis spawned out to the left. Our gorge was the main highway, both for travellers and the floods that pass through occasionally; some of the sporadic debris looked relatively recent. It was also the natural channel for wind, and we pushed our way upstream through the swirling gale. The wadi carved slowly through the coastal range that separates sea from desert, all the time enclosing us in an ancient natural corridor with few ways in and out. I thought back to walking in a maze at a country estate as a child, and to the growing fear of following that lined track around and around until finally being met with a dead end. I was glad to have Musallem with us.

He walked at speed, despite being nearly a foot shorter than me, and his legs took almost twice as many steps. A small rucksack was slung over his *thobe*, and on his head he wore a well-pressed brown-chequered scarf. Covering his feet were simple leather sandals that looked like they had seen many miles before. Austin and I carried day bags too; I had notebooks and snacks and water, and Austin's was mostly full of camera accessories. He carried his video camera in his hand and, as we trotted along, necks craned up towards the ribbon of sky above, he would run ahead to film us or ask us to stop while he attempted to scale the canyon walls for high-angle shots. His energy, for a man who had insisted he was going to be terribly unfit and a liability, was relentless.

'Every wadi has a name,' said Musallem. 'All of the Bedouin know them. This one is Wadi Melha, which means the salty canyon, and this one' – he gestured to a new alleyway of rock that had just opened up – 'is called Wadi Wishwashi. From the Arabic it translates to the Whispering Wadi.'

'Why is it called that?'

'It's hard to say. The best idea is that it is because of the songs that the wind sings when it comes along. Bedouin history is all passed down through generations by storytelling. Things get changed sometimes, or maybe forgotten a little bit. This is the beauty of oral history. We say here that if you have a question about the landscape, or maybe about anything, you can ask two Bedouin and get three different answers.'

Austin remained at the junction, desperate to film some of the rock formations, and Musallem led me on a there-and-back excursion along Wadi Wishwashi. We climbed over boulders and pressed through narrow, natural arches, and the rock around us changed from granite to limestone. A sheer drop to a cave below had been bridged by a small metal ladder, which Musallem smiled about as he recalled putting it there, and finally we hauled ourselves up a rope – another piece of his handiwork – to a large, circular, open space above the wadi.

'I want to show you the secrets of Sinai,' said Musallem. 'And to tell you how the Bedouin survive. People look at the desert and the rocks and think, how could anyone live there? How do they cross the mountains? Where do they find water?'

'Where *do* you find water?' I asked.

'This is a good question for you to ask to me now,' Musallem smiled. He led me farther into our rock clearing and there, suddenly apparent below, was a large pool of turquoise water, at least 10 m wide.

'We call this "the Plunge Pool"!' he said. 'When it rains, all the water gathers here, and also on the rocks above, which over years have formed angles and channels to bring more water here.'

Although we were still not far from the Red Sea, the memory of so much water had long since faded, and I thought how wonderful it might feel to find this after days in the heat and aridity of the Sinai Desert. There is water underground too, as we would see, but it can often be brackish and undrinkable. This pool, filled exclusively with surface water, could be a lifesaver.

'Are there more of these?' I asked.

'Of course!' said Musallem. 'They are all over. To those who know where to look. Nice and lovely, eh?'

We retraced our steps to Austin, who was delighted by what was fast becoming Musallem's new catchphrase. At least once an hour, Musallem would enjoy something so much that he'd describe it to us as 'nice and lovely', and Austin bounced up and down in delight at this. There were others, too; sayings that he had perhaps picked up from visitors over the years, or slight idiosyncrasies in his speech that were very endearing. Whenever he saw us smile at something he'd return the grin and say, 'Life is good!' Then, after pointing out a particularly impressive rock formation, or when witnessing a nice view along the wadi, he would turn to me and say, 'Lucky we, eh?' It was impossible to spend time with Musallem and not be impacted by his joyous love for the desert world.

In the afternoon we reached the head of the wadi and crossed a watershed into an open plateau where, in the recesses of the rocks, palm trees sprawled in small clusters like children relaxing in the shade. It was a jagged and barren landscape, and one that immediately swallowed us whole. It felt misguided to be walking away from the safety of the coastline, as it always does when one heads consciously into an inherently inhospitable place. It is these types of places, however, that have brought me the most joy and surprises over the years.

We rested under a palm tree, where an intense band of green climbed the side of the mountain, drawing water from a hidden spring to bring life in the face of the barren surface. I asked Austin how he felt.

'Well,' he said. 'I'm fat. There's no escaping that. I'm some sort of beached sea creature, dragging all of this extra blubber through the desert. And some of the skin is starting to peel off my feet. But I *feel* great! This is magical, isn't it? I've been writing a song in my head since we started. Do you want to hear it?'

I did, very much so. As well as motorcycles, filmmaking, spaghetti westerns and the 1970s, Austin's other true passion was music. Often, his music combined elements of all of the above.

'Okay mate. Here goes.' He began to sing a catchy bassline, not wholly dissimilar to 'Seven Nation Army' by the White Stripes. Musallem smiled, clearly utterly confused. Then Austin began to sing in a loud, booming voice:

> We've got a big bad desert, all covered in sand,
> And we're gonna get across it, got to have a plan,
> It's a pretty tricky trail but I think that we can,
> And that's the situation, facing [. . .]
> Two Bedouin, a camel and an [. . .] Irishman!

He bellowed out the last line, then went straight back into the bassline and hammered out the air drums. I cheered. 'I like this!' said Musallem.

'This is our caravan. Two Bedouin, a camel and an Irishman, and the musical Englishman too!'

We dozed in the shade of the oasis until the sun, which until now had raged furiously across an empty sky, fell like timber behind a mountain range to the west. 'I will tell you a story here,' said Musallem, 'before we go. This is how the history of the Bedouin is kept, by telling stories under trees while we eat dates.'

It sounded wonderfully civilised to me.

Many years ago a Bedouin stopped here to eat some dates, and he threw the seeds without thinking that a tree would grow up. Two years later he came and found the palm trees here, and he showed it to his children as a special place. Then he died, and his three sons grew up, and got married, and also had children, and so they needed more dates. Dates are very important, nature's sugars, for the Bedouin. They stopped here for the night, and the youngest boy saw the ghost of his grandfather telling him, 'If you are going to cut the trees to take the dates home, I will kill you!' The eldest brother ignored his warnings and, in the morning, one of them climbed to the top to cut three big bushes, and he fell down and died. The other brothers abandoned their plans and returned home and since that time, no one takes dates away from here. We can stop and eat them, but not to take them away. They are guarded by the ghost, and this story maybe 250 years old.

I thought about the story as we climbed a steep, winding pass over the next line of mountains. It had protected the oasis for many years, Musallem said, and, amongst superstitious peoples like the Bedouin, it would continue to do so for much longer. In Ireland we have many similar myths and legends, and they too have a basis rooted in pragmatism. Most also act as some kind of a safeguard: to stop a natural area being exploited or destroyed perhaps, or to caution against foolish acts. I asked Musallem if the same was true here and he smiled. 'It depends if you believe in ghosts or in good intentions,' he said, and laughed, skipping off along the trail.

Just before nightfall we passed through the Coloured Canyon, named for the marbled mixture of reds, yellows and whites that swim in layers along the walls of rock. Partly, Musallem said, this was because of the way in which the sandstone and the granite interacted – the granite was at the bottom as the hardest rock, while the sandstone was much more malleable, allowing water to carve channels through it and shape its features.

'The colours are also mixed up from a volcanic situation, when they were like liquid,' Musallem said. 'The red is iron, and the yellow is sulphur. It's like nature's photo art. Nice and lovely, right?'

The colours swirled around us like stars in the sky, until finally we climbed out of the canyon and walked past an abandoned hut on the plateau. 'What's this?' asked Austin.

'For the tourists,' replied Musallem. 'There used to be hundreds a day here. They'd come on day trips from Sharm el-Sheikh. It was a restaurant and a place for parties, and you could drive a 4 × 4 in from the road. But now there's no need for this place.'

The empty building, still in fine condition, sat proudly atop the hill looking down on the once thriving avenue of rock below. It reminded me of the *qasr*s in Palestine and Jordan, harking back to a better time.

We stopped for the night in the lee of a granite boulder where Suleiman and Harboush had been relaxing since mid-afternoon. Austin peeled off his socks to reveal broken skin on a total of four toes. A fly landed on the soft, red exposed flesh. He winced ever so slightly.

'How far did we do?' he asked.

'Twelve miles.'

'And was I going too slow?'

'No, you did well.'

'Great! Well, if I can keep this up, it might not be a total disaster.'

Musallem listened in. 'There are no disasters amongst friends,' he said. 'We will go at the best speed for all of us. Now, let's eat pasta. Nice and lovely!'

# Life Is Good

Departing in the morning is not necessarily a swift process for either camels or the Bedouin. I soon learned that there was a very distinct routine, and nothing could or should rush it. This was very much in keeping with every other aspect of Bedouin life – efficient, methodical and unrushed.

Musallem rose from his sleeping bag at about 5 a.m. and began tending to a small fire using wood that we'd gathered the previous night. Coffee was brewed in one kettle, tea in another, and he crouched on haunches warming his hands in the soft, red heat from the cracking branches of scrub. Suleiman and I joined him around 5.30 a.m., then Austin, and in relative silence we ate bread and long-life hummus, which we squeezed out of a cardboard packet. By 6.30 a.m. our camp was disassembled, each man taking care of his own corner. It took another 45 minutes to load everything onto Harboush. He was not at all impressed, uttering his guttural cries and destroying the calm of the early hours as we prepared the pack.

'Don't worry about him,' said Musallem. 'He is grumpy because Suleiman caught him trying to eat our cucumbers. They had a bit of an argument and now he is not talking to Suleiman.'

The various layers were added slowly to his back. First was a large and square rug, on top of which a softer animal skin was added. A girth made of cloth held these in place. Next, the saddle was added and it was a work of art, made of rich brown leather with one horn on the front and another on the back. Long, braided tassels hung from the sides and, attached to the front was a piece of fine blue silk with multicoloured sequins woven in amongst dashes of reds and blues; in the centre was a fine embroidered letter 'S' in bright red, surrounded by a square of pure white.

'What does this letter mean, Suleiman?' I asked. He looked confused.

'It is for Suleiman,' he said.

'Of course!'

On top of the saddle was placed another sheepskin which, had there been a rider, would keep him or her comfortable. Suleiman said that, were he to do this trip on his own, he would probably ride most of the way. In fact, this would be Harboush's first trip solely as a pack animal. 'He is as inexperienced with you as you are with him,' said Musallem with a glint in his eye.

Either side of the saddle were placed vast cloth sacks, expertly sewn together before we left. Our bags and food were placed inside and the extras – like the Bedouin sleeping arrangement, which was simply two large blankets – were tied to the top. Small twigs, gathered each day, were placed either side of the front and back horns of the saddle, acting as non-weight-bearing fasteners to keep the pannier bags level. Everything about the system was simple but effective, and finally a second girth was stretched around Harboush's belly to hold the final additions in place. By 7.15 a.m. we left, just as the morning light crested the limestone peaks and flooded the valley with a rich and deep orange hue.

Musallem walked with a straight back and arms at his sides, always fast. Suleiman led Harboush, his pace dictated by the camel's loping stride, and it was only when Musallem fell into conversation with Suleiman that he slowed. My natural pace was somewhere in the middle and I mostly strode alongside my Bedouin companions, occasionally taking my turn with Harboush's roughly hewn lead-rope. Austin would run ahead to film, then drop behind, always humming gently to himself, and we'd know he was approaching because the wind carried his songs to walk beside us long before his body arrived.

We travelled downhill, along a broad wadi called al-Abraq, and as we neared its terminus, Suleiman led Harboush in a large loop around two large piles of barbed wire that lay collapsed in an untidy heap by the rocky walls. The sight of anything man-made felt incongruous with our wild existence, especially something created with the inherent intent to cause harm.

'What are these here for?' I asked.

'Oh,' Musallem said, nonchalantly, 'this used to be a minefield, maybe 40 years ago when Sinai was occupied by Israel. Don't worry, all the mines are cleared now. Here, at least.'

Egypt has endured successive occupations throughout its history. For 400 years the Ottomans reigned over the region although, like many before and after them, they largely ignored the Sinai. That was followed by a rather shorter stint of British control during which the Arab uprising pushed the Ottomans out completely. The British were spread too thin to keep control of such a large area, however, so Egypt was granted independence in 1922 on the understanding that the Suez Canal would remain in British hands. This, after all, was surely the reason for their involvement in the first place.

After the creation of Israel in 1948 and Egypt's own internal revolution that saw the nationalist General Nasser take control in 1956, the British were expelled from the Suez Canal. Then, in 1967, Nasser and Egypt prepared to launch a decisive strike on Israel with backing from a coalition of Arab nations. Israel, however, knew what was coming. They launched a pre-emptive strike, bombing into oblivion Egypt's still-grounded air force. Sinai – like Gaza, East Jerusalem, the West Bank and the Golan Heights – fell to the Israelis during what they called the Six Day War.

Sinai soon became a functioning extension of Israel, despite Egyptian attempts to retake it, and not until 1982 did the last Israeli tanks withdraw from the peninsula. It had become a diplomatic bargaining chip; for the return of Sinai, Anwar Sadat, who served as president from 1970 until his assassination in 1981, had to recognise Israeli statehood and normalise relations. Today, memories of the Israeli occupation are slowly fading, yet there are some legacies which will take longer to dissipate. Roads built during that period still carry Egyptian traffic, and many of the contemporary resorts along the coastline were constructed with Israeli money (originally for Israeli tourists.)

More difficult to read is the residual influence that's left behind. For many Bedouin, Musallem told me, the occupation was a prosperous time. They had little love for the Israelis but they did have jobs and money and security in the more stabilised economic environment, all of which can buy a great deal of understanding. Bedouin, he said, are a pragmatic people at heart, and they enjoyed the removal of many of the hardships in life. Now, at an all-time economic low and amidst rising tensions with the central government once more, the days of occupation even evoke nostalgia from some – not quite the 'good old days', perhaps, but far from the bad ones.

There are few roads now in Sinai, particularly so in the interior. It is simply too difficult to maintain them in the ever-shifting desert. At a spring called Ein Furtaga, where multifarious jagged wadis succumbed to a large clearing, there was one such attempt at building a thoroughfare. The ribbon of tarmac wound its way in and out of the oasis admirably, using narrow wadis to the east and west, and although the ground crumbled at its sides, for the most part its entry and exit were intact. At the oasis itself, however, the road was lost. Yearly floods had eaten away at its existence, exposing layers of concrete underbelly, until finally a large section had been washed away entirely.

Beyond the failed road lay a house, on higher ground, and two small outbuildings. An overweight Bedouin in a grubby shirt sat sweating in the shade of a wooden pavilion. The only other account that I had read of Ein Furtaga was in a book about the 1956 Suez War, when an Israeli general named Yoffe reached the spring with his Ninth Brigade to find it completely deserted, save for one Bedouin with tuberculosis. It is perhaps slightly more prosperous now, but only just.

We drank tea with the man, and Musallem filled him in on news from the coast. Goats and their kids wandered around in the sunshine, and Austin found himself smitten by the sweet faces of the youngest ones. Two women joined us briefly, their every patch of skin covered from the heat and the roaming eyes of visitors. Aside from black gloves, however, their other garments were rich in colour, with reds and purples gleaming in the midday sun. They were two of the man's three wives. The location of the third was a mystery.

'How is life out here for this man and his wives?' I asked Musallem. He relayed the question.

'Hot!' came the man's reply, following by a lot of laughing. Another burst of Bedouin Arabic came like rapid fire, and Musallem thought for a minute before translating.

'He say they are OK. They have all they need, and they go to the coast to get more supplies. Life is peaceful, but he would prefer to be rich.'

'Is he happy with three wives?' I asked.

'Islam says he can have up to four wives, but he told me earlier that four is too many wives. He also said three is too many.'

'How many would he like?'

'Two,' said Musallem. 'He says two is the perfect number of wives.'

In the next valley, Wadi Ghazala – Valley of the Gazelles – we found another herd of goats and, from the folds of a rock, there emerged a hunched, skeletal figure. From the black robes I could tell it was a woman, but nothing more, and it was not until she got close that I could see she must be at least 80 years old. She reached out to shake my hand, then Austin's, and then embraced Musallem in a warm and lingering hug.

'She calls me her son,' said Musallem, smiling broadly again. He fished out some hummus and bread for her, and they talked briefly before she retreated back to the rocks.

'She looks after the little goats out here while they're young,' he said as we continued along the valley.

'Where does she live?'

'While she's out here, she stays outside, under the stars. If she needs anything, she can go to Ein Furtaga. She is from the old generation. You see how she did not mind to touch your hands? She is a Muslim, of course, but the older Bedouin from the mountains sometimes do not mind about some of the rules.'

'What did you talk to her about?'

'I just asked how she was. I see her when I walk past so I make sure she is OK. She said there is another family in the valley somewhere, and they have animals that are grazing. They are not Tarabine, so I will need to look at this sometime.'

'What do you mean?'

'People are welcome here, but we have to know who they are. Next time I am there I will ask some questions to see where they have come from, and, if they are passing through and bring no problems, they are welcome in the Tarabine area.'

We camped in the middle of a valley, watching the satellites pass by overhead as the stars and planets flickered into life. Austin tended to his feet, which were bruised after an 18-mile day. Suleiman reclined on one elbow and smoked a cigarette, and Musallem watched the fire. 'This is great,' said Austin. 'This is wild camping at its absolute best.'

'No mosquitos and a nice breeze,' agreed Musallem. 'I like it here. This is maybe one of my favourite places on earth. When I'm here, I think "Life is good."' It was hard to disagree.

# Footprints

The rhythm of our journey became as natural as breathing: wake, eat, break camp and walk. Each morning Musallem would bake fresh *libba* bread, kneading flour, salt and water in a metal pan and then pushing the dough under the ashes of the fire to bake. During the hottest part of the day, around noon, we would sleep under a tree or by a rock for a few hours then walk until sunset and choose a bedroom for the night in the sands of the wadis. At times we would not talk for hours, simply watching the landscape around us morph in time with our plodding progress. On other occasions we'd speak incessantly. Austin told us about the Pyrenees, where he ran off-road motorbike excursions each year, and he talked us through the history of the spaghetti western. I spoke of Palestine and Jordan, and about Ireland and other places that I missed. Musallem was our glue, translating odd snippets of wisdom from Suleiman (watch out for scorpions when you pee, for example) and using his own thoughts to sketch pictures on the canvas of Sinai.

We stopped at a spring by a mountain called Jebel Milehis. 'It means, the mountain of the place where you lick,' said Musallem. 'Come, I'll show you.' Nestled under a sandstone overhang was a small pool of water and, above, a narrow crack feeding it. Three palm trees marked the spot from the outside, and a small fig tree grew in their shadow. Where Musallem crouched, the edges of the basin for the water had been sculpted by hand. 'Who made this?' I asked.

'We did!' he said. 'The Bedouin. Otherwise the water would be wasted. Someone has come here and carved it so it catches the water, and now animals can come and drink here. This is why we say *Milehis* – the place where you lick, to get the water.'

Sandstone now was beginning to dominate the rock formations around us. There is a chaos to sandstone, the rock giving way to the elements in a wild and unpredictable way, so that to look at it for any length of time is to see a physical rendering of its history; each rainstorm and gale and pair of feet that have climbed there etch their stories into the soft and forgiving exterior.

Musallem, Austin and I climbed to the summit to look out at the route ahead, while Suleiman and Harboush plodded on along the valley. I watched Musallem scale the heights in his flat sandals and thought how he must feel the trek, and sense it, in a much different way to Austin or me. In thick desert boots, as comfortable as they are, one loses the texture of a walk. Those who wander barefoot talk of the sensation of shifting earth beneath toes, and sandals cannot be far off this experience. The ground that Musallem trod upon made as much of an impression on him as he did on it, and the relationship was much more symbiotic than I could ever achieve.

It took us over an hour to ascend 400 m, and at the top shingles of granite crumbled away to reveal a breathtaking view across the plains. From down below the surrounding wadis felt intimidating, tall and impenetrable, but now we could look out across numerous scars of sand cutting through jagged rock in something approaching a predictable manner, and perspective was regained. We noted how one led to the other, how this one fell and that one rose, how the sand was thicker in one side of valley because it was a channel for the prevailing wind. Not content with being on the plateau, Musallem led us across loose rock and terrifyingly narrow ledges to the highest point visible, and there we sat on a space only big enough for three bottoms, tossing bits of rock down the precipice and giggling as they rolled, smashed and exploded on impact below. We were, for a brief moment, children once more, enjoying the simple pleasures of life, on top of the world.

'How long have you been walking in this part of the desert?' asked Austin as we slid down the other side of the mountain.

'Forever,' Musallem answered. 'I used to bring tourists into the desert after I set up my camp at Ras Shetan, but there have been very few people since 2005.'

'Is it difficult to get licences to be a guide?' I asked.

'Impossible,' he smiled. 'I don't have a licence. The government won't give me one. I tell some people where I'm going and who I'm with, but it can never be properly official.'

'Why is that?'

'The government are more scared than the tourists, I think. They don't want anything to go wrong, and they don't trust Bedouin. Bedouin don't trust the government either. They think they are stupid. So it goes in circles.'

'What could go wrong?' Austin asked.

Musallem shrugged. 'Who knows? But it's the desert, so they won't take any responsibility.'

Between 2007 and 2009, Musallem began charting some of the routes in the Tarabine territory that he'd spent his life walking. Together with a British friend and with a small amount of EU funding, he retraced his footsteps and created trails and itineraries that hardy tourists could walk in a few days or a week. Over the years his vision grew and he found kindred spirits from the other tribes. Faraj Suleman of the Mozeina and Faraj Mahmoud of the Jebeleya, both respected outdoorsmen, joined his efforts and brought with them similarly encyclopaedic knowledge of their own area. A British hiker and writer, Ben Hoffler, who knew the Sinai as intimately as any foreigner, began to work with this Bedouin co-operative, and in 2015, after years of development, they launched the 'Sinai Trail'. This is a Bedouin-run long-distance hiking trail from the Red Sea to the High Mountain Region, an area centred around the town of St Catherine, boasting rows of jagged peaks well above 2,000 m high.

Like the Masar Ibrahim and the Jordan Trail, it is still in its infancy, and it too is designed to connect ancient routes with the whims of modern recreation, taking locals and tourists alike through the history and wildernesses of the wild peninsula. The aim of the co-operative is also to strengthen the economy, creating jobs and opportunities along the trail which, after the Metrojet bombing, is an increasingly difficult challenge. I told Musallem that I thought it was an admirable but audacious project – did he think it would work?

'Of course!' he said. 'Life is good. I like to be ambitious. We make the trail to build jobs and show people Sinai, but it's also for us too. It protects the heritage of the Bedouin too. You see when we walk, how I talk about the names of the wadis and the mountains? I see you writing them down too. This is a document of our lives and history here, and it helps everyone to remember that it is important to look after it. So if we even do only that, then it will have worked.'

At the foot of the mountain was a collection of Bedouin huts which Musallem referred to, collectively, as 'Sheikh Salem's tent'. We drank tea with Sheikh Salem – a big man, with a face that wore each of the storms it had weathered – and as he spoke with Suleiman and Musallem I looked out at his small lot. Two camels stood in the shelter of an upturned car chassis, and a small boy maybe three years old fed them grain from a cloth bag. By the farthest hut was the shell of another old jeep which had been converted to store jerrycans. Two of the huts were made of wood, with supporting beams holding up a thatched roof and an area that one might describe as a 'porch' being separated from the interiors by squares of material sewn together to make a partition. Small fig trees grew sporadically, protected by wire mesh; presumably the wandering camels were as big a threat as the wind and dust storms. Finally, there was an ancient-looking acacia tree with a rope swing made of an old grain sack. Sitting in it, holding tight to two bound ropes, was a small boy, and beside him a collection of rusted tin boxes with a pigeon in each. Strips of corrugated iron patched up holes in the huts, and when the wind blew through, as it did regularly on the plain, the whole camp shuddered. It felt like a scene out of *Mad Max*.

Sheikh Salem told us to look out for petroglyphs, which he said were everywhere along the base of the mountain, and we climbed back out of the valley across a sprawl of multicoloured natural stepping stones of rock. In the spirals of sulphur and iron and volcanic ash in the stone we thought we also found the carved animals of the Nabateans; perhaps – they certainly looked like those in Wadi Rum. They were faded almost beyond recognition, but as ever the humps of camels became clear, and simplistic human figures flanked the roaming animals.

There were other carvings too: Christian crosses drawn by early pilgrims from Europe who came to see the places where Moses and the Israelites had trod. Pilgrims had been arriving from as early as the fourth century, though relatively little is known about those first tourists, and the volume of travellers was much less too. Many of the inscriptions that we found were made by Armenian pilgrims, probably between the seventh and tenth centuries – a time when Sinai was under Muslim rule, which is interesting to note since it did not diminish the zeal (nor affect the success) of the travellers during that time.

Beside the crosses were outlines of tiny footprints scraped into the sandstone, and Musallem studied their juxtaposition.

'The Christians were here and left their mark, for sure,' said Musallem. 'We walk in their trail now, and also of the Muslims on Hajj sometimes, but there are many more Christian reminders here.'

'And what are the footprints?'

'They're from the Bedouin, and it's kind of romantic. If a man wanted to marry a woman, he'd make the shape of his foot on the rock. If the woman agreed, she'd carve hers next to it. It's a kind of love memory. You can also see where the family approves, because they make a circle around it.'

We were surrounded by love, both mutual and unreciprocated. Most prints were together, one always slightly larger, and many had the circle of approval sealing the marriage. The sad ones were the lonely feet, destined to walk alone and, equally unfortunate, the uncircled pairs: young lovers whose parents would deny them a future together. I thought of the modern-day graffiti of young love – of hearts on school walls and names intertwined on street corners. I thought too of the padlocks that are attached to bridges around the world as a symbol of everlasting commitment. Love, endorsed or forbidden, is an equaliser.

Here, in the rock of Sinai, the Bedouin were marking their own rituals of courtship and of love lost, found and desired.

We found more petroglyphs that afternoon, in a closed box canyon which wound its way uphill out of a sandstone plain. Harboush was shackled and he hobbled off to munch on some small dwarf plants, and the human contingent of our team followed the narrow wadi to its terminus, where a large sheer cliff face blocked onward progress. At times, the walls were so narrow that we had to turn sideways; our shoulders were too wide to fit. The sandstone was smooth where the water ran through in flood times, and above the watermark the rock conjured wind-blown gremlins and ghouls.

We rested on a high perch and looked at the fortress of stone around us. At one point, it had been popular with tour groups who would come north from Sharm el-Sheikh. We knew this because hundreds of these tourists had scrawled their names into the soft rock all around us. I read some of the entries in this requisitioned physical guestbook.

'Jeffrey wuz here, Sinai Tour 2001!!' said one by my left shoulder.

'Mohammed is cool!' screamed another in big script. Then 'No he's not!' countered a joker, before someone else, presumably Mohammed again, defended his honour with the inarguable 'He is VERY cool. Cooler than Ali.'

There was no response and so, etched into history in the closed canyon, Mohammed's coolness was made permanent.

There were love hearts and, of course, penises – probably drawn by British teenagers – and lists of names of travellers who seemed less inspired and enthusiastic than Jeffrey, and 'Hendrik Grubber, 2003' said one. He had underlined his surname to make sure it was obvious. 'Pete G', said another; a third: 'Geordie George'. I asked Musallem what he thought of them.

'It's not right,' he said. 'This graffiti is not needed here. There is already some before them. Look here.'

He led onto another perch where, only just discernible on the darkened rock, there was the unmistakable shape of a camel. 'This is ancient,' said Musallem. 'Bronze Age, I think.'

I wondered if Mohammed or Jeffrey had simply scratched it in and fooled everyone, but Musallem pointed to the location, colour and style of the carving as proof of age.

'It's ancient,' he said. 'We've had people study it. Before this, they thought that camels were not used by humans until the end of the second millennium BC. This shows that they were probably used in the Sinai long before that.'

It was odd to think that this canyon, with its terrifying high walls and tight squeeze, had been home to early nomads, then to Nabateans, then Christian pilgrims and, hundreds of years later, to stag parties from Newcastle in the nineties.

That night I slept poorly. My stomach cramped irregularly through twilight hours, and my temperature fluctuated wildly. By the time we had risen and packed away in the morning, I found myself unable to stand straight. Nonetheless we departed on time, and I skipped breakfast, making an excuse and keeping any concerns to myself.

Our caravan departed before the sun breached the cliffs and we headed now for the oasis of Ein Hudera, which it has been suggested is the site of Hazeroth where Moses and his Israelites paused during their 40 years of wandering. Before that it was part of the Nabatean trade route between Egypt and Edom (and on to Damascus) and subsequently became part of the pilgrimage trail between the coasts and the holy mountain. As with so many patches of earth that I had walked upon, this was a place regenerating time and again to fulfil a new use by the movement of walkers. Now, it was on the fledgling Sinai Trail, and the camp would be our home for the night.

It was not a long way to the oasis but I struggled. Each footstep was an agonising effort and I lagged far behind the rest of the group. For four hours I hauled myself through deep sand, sinking backwards with each step, until finally the rich green of the palm trees came into sight. Ein Hudera lies in the territory of the Muzeina tribe, and a number of families live in the settlement. A rickety wooden fence separated permanent habitation from wild desert, and as we crossed into the encampment I noticed, briefly, that there were even a few concrete structures. In the centre was a large social area, where wadi mats were laid out around a fire and pots of tea simmered in the ashes. A thatched roof provided shade, and three men stood to greet us. I shook hands, and then slumped onto a mat.

Later I awoke, now in the dark shade of a back room that was covered by corrugated iron. Austin sat with me. 'You passed out, mate,' he said. I tried to sit, and vomited onto the sand by the mat.

'Lie back down,' instructed Austin. 'Close your eyes and try to sleep. I'll get water.'

For hours this was the pattern – I'd slip in and out of consciousness and then, every 20 or 30 minutes, violently purge the contents of my stomach. I only recall having one thought: I was a long way from anything. Austin would dutifully clean up after me, pass me more water and tissues, and then I'd pass out again.

At some point in the night, Musallem decided that I needed the help of a Bedouin. He arrived with a glowing green drink in a teacup, which he said was a local remedy. I hadn't the energy to ask what was in it, and it seemed perhaps better if I didn't know.

'You must drink it in one go,' he said, and I did. It was sharp and bitter and tasted like water from a bog, and I immediately felt like throwing up once more.

'Now we do the next stage,' said Musallem. 'It will be painful but good.' I only believed one of those things.

I was instructed to lie on my front, and Musallem performed a vicious form of massage therapy on my back, pinching skin and muscle and pummelling my spine. He hammered away with a gleeful look on his face for a seemingly interminable amount of time, then took off his keffiyeh and tied it in a knot around my upper left arm. He paused, then pulled it so tight that I yelped in pain.

'What's this for?' I asking, pleadingly.

'This is to stop the blood flow,' said Musallem, as if it was obvious that he would do such a thing. 'Now we cover you up.'

Four thick Bedouin blankets were placed on top of my limp body, and underneath I sweated and bit my lip with the pain of the tourniquet. Minutes passed and they felt like days. I was only vaguely conscious, and the world was dark. Fleetingly, I saw Austin's face looking down at me. He had been watching over me for nearly a full day. It was good to know he was there. I was quickly going off Musallem.

I awoke the next morning in another part of the camp, with little recollection of the intervening hours. Austin, as ever, was there.

'How do you feel?' he asked, softly.

'Better, I think.' I stood and took a few teetering steps without collapsing or vomiting. Austin accompanied me outside, where the sun was just beginning to light up the camp. I recoiled from the intensity of the light and Musallem and Suleiman, who were sat by the fire, came to check on me.

'I think I can walk today,' I said.

'Good!' said Musallem. 'I'm sorry for the sickness. All journeys have their difficult parts. And now you will not get sick again, because you know how painful it is to be treated by a Bedouin!'

He clapped me on the back and went to ready Harboush for the day ahead. Suleiman shrugged and smiled his half-grin. Then he lit a cigarette and nodded at me. It was time to go.

# Slowing Down

It was not the visit to Ein Hudera that I had hoped for. I had looked forward to seeing living history in action: the date palms and olive trees, the cultivation of life and hospitality in the desert. As we left, I had instead to comfort myself that I was surely following in a long line of other travellers who had succumbed to ailments there on the road to Mount Sinai.

The greenery was quickly swallowed by the folds of the valley, and we continued along the broad and sandy Wadi Hudera until our way was blocked by a pass called Naqib al-Shal. Here Harboush was unburdened to give him more freedom on the loose rocks and Suleiman led him up the narrow, switchbacked trail while Musallem, Austin and I shuttled the load to the top. Thick rain clouds gathered rapidly as we did so, blown in from the east by a swift wind, and at the summit they burst dramatically, drenching the sand with fat drops of rain and turning the dust of the wadi into a river of mud. We ran to a small and abandoned building which seemed positioned by divine intervention and there we watched the storm roll across the sky. As quickly as it arrived, the clouds dissipated and we crossed over the main blacktop road that led across the southern part of the peninsula to the Monastery of St Catherine. Soon we were alone, back in the arms of the desert.

Ein Hudera had been a natural stopping point for rest and change. In normal circumstances Musallem would have returned home and we would have been passed on to the stewardship of a representative of the Muzeina. It was unclear right up until the last moment whether this would happen for us. When we walked out of the oasis together, Musallem said only that he had agreed with the men there that he would stay with us. It was an exceptional circumstance, he had told them.

'I want to finish this journey with all of us together,' he said. I was touched – I presumed that our relationship consisted mostly of a one-way admiration, but he insisted to Austin and me that he enjoyed our stories and company. 'You love this trail, and I love this trail. And I love showing you the trail. Life is good, brothers!' he said, in his inimitably endearing way: part Sinai Bedouin, part Californian surfer.

These were to be the final days of my journey. I was into my fifth month of travel, and by the time I stopped walking, the soles of my boots would have seen a thousand miles pass beneath them. With time to think as we walked, I tried in vain to concretise my feelings on being so close to the end; it was very hard to relate the walk to Mount Sinai with what came before. I was surrounded by a new group of people, in a new landscape. The pressures of previous months – of finding places to sleep, and of navigating and explaining myself to new people on a daily basis – were now gone. It was somewhat ironic therefore that the closest I'd come to having to halt the trip was from the mystery illness at the oasis, but otherwise the concerns of Palestine and Jordan were only a memory.

The journey as a whole had no doubt been a disjointed one. Yet with the end in sight, I could now see connections much clearer than the divisions. These were lands that were intrinsically linked physically, culturally and historically, and even contemporary geopolitics could not diminish that. The migration routes, and trade routes, and pilgrimage trails and Bedouin paths and hiking trails all worked to create unavoidable thoroughfares – much more powerful than any paved highway – that channelled travellers though the identities and faiths and ethnicities of the Holy Land. In my head I was building up a map of the journey, but one that was not based on landmarks; instead, I had a representation of the walk through faces, conversations and acts of kindness. To walk is to meet people on their level, face to face and shoulder to shoulder, and it serves more powerfully than anything else that I have found to highlight a shared humanity among all.

The time in Sinai had instead become an experiment in slow living. Our group adhered to a basic routine, and the days took a similar pattern. In this way, I felt I could travel forever – combining the calm predictability of the Bedouin schedule with the opposing and inherent fickleness of a long journey, where the only certainty was constant change. In the past I have reached the end of lengthy voyages desperate for the end, but not this time.

We passed a well, dug deep into the earth by the Muzeina and covered by a sheet of metal. Large boulders marked the outline of a trough, and above the well itself three rusted iron girders were placed in a triangle suspending a pulley and bucket. Harboush drank long and noisily, and I asked Musallem about the etiquette for using the water.

'It is for everybody,' he said. 'Anyone passing through can use it for themselves and for their animals. We will fill this trough now so any other animals have it to drink also.'

'So the Muzeina don't mind Tarabine or Jebeleya or foreigners using it?'

'Of course not, but as long as we just use it while we travel. If we try to live here or to make a garden, then no. It is too precious for that.'

I said that I supposed they would never know who might use it as they passed through. Musallem laughed. 'But they always know!'

'What do you mean?'

'They are always watching. At the oasis [Ein Hudera] the men I spoke with could tell me everywhere we'd been. They knew all our camps, and where we stopped for lunch. It's the Bedouin security system. We are always watching.'

The Bedouin CCTV was all-seeing and all-powerful. It was how they protected their homeland, said Musallem, and it was something to bring comfort rather than fear. I still found it an odd and slightly disconcerting thought, however, that even when we might have felt like we were alone in the desert, we rarely were.

We spent a night in a cave, deep in the belly of a sandstone chamber, and in the morning Musallem and I climbed an adjacent mountain with first light.

'I wish we were birds, so we could fly out over this!' he cried into the wind as we summited. A pale red orb grew out of the haze to the east and brought the layers of brown to life in front of us, and Musallem built a cairn to welcome it to the day. We agreed that there was little in life that matched watching a sunrise from the top of a mountain. Back at camp, Austin patted his belly and said, 'I feel the fittest that I've done in about 20 years.' Suleiman laughed, and lit another cigarette which he smoked as we began to walk.

As we walked, Musallem and Suleiman would sing long tales of camels and women and travelling. Suleiman said the stories marked the passing of time, and I wondered if this might be a Bedouin version of the Australian Aboriginal songlines, charting distance and movement through the verses of song. Certainly, navigation seemed to happen on a separate plain of consciousness from what I was used to. Unlike in the north of Sinai – and in other vast sand deserts like the Empty Quarter or the Sahara – a reading of the shifting of the sands and the movement of the constellations was not needed. Instead, Musallem's skill came from his experience, and sensory attachment to the memories. Inside his head was a map of our route more detailed than any physical representation in existence, and although his knowledge seemed at times to be ethereal, it is based in a recognition of immovable physical markers. Thus he would simply look to the wind, and sing his way towards Mount Sinai, and in his subconscious and periphery the route would reveal itself ahead like an illuminated trail.

We had been climbing slowly from sea level ever since leaving Sahara Beach; now at well over 1,000 m the margins of the day were cool, and the nights glittered with frost. Musallem took us on a detour to avoid an army camp that he had been told about at Ein Hudera and reminded us about his lack of a licence.

'If anyone finds us, say you are on a day trip from St Catherine,' he instructed us. There was the faint noise of light artillery from an

Egyptian military camp in the distance – training, we hoped – but it seemed improbable that we'd be discovered in the wadis.

The High Mountain Region began to beckon us in and, in the foothills of the granite slabs, we passed by two large square areas of cultivated land. They shone with an unnatural brightness in the sea of brown all around, and between rows of plants ran water pipes, pumping precious liquid onto the roots. These were poppy fields, and they were at the heart of Sinai's illicit drug trade. Up close I could see a shock of bright purple and pink flowers beginning to bloom, but most of the pods were still fused shut. In time, they would be sliced with a razor blade so the milky substances inside could ooze out. It would dry in the sun and, ultimately, be sold as opium either locally or across the border in Israel and beyond.

'Don't film anything,' said Musallem. 'The men who work here are very cautious and do not want to be caught.' I noticed how the poppy fields had been created within the shadow of a large rock face, presumably so that Egyptian aircraft could not see them. According to my map, and Musallem's warning, we were only a mile away from the army checkpoint from where the sounds of military training still sounded.

Beside the second garden we were spotted by two teenagers and, after a brief moment of standing still like rabbits caught in headlights, they glanced at one another and approached us. Musallem greeted them warmly and they quietly sloped over to shake our hands. Both looked exhausted and their clothes were dirty and torn. Behind them, perhaps 100 m away, was a single small hut made of wood and cracked sheets of iron.

'They would like us to go for tea in their home,' said Musallem, motioning to the shack. We sat with six opium farmers and drank sweet, viscous tea. One of the farmers was an old man, his slight frame dwarfed by a large fleece jacket. Another said he was around 40, though his face was drawn in the manner of someone much older, and the remaining boys were no older than 18. The men used to have jobs in the tourism industry on the coast (Musallem translated as they spoke), but there had been no work for years. This was now their last resort. None of them wanted to grow opium, but they could not get permits for legal crops. One of the boys told Musallem he thought it was probably haram – against Islamic law – but there were no other options. Desperate, they lived out in the desert, tending to the poppies and hiding from the military.

'They work here all hours of the day, and they sell the stuff for maybe $30 or $40 per ounce as opium.'

'How much does it sell for when it reaches the cities?'

Musallem consulted the men. 'In Cairo, maybe $300. In Tel Aviv, $500.'

Suleiman took some of our remaining bags of pasta from Harboush and left them with the men. 'They are very hungry,' Musallem told me. 'They are nearly starving, in fact, and the work is very tiring, but they said we can see where they work with the wells, if you like.'

We followed two of the teenagers to the back of one of the poppy fields, and in front of me appeared a great gaping void in the earth. Perhaps 10 m wide and 40 m deep, it was quarried out of unforgiving ground. A generator sat precariously on a small slope by the lip, and a single pipe ran into the darkness, drawing water up from the subterranean aquifers below.

'It's huge,' I said.' 'How long did it take to dig this?'

'Two months,' said Musallem.

'All by hand?'

He nodded. 'But at least this one had water. They dig wells all over like this, hoping to get lucky. Many times there's nothing there, so they start again.'

The boys scurried back to work, flooding basins to feed the illegal crop that would allow them to subsist. We untied Harboush and began to walk. Before we left I had asked the boys what they would like to do when they were finally able to leave the farm. Musallem translated their answer with a wry smile. 'They'd like to be tourist guides,' he said. 'And to walk with people like you through the desert for fun.'

The poppies were not the only plants that we saw in the desert. To Austin and me, who were largely ignorant, the few plants that we saw all looked relatively similar, but Musallem gently reprimanded us when he heard us talking like this. There are, he claimed, over 800 species in Sinai, split between those found in the desert plains, and those in the mountains. At higher altitudes, he would point out the shrubs and their various uses: Judaean wormwood was the key ingredient in a remedy to relieve diarrhoea, while horsemint meant water was close by. Some of the plants were edible, like the pink leaves of the bladder dock, which Musallem said he often ate and described as 'the insurance policy'. What did he mean, I asked?

'No one will come here to find you for a long time, maybe if you're in trouble. So we have to know everything. I know how to look for water, and I can see a flint on the ground to make a fire. I find shade and then pick some of the right plants to eat. I would be OK here for a long time, maybe forever. This is the insurance.'

There were also many plants that should not be consumed but served other purposes. The bulbous stems of the Jointed Anabis, for example, could be crushed to make into a type of soap that the Bedouin used. Others were less useful: one with polka-dotted purple flowers was very poisonous, while another, with pink buds that looked very like the edible bladder dock, was hallucinogenic. 'We have to be careful of Harboush,' joked Musallem. 'He might eat it and have a party on his own.' In truth, however, Harboush took no interest in the many varieties of flora that dotted our way. Instead, he focused mainly on the thorny Spiny Zilla, crunching happily through the spikes as a human might with a packet of crisps. The only other thing that made him raise a bushy eyebrow once in a while was when he heard the rustle of cardboard, which he loved above all else. I had become very fond of his gentle presence and reassuring stoicism, and would be sorry to leave him behind.

# Many Roads, Many Ways

It is often said that there are many paths to God, which in Sinai works both as a metaphor and as practical advice. We were approaching Mount Sinai from the northeast and, on our final night of the journey, we paused in an area called the Blue Desert. It was an odd place; a vast plain between the mountains where the ubiquitous red rock that I'd come to know so well had been artificially coloured using masses of blue paint.

The story, which Musallem told me as we arrived, was that a Belgian artist called Jean Verame was responsible. In the 1980s, to celebrate Egypt's peace treaty with Israel, he set out to cover many of the large boulders in the area in blue, working with the personal approval of Anwar Sadat and 10 tonnes of paint supplied by the UN. The result was undoubtedly striking, yet a little strange. The turquoise sat at odds with the soft colours of the desert and, where the paint had begun to peel off, it left only dappled marks of the grand idea. The local Bedouin were very fond of it, said Musallem, and I'd heard it touted as one of the main tourist attractions in the area (back when there were tourists), but, as is usual in these cases, even the finest efforts of mankind were no match for the colours, beauty and art of the desert itself.

We were now less than 10 miles from the town of St Catherine at the heart of the High Mountain Region, and we had crossed into Jebeleya territory (indeed the name Jebeleya means 'people of the mountains'). Suleiman was almost home. Not long after we had set up camp in the shadow of a bulbous blue rock, a truck appeared on the horizon, heading our way. We watched it arriving for 30 minutes. I began to get some notion of how easy it might be for Bedouin to survey their land when they knew the right spots to watch from.

The truck delivered two guests. One was Suleiman's father, who was elderly and walked with a bowed back but a broad smile. The other was Nasr, who wore a fine clipped moustache and worked as a guide in St Catherine and the surrounding mountains. He would travel with us to Mount Sinai, he said, and he did not come empty-handed; from the car he produced two plucked chickens, and from his pocket a metal tin of jazzy cigarette tobacco.

Nasr prepared the chickens by carving them up and marinating the pieces with homemade spices. He dug a circular hole in the sand, perhaps 30 cm deep, and set a new fire on the base. Once the ashes were red hot and the flames had died down, the chicken was placed in a metal container and the hole covered over from the top. An hour later, our slow-roasted chicken feast was ready, and we gorged on the succulent meat. It had been two weeks since I had eaten anything fresh.

We watched the stars together for the final time, and as the Big Dipper moved across the sky, a pale moon lit up the desert floor.

'You know,' said Nasr, 'there are Bedouin somewhere in these mountains who are still cut off from the rest of the world. Some of them don't want to be part of the modern world.'

Musallem told a story about the first car in Sinai. It had come from England and all the Bedouin came down from the mountains to marvel at it passing through. They had little idea what it was for, but when it drove through a section of the desert they commented most on the smell that it left behind. For a month they could still sense traces of the petroleum, and that was the impression that left the longest legacy.

Nasr then told me that when his uncle first saw a radio being used in St Catherine in the 1970s, he was desperate to have one. He ultimately sold a camel to afford one, only to realise that he didn't have the requisite power source to run it.

'The Bedouin are very clever,' he said. 'But modern things are not natural for people here. Sometimes it takes a long time. I think it's good, probably. We have things here that don't need updating.'

Suleiman's father left after dinner to drive home. When everyone else had retired to their sleeping bags, and the only glow came from the waning moon and the dying embers of the fire, I took one last chance to speak with Musallem before our journey ended. I wanted to ask him about religion. He occasionally mentioned Allah, but I had not seen him praying.

'Are you a religious man, Musallem?' I asked finally. He smiled, his teeth reflecting the light of the moon.

'Are you?' he asked in return.

Almost without exception on my journey from Jerusalem, I had lied when asked this question. To the vast majority of people that I met in the Holy Land, it was almost unthinkable to not have a religion, and so I identified as a Christian.

'I am not religious,' I told Musallem. He waited, encouraging me to elaborate.

'My parents weren't either, but I grew up in a very religious environment in Ireland. I think about it a lot, I suppose, and when I was younger I thought at one point that maybe I'd found God. But in the last 10 or 15 years I just feel like an observer. I don't pray and I don't follow any doctrine, but I do feel like the planet we live on is much too intricate and diverse to be an accident.'

'Maybe you go on adventures to try and find an answer for this,' he replied.

'Maybe,' I said. 'Probably.'

There was a long pause. Nothing moved save the stars above us.

'I am a Muslim,' said Musallem after a while. 'When I was younger I was very strict. I studied the Qur'an a lot, and when I was 16 I was very in love with it. I would go to the mosque to pray with my father. He was a lawyer and a big sheikh for Tarabine, and a very religious man.'

'And now?' I asked.

'I still pray, but I do it in my own way now. Islam is a very special religion. It is a peaceful religion, and it's important to remember this when Da'esh is destroying its name.'

'What do you think is the real relationship between Da'esh and Islam?'

'Nothing. They are nothing. Islam is peace. The Qur'an does not tell me that I can kill people. It does not encourage it. There are complicated parts of the Hadith, but it always says that peace is best. Maybe if you kill my brother, for example, I am *allowed* to kill you. But, if I choose to *forgive* you, it's even better. There are scales of justice, you see? It encourages the peaceful option.'

'Do most Bedouin think like this?'

'I think so, and I hope so. For me, I learned from my father. He was very wise. He died of a heart attack some years ago, but from him I inherited a love of coffee, cigarettes and religion. Through those things, I remember him.'

We could have talked all night; Musallem never seemed to tire. But I was exhausted, so I thanked him again for our time together and climbed into my sleeping bag. He was the perfect ambassador for the Bedouin, I thought, and for the fledgling Sinai Trail. Anyone who came here to walk would get much more than a simple hike in the wild if they were fortunate enough to have Musallem for company.

We rose early for the final push to the summit of Jebel Musa. My Bedouin companions referred to it either by this name or by the direct English translation, Moses Mountain. Mount Sinai was not used by anyone there, except me. I even heard Musallem call it by the Greek name – *Hagia Koryphē*, meaning the 'Holy Summit' – or *Horeb* – the Hebrew name for the mountain upon which Jebel Musa and four other peaks stand – before he used 'Mount Sinai'. This term, Nasr told me, was mainly useful for tourists, and also as a shorthand to identify it with the Biblical narrative, but it was not used by Bedouin to denote the contemporary location.

There are five routes by which to ascend the mountain – the Path of Moses, the Path of the Pasha, the Path of Egeria and two others whose names I could not discover. We would follow the first of these, the Path of Moses, which is set with 3,750 steps, built by industrious monks in the sixth century (I heard a few versions of this story, and one said that over the course of 50 years the steps were created by just one painfully repentant and mysterious monk, but I could not verify this.) Pilgrimage accounts from the Byzantine era refer to this pathway as the main route even then, and today the so-called 'Steps of Penitence' still carry weary pilgrims upwards towards the site where Moses received the Ten Commandments.

It took us most of the morning to reach the flanks of the great mountain, and for hours we walked directly towards the distinctive triangular summit of Jebel Musa, as if it were our very own North Star. On the high pass of Naqb al-Dhirwa, the entrance to the highlands, Nasr pointed to a small doorway set within a pile of rocks to one side of the path. 'This is a leopard trap,' he said, by way of explanation. Leopards, while beautiful to the outside observer, were to many Bedouin simply a threat to the livestock in the valleys, and their hides a potential source of income. 'There have not been any for maybe 70 years, but the Bedouin used to catch them here. A goat would be put into the trap, and then when the leopard came to eat him he would run away, and a string on his leg would pull down a rock to catch the leopard.'

In the afternoon, at the confluence of two great wadis, we came upon a small village called Sebaya with perhaps ten houses clustered together below the bulging peaks above. One of the houses was Suleiman's and, in the scrubland behind it, Harboush too found that he had returned from whence he came. I helped to unload him for the last time and Austin slipped a celebratory nosebag of grain over his ears. I gave him a final ruffle of the flanks and we left him to rest. Suleiman decided to accompany us to the top of the mountain as well, despite having tasks to attend to in Sebaya. 'Why not?' he said in English, grinning. Cigarettes were lit all round.

'There is a spiritual feeling here,' said Musallem as we climbed, the gradient increasing exponentially once we left Sebaya. 'You can sense the others who walked here before.'

There were certainly large numbers of other travellers who had made this journey throughout history, and many of them did so along the very same track upon which we stood. It was in the early Christian period in the sixth century that the narratives of the Old Testament became almost inseparably attached to the landscapes and mountains of Sinai – the holy mountain, the burning bush and the caves of Moses and Elijah all took on a literal form that was widely accepted, and the prayerful could visit these places.

The Old Testament itself is rather vague on the location of the mountain from which Moses received the Ten Commandments. Deuteronomy locates the event in Horeb, which is understood by many to mean Sinai, but those who are sceptical point to a verse from Galatians (4:25) which states, 'Hagar stands for Mount Sinai in Arabia',[66] indicating, perhaps, that the mountain was in the Arabian Peninsula. Jewish tradition does not point to any specific location, and there is no evidence of pilgrimage to Sinai before the Christian journeys. Some sceptical scholars argue that the mountain was variously in northwest Saudi Arabia, southern Jordan or the Negev Desert in Israel.

The story of Moses receiving the Ten Commandments is, regardless, familiar to most in the West. According to the Book of Exodus, Moses, having already survived a Pharaonic purge of Hebrew children as a baby,[67] fled to the Sinai Desert after being sentenced to death for killing an Egyptian foreman whom he saw assaulting a labourer. He lived in exile there for 40 years until, in the form of the Burning Bush, God appeared and asked Moses to save the Israelites, who were the descendants of Jacob the Patriarch (who himself was the grandson of Abraham). With God's help, the Red Sea was parted and 600,000 Israelites came to Horeb, where Moses stayed on the mountain for 40 days and 40 nights. He descended finally with two stone tablets bearing the Ten Commandments but found, to his horror, that the fickle Israelites had built a new idol to worship. In anger, he smashed the tablets and returned to the mountain where God, graciously, provided him with new ones. This time the Israelites remained true, and the Ark of the Covenant was constructed to house the new commandments. The rest, as they say – particularly the basis of Christianity and Judaism rooted in these God-given directives – is history.

As we walked, Musallem pointed to inscriptions in Greek, Coptic, Georgian and Armenian lining the trail. 'There are many here, from all the other pilgrims,' he said. 'We are the latest in the line.' He said that Sinai had perhaps been a holy place even before the early Christians adopted it.

'Why do you think that?' I asked.

'The Nabateans came here for rituals, some people say. You can see their artwork on the rocks in places. I've heard stories about people here before them too worshipping other gods. So maybe it has always been a holy place. It is hard to say. Now though it is special to everyone. Christians, Muslims, Jews, and especially the Bedouin, for whom it is home.'

Whether because of or in spite of its sacred claim, over the centuries the mountain has created its own aura. I am quite sure that spirituality can be cultivated, and I have felt it in many places – by the Western Wall in Jerusalem, or St Peter's Basilica in Rome, or indeed in humbler but highly venerated village mosques and Sikh, Hindu or Buddhist temples. When enough people of faith gather in a spot for a long enough time, there is something intangible that happens to that place. It is one of the many things that give me pause for thought as an agnostic, but I am certain that there is, on Jebel Musa especially, an imbued religiosity, set there by the many feet which have carved a path to the summit over millennia.

I had tried to read as many of the pilgrim accounts as I could before I reached the summit, but the volume of them was intimidating. The earliest description was written by a woman called Egeria, who was probably a Spanish nun.[68] Her detailed description of the path to Sinai, through the rugged mountains, is still familiar to the modern-day pilgrim. She writes:

These mountains are ascended with infinite toil, for you cannot go up gently by a spiral track, as we say snail-shell wise, but you climb straight up the whole way, as if up a wall, and you must come straight down each mountain until you reach the very foot of the middle one, which is specially called Sinai. By this way, then, at the bidding of Christ our God, and helped by the prayers of the holy men who accompanied us, we arrived at the fourth hour, at the summit of Sinai, the holy mountain of God, where the law was given, that is, at the place where the Glory of the Lord descended on the day when the mountain smoked.[69]

Little has changed in some regards. Everything that I read, in fact, restated many of the same early impressions; from devout bishops and wandering monks to the later, intrepid tourists like John Lewis Burkhardt of Petra fame, and Thomas Cook who, in 1868, put Sinai on the itinerary of his Holy Land Tours for the wealthy British holidaymaker.[70] What they all agreed on was this: there was always a church of some form built around the site of the Burning Bush (this is now enclosed in the Monastery of St Catherine) and the way to the summit was invariably challenging, regardless of travellers' abilities. The writers also mention the presence of a small church on the summit – we hear about it as early as the fourth century, and since then various incarnations have come and gone until the Greek Orthodox chapel that stands today was built in 1934 – and just as prevalent are notes on the pleasant company that they all kept; namely, the 'Saracens', those we now call the Bedouin.

According to Eutyches – a ninth-century writer and patriarch of Alexandria – the Byzantine emperor Justinian I, who built the Greek Orthodox Monastery of St Catherine at the foot of Jebel Musa, settled 200 families from Anatolia and Alexandria to protect the monks. In the seventh century, as Islam swept across the peninsula, these families outside the walls of the monastery converted to Islam and began to share the customs and lifestyle of the Bedouin. Today, the Jebeleya tribe of the High Mountain Region are directly descended from those Greek and

Roman immigrants. If true – and Nasr confirmed to me that this is what most Jebeleya believe – it makes them unique amongst the Bedouin, and an anthropological anomaly (the other tribes are all descended from ancestors who came from the Hijaz). As such, the tribe has always worked to protect both the monastery and the more intangible sacred nature of the area, and for 16 centuries Christian pilgrims have lauded the hospitality and hard work of the Bedouin guardians of their holy site.

We passed a dam, built to calm flash floods in the wadis, and as we wound our way around the flank of the mountain I finally saw the monastery for myself, nestled in the mouth of a gorge. It was a long, sprawling network of buildings, built from beige brown stone that blended into the desert monochrome. A fortress-like wall snaked around the compound, keeping it safe from harm. During his visit to the monastery in 1822, Burkhardt recorded the words of a monk, who said that, 'had [the monastery] been subject to the revolutions and oppressions of Egypt or Syria, it would have long ago been abandoned; but Providence has preserved us by giving us Bedouin for neighbours.' This seems to slightly overlook the effectiveness of the Bedouin soldiers, but, whatever the reason, the monastery did indeed survive against improbable odds.

St Catherine's is, famously, the oldest working Christian monastery in the world, and its library houses the Syriac Sinaiticus and, until 1859, the Codex Sinaiticus.[71] It also contains a living version of the Burning Bush – believers say it is the very same from which God appeared to Moses – and the remains of St Catherine, an Alexandrian Christian who was tortured and beheaded for her faith in the fourth century at the behest of the Roman emperor Maxentius, and whose name is now borne by the monastery. Angels are said to have carried her remains to Sinai, where they were discovered by monks 400 years after her death. Today, a small number of monks continue to be in residence; a workforce of 400 Jebeleya still look after the compound, and the nearby town of St Catherine has grown to a population of 5,000, servicing the needs of pilgrims and tourists.

As we climbed, we passed occasional huts selling drinks and snacks to those on their way to or from the summit. Only one was open, and inside we found Suleiman's brother and two friends slumped behind a row of Mars bars. We bought some coffee and I looked at the walls, which were plastered with postcards, stickers, photos of visitors to the mountain and two enormous flags: the green and yellow of Brazil and the less familiar red, yellow, black and white of East Timor.

'I remember when there were 700 people here a day,' said Nasr.

Musallem nodded. 'There was more work than we knew what to do with. I would even bring people up here myself when the Jebeleya guides were too busy.'

'For the millennium, we had 7,000 here, in one day!' Nasr recalled with a smile.

'How many have been here today?' I asked, and Suleiman put the question to his brother.

'Ten,' came the answer. 'Including the five of you.'

I bought a handful of Mars bars and stashed them in my backpack. I didn't expect it would help much.

We walked on, past a sixth-century whitewashed Byzantine church, beyond which were two arches to pass through. First was the Gate of Forgiveness, where pilgrims were once asked: 'Who shall ascend into the hill of the Lord? Or who shall stand in this holy place?'

The pilgrims would respond by continuing the recital of Psalm 24:

He that hath clean hands, and a pure heart; who hath not lifted up his soul unto vanity, nor sworn deceitfully. He shall receive the blessing from the Lord, and righteousness from the God of his salvation.

Until the 1880s, a certificate was presented and the journey could continue, but now the arch was abandoned. So too was the sixth-century Elijah's Gate, the arch farther along which had a faint inscription that read 'John the Abbot' along the top.

We approached the final 750 steps of the ascent, where many of the various routes around Jebel Musa meet. The rocks were rough and uneven, each pressed deep into the mountainside by 1,700 years of piety.

We walked in single file and in silence, counting our steps until Nasr, who led the way, crested the summit at last. In front of us lay a twentieth-century church, created using the blocks of its ruined Byzantine predecessor. It was small but seemed to grow out of the granite, with a large wooden door and two small metal crosses on top of a sloped roof. Opposite, across a flat and well-kept area laid with red bricks, was a rectangular mosque. Underneath, Musallem said, was the cave where Moses took shelter during his time on the summit.

We were alone, though it did not feel like it. The mountain top seemed to carry with it the stories of the past and the echoes of the hundreds of thousands of people for whom attaining this summit had been the integral defining spiritual moment in their lives. As I walked from the church to the mosque, a fiery sun was sinking to the west, a red orb growing richer and rounder with every second that it fell. The Sinai was laid out all around me, and it had saved its greatest panorama for the last moment: titanic, jagged jawlines of ancient mountains, bulging and swollen summits and, sculpting the edges of each massif, curved and pale wadis, each leading to another as if creating a vast spider's web across the land. To the east, the Red Sea shimmered in the dying light and below the setting sun was a faint trace of the Gulf of Suez. Beneath me was 2,285 m of red granite, 800 million years old, and above – or perhaps all around – the God that everyone came here to find.

Egeria had been similarly awestruck by the scale of the view:

From thence we saw Egypt and Palestine, and the Red Sea and the Parthenian Sea, which leads to Alexandria and the boundless territories of the Saracens, all so much below us as to be scarcely credible, but the holy men pointed out each one of them to us.[72]

My version of the 'holy men' was Nasr and Musallem, and they too dutifully directed my gaze to various points across the land.

In 1885, fourteen hundred years after Egeria, Edward Hull, a geologist from Antrim – a town in Ireland just 15 miles from where I grew up – declared that:

> Nothing can exceed the savage grandeur of the view from the summit
> of Mount Sinai. The infinite complication of jagged peaks and varied
> ridges, and their prevalent intensely red and greenish tints.[73]

I, for once, had little to say. Certainly nothing that had not been said before. I was finished, but of course the end never feels like the end; it was just another day and another trail, albeit one that ended on a sacred mountain. The longer the journey, the more time it takes to acclimatise to it and then to let it go.

Austin embraced me, and soon Nasr, Suleiman and Musallem joined in. We celebrated together both our individual achievements and our collaborative success.

'You've made it. 1,000 miles,' said Musallem, shouting as the evening wind began to blow. 'Life is good!'

Nasr wrapped up in a thick Bedouin jacket, and put his arm around me. We sat on a low brick wall to watch the sun make its final dive for cover. Soon it was swallowed whole by the Gulf of Suez, and immediately the sky exploded in a purple haze. The wind howled and the long shadows of evening died, giving way to the black voids of night.

'*Khalas*,' said Nasr. 'It is done. Now, we can go home.'

# Epilogue

It is good to know the truth and to speak the truth. But it is better to know the truth and to speak about palm trees.
    (Arab proverb, as quoted by Freya Stark to G.W. Murray in
                                    'The Land of Sinai', 1953)

The day after we summited Jebel Musa, Suleiman and Nasr returned to their homes while Musallem spent a night in the town of St Catherine with me and Austin. We stayed at a Bedouin hostel called Fox Camp, run by a man called Faraj Mahmoud. He seemed to know even more about the history of the Jebeleya and Sinai than Nasr and Musallem, and it was a shame to have so little time with him, but our brief encounter was a reminder to me about just how many people had been involved in the conceptual and practical setting-up of the Sinai Trail.

Eventually Austin left for Sharm el-Sheikh and from there flew home to London. Musallem returned to Nuweiba and I was alone once more. I had made no solid plans for how to end my journey. The sensible thing would have been to hire a taxi to the northern border and from there head to an airport in Tel Aviv or Amman, but I wasn't quite ready for that. Something had been niggling at me since

I left the West Bank, and this was my only chance to indulge it before I went home.

This journey was never meant to be about the Israeli – Palestinian conflict. Neither was this book. After my time in the West Bank, Jordan and Sinai, however, it became clear to me that it would be remiss to leave the region without also spending more time in Israel. Its very existence permeated so many of the conversations and interactions that I had had, and I was curious to see life from the other side of the wall, so to speak. Israel was the proverbial elephant in every room that I had walked into for five months.

I briefly considered walking all the way back to Jerusalem, but quickly dismissed the idea. Firstly, and primarily, I didn't really want to. I have learned by now that to try and force a journey without enthusiasm is a pointless and thankless task. I was tired, and would have needed a long rest before I could take on another 500 miles. Another reason for my apathy was that it would also have been unwise – perhaps impossible – to walk through northern Sinai to the border with Israel. At the very least I would risk kidnap or arrest – unlike in the south, there are a number of jihadist groups affiliated to Al Qaeda, and others to Da'esh, who operate in the north. Instead, I got a taxi to Taba, the northernmost of the Red Sea resort towns in Sinai, and from there crossed to the Israeli city of Eilat. I allowed myself three weeks to get back to Jerusalem; some of it I would walk on trails like the Israel National Trail, some I would hitch-hike and, when I felt lazy, I would take a bus. My route would take me from Eilat through the Negev, stopping in some of the small towns and villages in the desert and, ultimately, to the administrative capital of Beersheba. Finally, I would walk back through the southern part of the West Bank, via Hebron and Bethlehem, to close the circle, where I began, in the Old City of Jerusalem. What follows is a truncated version of that journey, which I hope holds relevance for the earlier part of this story.

Crossing the border into Israel was an unpleasant experience. At the entrance to immigration control I presented my passport to a young blonde Israeli who looked thoroughly unimpressed with my dirty clothes and Indiana Jones hat. Whether because of this, or perhaps because of the Iranian and Saudi Arabian visa stamps in my passport, I was asked to step aside and wait by a low table with two dusty chairs. There was no one else there and the Israeli holidaymakers returning from Taba shuffled past in quick succession, avoiding my eyes.

I waited for two hours, and was questioned for another two by three immigration officials who took it in turns to ask me the same questions. I stuck to my story – I would be walking along the Israel National Trail. I did not mention that I would enter the West Bank. It is, for the most part, inadvisable to tell Israeli immigration of any intention to visit the Palestinian Territories and, although it might seem unwise, the general advice then is to lie, or at least to withhold the truth. There was partial reality in my claim, of course, and I hoped that would carry me through.

'Do any of you hike?' I found myself asking my interrogators at one point. 'Israel has one of the most extensive trail networks in the world.' My words fell flat. 'It's really very special in that regard [. . .]'

'Oh it is, is it?' growled one of the men. 'And what are the trails like in Iran?'

When I was finally cleared, I assumed the whole affair was pretty standard practice for grubby-looking men crossing into Israel with oversized backpacks and questionable hats. I stepped out into a no man's land. The city of Eilat curved around the coastline, with its high-rise buildings glinting in the sun, and, although it took me about an hour to reach the centre, the difference from Sinai was palpable. I had left a run-down town on the Egyptian side where manual workers lounged in the shade of palm trees and Bedouin women in abayas shuffled past a market stall filling baskets with questionable packaged produce. The roads were rutted, crumbling back into desert, and the buildings worn and peeling. Just a few hundred metres away, however, the cars were gleaming, new and big; many were American-brand sport utility vehicles that might have dwarfed the roads had they too not also morphed into four- and eight-lane highways, smooth as a racecourse. A row of advertising hoardings stood between me and the beach, which was covered with scantily clad Israelis enjoying sun, sea and sand. I could not remember the last time I had seen a bikini. Everyone was deeply tanned, and roadside shacks sold bottles of beer from ice buckets. From a booming stereo somewhere came a deep, pounding bass beat; the soundtrack to a new world.

Using a free Wi-Fi connection in a Starbucks café – both relative novelties – I found details for a cheap hostel and walked to the address. I arrived 30 minutes before check-in and the owner refused to let me in, so I sat on a curbstone drinking lemonade that cost six times more than the same bottle in Sinai. That evening, with no inclination to stay in my clean but characterless room, I wandered around the various districts of the city, always ending up back at the beach, which had by now transformed into an open-air nightclub. This was a strange transition, and one that I usually did not experience until I returned home; I had lost my unique selling point as a curious-looking Westerner in places like Sinai and now was simply a grimy, bearded tourist. I found it hard to engage with anyone – it felt like trying to approach strangers in a big city in the UK or the US where, without a good reason for initiating a conversation, most people will ignore you. Finally, feeling lonelier than I had in months, I retired to my hostel.

I caught a bus headed for the Negev Desert. The Negev, or *Naqab* in Arabic, covers more than half of Israel's land mass, and it was where many of the Bedouin that I met in the West Bank said their family had once roamed prior to the *Nakba* of 1948, when as many as 700,000 Palestinians were forced out to the West Bank, Gaza, Jordan, Lebanon and Syria. It is rocky and arid and, in many places, possessed of a lunar-like beauty in its landscapes. Dotted through this vast region are a variety of mountains, wadis, oases and craters, as one might expect, but there are also five enormous *makhteshim* – huge depressions in the earth with steep walls that, as they descend, reveal the rock strata and, with those, the passage of time. They are a hallmark of the Negev, and a major tourist draw.

There are a number of towns in the desert, many of which were inspired by the first Israeli prime minister, David Ben-Gurion (1948– 63), who sought to populate the Negev with centres of learning, espousing the particular benefits of the desert to tease creativity out of scholars. Today, despite the exodus of many Bedouin after the *Nakba*, there are still scattered communities of semi-nomads in the Negev. Their lives are tough and they face constant obstacles to the traditional Bedouin way of life. The Israeli government has consistently tried to move Negev Bedouin into government-approved townships, and it is estimated that 40 per cent of the population now live in unrecognised villages,[74] with no access to state-supplied electricity, water or refuse collection. Despite this, they remain, refusing to leave their ancient homeland.

The Negev is also a military zone, one of the main training grounds for Israeli youth completing their military service.[75] As I waited in the Eilat bus station, I watched hundreds of teenagers in khaki uniforms bundle into vehicles heading north. They all carried large, army-issue backpacks and strode around in high, black desert boots. Most carried weapons, and I was the only passenger on my bus who was not headed for a military base.

I chose a seat by a window towards the back of the bus, squeezed next to an overweight soldier of about 20, who adjusted his spectacles and avoided my gaze. He carried an automatic rifle which, initially, he wedged in between my legs and his. Then, after examining the positioning for a while, he lifted the rifle, swinging it around with abandon, and placed it diagonally across his lap so that the barrel of the gun jabbed me in the ribs. I asked gently if he might remove it, which he did in a fluster of mumbled apologies, and eventually stowed the weapon under his seat.

In front of me, a moody teenager threw himself dramatically down onto two seats. He elbowed my knees aggressively through the soft fabric, and I exclaimed in surprise. Quickly he turned around and spat, 'What's your problem? Fucking tourist. Do you want to make a problem?'

For a second I was sure he meant to hit me, until two of his acquaintances stepped in and pulled him away. One of them apologised as they did so. The soldier beside me stared straight down at the floor.

We left the station, and the teenagers settled into their seats; boys flirting with girls, some sleeping, most engrossed in the screens of their smartphones. It reminded me of field trips from high school, where all the cliques became slowly evident as groups rotated: cool kids at the back, quiet kids at the front, loners on their own. No one seemed particularly excited to be there.

Every 15 minutes or so the bus stopped at an improbable-looking spot in the desert, where small army camps were marked by a row of tanks or a single high-walled barbed wire building. Two or three bodies would slide off the bus and we'd move on. I asked the boy next to me where he was going.

'Not far from here,' he said. 'You?'

'Into the desert, to hike. Where are you from?'

'Eilat, and you?' He had a soft voice and an endearing smile, but he was still too nervous to make eye contact. When I was a little younger than he was I too wore thick glasses and carried a lot of extra weight around my middle, and I warmed to him quickly as we spoke. I told him that I was from Ireland.

'That's cool!' he said, a thick accent coating his perfect English. 'My cousins went backpacking there.'

'How long will you be in the desert?'

'Just six weeks, but I still have a little over six months left of my military service. I've done two years so far.'

'Where else have you been sent?'

'Hebron, Jerusalem, other places in the desert.' I thought of him in Hebron, in the heart of the West Bank. He smiled weakly, noting my silence. 'It was OK,' he said. 'I mean, I didn't enjoy it, but I got through.'

'What will you do afterwards?'

'I want to go backpacking and travelling as well. Probably to South America. Argentina looks great.'

I told him Argentina was indeed lovely, and he smiled at the thought.

'You'll have to excuse me,' he said. 'I get travel sick, and it helps if I close my eyes.'

Ten minutes later he got off, bashing his gun against every seat on the way out.

I spent a night in Mitzpe Ramon; a pleasant, small town built on the rim of the 'Makhtesh Ramon'. It is the largest *makhteshim* in the world, and the tourist literature that I collected in Eilat compared it to both Tatooine – the lawless and harsh desert world from *Star Wars* – and the Grand Canyon in Arizona. The views from an outlook spot high above the town were spectacular, and I was joined by tourists from all over Israel who came to watch the sun set over the vast depression in the earth.

In the evening I drank beer in the garden of a makeshift hostel with six Israelis, all of whom had made their home in the desert. One of them, Roni, owned the small house where I stayed, and he told me that he was born in Sinai when it was under Israeli occupation.

'I miss the sea,' he said. 'But I love the peace of the desert. This is the next best thing.'

He admired the Bedouin there, he said, and he valued their skills and knowledge above all else. I asked what he thought of the Bedouin in the Negev.

'They're very special too. But they have many problems, and some of them they cause themselves.'

'How so?'

'I'll tell you the secret. All they need to do is say that they are happy to be part of Israel. I know a lot of them, and I tell them: put an Israeli flag outside of your camp, whether you believe it or not. Then you will be left alone.'

'Do they listen to you?' I asked.

'Sometimes, but mostly not. And so they suffer.'

Domingo, a native Chilean who had emigrated to Israel in 1968, chipped in. 'Statehood matters most of all,' he said. 'I'm all about peace and love and everyone should be happy, but Israel's existence needs to be recognised.'

Miriam, a West Jerusalemite in her mid-30s who had been quiet up until this point spoke now.

'There has to be peace, though. That's the most important thing. I travel a lot too' – she looked at me – 'and I know Israel sometimes has a bad reputation.'

'Where have you been?' I asked.

'All over Europe, America, South America. China too. But do you know where I want to go most of all?'

'Where?'

'The West Bank,' she said with a sigh. 'And it is the place I can never go. It makes me very sad.'

'Many Palestinians would like to visit Israel too,' I said, choosing my words carefully. I did not point out – though I wanted to – that she could go just about anywhere in the world with ease, while, for Palestinians, just leaving their home town or city was potentially problematic.[76]

Roni cut in again. 'Look, there are problems in the West Bank. I don't know the solution, but until it's sorted out we cannot take any risks. There is a threat to all of us there.'

'Do you feel unsafe here?' I asked. They all shook their heads.

'With Mossad,[77] I never feel unsafe,' said Domingo. I smiled, but it was not a joke.

Shortly afterwards, a man called Leo arrived wearing a metal Star of David and a carved wooden lion's head around his neck, both of which hung low over his open-chested tie-dye shirt. He said he had been born in Tel Aviv to African-American parents who had immigrated to Israel on a spiritual quest. Like everyone else that I'd been speaking to all evening he was high as a kite, and he came bearing more marijuana in a small box with a picture of Bob Marley on the front. They were an easy-going and fun crowd, if opinionated – hard-line hippies perhaps – and I had enjoyed their company, but eventually being the only sober person at the party wore thin. At one point, Roni began to tell me about the aura of the desert, and the difference between regret and remorse.

'It's, like, one of them, you know it man, you feel it right inside of your heart, but the other one it just comes and fucking takes you out in the night, y'know?'

I went to bed.

For four days I walked through the Negev, and it was some of the most enjoyable hiking that I have ever done. The trails were clearly marked – and there were many of them to choose from – and each night I could pitch my tent wherever I liked. I wound through canyons and along high plateaus; buzzards swooped overhead and, in the arid hills above me, Nubian ibexes leapt with impossible grace between promontories. I regularly met other hikers, most of them young Israelis who had recently finished their National Service. They dressed casually in shorts and T-shirts, and wore brands like Patagonia and North Face. We chatted in English and shared food, and I liked every one of them. Politics was not discussed much, and neither was religion. When it was, there was a mixture of views, and no one pushed an agenda. We were simply hikers enjoying the communal nature of a good trail, and I felt very much at home in the company of just about everyone I met.

On the rare occasion of crossing a paved road, I stopped at an American-style gas station to eat ice cream and tend to my blisters (in that order). A military Humvee stopped and two male soldiers sat at the table beside me, drinking Coke and punching each other in the arm. One asked me where I was headed and I said simply, 'North.'

'That's cool,' he said. 'What do you think of Israel?'

'I love the hiking here. And people on the trail are friendly.'

'Really?' he asked, surprised. 'Sometimes Israelis can seem a bit, maybe, closed. I'm glad you've found friendly ones. We're just reserved sometimes, I guess.'

'Where are you going?' I asked.

'We have some training near here, then I'm posted at one of the checkpoints.'

'Into the West Bank?' I asked. He nodded.

'How is it there?'

'It's a pretty shitty job, to be honest. Everyone hates you. They stare at you and they're scared of you. And I'm scared of them a lot of the time. I want to trust them and to help but, y'know, you hear all these stories. I feel bad a lot of the time.'

His friend nudged him and they moved to go. The soldier wasn't all that much younger than me, and he told me that he'd already hiked the entire Israel National Trail. He came from a middle-class family on the coast, and he liked the Red Hot Chili Peppers. I grew up in a comfortable family by the sea and I liked the Red Hot Chili Peppers too.

As he left I thought: that could be me. How would I feel in his place? What would I believe? For the first time since I left Jerusalem I had begun to appreciate the fear that was felt by many Israelis, and to see their desire to protect themselves and their country. But as an outsider I could never fully understand, just as I could never fully understand the plight of Palestinians that I'd met.

I realised too as I walked that part of the reason I had come to Israel was because, more than just being curious, I *needed* to see some of the humanity in the country. I had spent such a long time hearing the opinions of others on the Israelis, and it was important for my own processes to put a human face to the population. I had heard enough of the invisible, all-powerful authorities. I had found the first days in Eilat and on the bus unsettling because, for the most part, my expectations – that it was a place that would feel alien – were being reinforced. As ever, though, walking provided the time and space for reality to slowly creep in. At times, all we have is hope, and much of mine is based on an inherent goodness in humanity that I have found all over the world. To have that reaffirmed is always welcome.

In a pretty university town called Midreshet Ben-Gurion,[78] I stayed with Shai Yagel, a guide who met me off the trail. He arrived riding one fat bike and wheeling another alongside. I dumped my pack at his house and we took off across the desert, bouncing with abandon over rocks and crevices on the trails, the wind howling in our faces.

Shai was in his mid-30s with a rough beard and long hair, and I enjoyed my time with him greatly. He had a garage full of bikes and climbing gear, and he spent his days working in trail development in the Negev. For a long while we talked about the perfect trail: what it required, where it would go, and how the route should interact with the walker.

'Trails have authors,' said Shai. 'They're like anything creative. We think of them like this physical thing on the ground going in whatever direction, but someone designs them. If it goes up a mountain, that's a choice. If it goes through one community and not through another, that's a separate choice. That's one of the issues with trails in Israel –

they'll often avoid places which don't fit in with the bigger message or picture like, for example, Bedouin communities.'

Shai had scouted and marked a number of trails in the Negev that included such communities. He said he had spent a lot of time with the Bedouin, and I knew from mutual friends that he was universally respected for his work in the desert.

'I want to make trails, and I want to help,' he said. 'But I find it hard to keep quiet about things I don't agree with. I mean that in every sense. Problems that I have with Israelis and the government, but also in the Bedouin communities. Like, I don't agree with having multiple wives and making them stay at home. I say to those guys sometimes, "Hey, come on. This isn't right." And I guess we agree to disagree.'

I asked if he thought that efforts to connect trails in Israel and the West Bank could be a success.

'It's difficult,' he said. 'If the primary goal was conflict resolution, then maybe. But just to call them hiking trails and try and join them up is difficult. What I have noticed, though, is that trails are a great way to break down a bunch of other barriers. I work with a lot of Palestinians, right? When there is money involved and the economy is good, politics goes out the window. So if trails can bring income to the West Bank, that's a good start.'

'What happens if there's not a lot of money in it, at least to begin with?'

'When there's not much money around, people cling on to other things. I notice it here in Israel and also among Palestinians. When things are hard, people get more religious. And that becomes a problem eventually.'

I walked north to Beersheba, which in the Hebrew Bible, or *Tanakh*, was named by the patriarch Abraham. It survived through Persian, Hasmonean, Roman and Byzantine rule, and in the early twentieth century, under Ottoman control, it became the first battlefield of the 'Southern Palestine Offensive', the British military push to break the Ottoman line during World War I. Now it is the northern gateway to the Negev Desert, and the modern city is home to over 200,000 Israelis. The population is a melange of immigrant Jewish families, many of whom came from Arab countries such as Iraq and Yemen in 1948, while smaller communities of Jews from the ex-Soviet Union, India and Ethiopia have also made lives there.

I was met in the city by Abbey, a young Israeli who worked as an educational support assistant at the university and who, with her husband Noam, let out the spare room in their rental apartment to travellers, like me, who are passing through.

She helped out at a local community venue on weekends, and in the afternoon we walked around the Old Town putting up posters advertising an upcoming gig. 'What kind of music is it?' I asked.

'Sort of folk and rock, and a little bit of Americana.'

We plastered the image of the band up on the windows of at least ten bars and cafés, and each reminded me of somewhere one might find in East London; stylish décor, artisanal beer and handsome, well-groomed clients with clipped beards and skinny jeans. By the time we returned to the house, Noam was back from work. I saw him through the patio doors wearing his prayer shawl and *kippah*, and rocking back and forth with a *siddur* – Jewish prayer book – in his hands.

'Leon!' he said, in a deep voice when he finished. 'I'm so glad you made it!'

We ordered pizzas and ate together, and I told them of my journey. 'Where will you go next?' asked Noam.

'From here I'll walk through a village called Lakiya, then north.'

'Why are you going through Lakiya?' asked Abbey. 'You know it's a Bedouin village, right?'

'I do. I guess that's why I'm going. I'd like to see it.'

She glanced at Noam, who continued smiling. 'Well, just be really careful,' she said. There was genuine concern in her voice for my well-being. 'I haven't been, but I've heard it can be dangerous.'

'I'm sure it'll be fine,' I said. 'I'll go to the West Bank after that.'

There was silence. 'Do you think it's OK there at the moment?' I asked them.

'I don't know. Maybe for you, but not for us.'

'I hope you don't mind me asking, but what do you think of the situation in the West Bank?' That week, there had been news of another attempted stabbing at a checkpoint.

There was more silence, and I felt immediately like I'd crossed a line of acceptable conversational etiquette. Noam spoke first.

'I don't know,' he said. 'It's hard to speak about. It's very difficult, and I know there are a lot of problems. Many of these people don't recognise the existence of our state of Israel. There's a lot of hatred and dangerous people there, and it's a hard situation. I feel bad for how difficult life can be for people there too, though.'

Abbey continued. 'All of us know people who have been victims of terror attacks. There's a threat that means we can never really relax from it. We aren't in a position to know what to do about it. The IDF and Mossad keep us safe, and we can't think about it. It will be resolved someday but until then, it's out of our hands.'

'Would you ever live on a settlement?' I asked, pushing my luck.

'I think so,' said Noam after a moment. 'Yes, because they offer very good value. I mean, of course, our jobs are here at the university. But if the city became more expensive or we moved, or when we have a family, then I'd have no problem with that.'

I wanted to ask if they supported Netanyahu and his government, but I had already pressed too much.

'Tell me more about the bands that visit here,' I said.

'Oh,' said Abbey, smiling again. 'Well there's so many!'

It took just under a week to walk from Beersheba back to Jerusalem, and the day after I left Abbey and Noam, I slept in a grove of olive trees near the Meitar Junction checkpoint. The following morning, I walked back into the West Bank. Beyond the armed guards and the identity checks, the quality of the road deteriorated immediately and the colour of the earth changed from the rich, emerald green of the well-irrigated Israeli side to a dull beige on the arid Palestinian side. In the company of friends, I walked through the South Hebron Hills and into the city of Hebron itself, the largest city in the West Bank and one which might well be the nadir of the whole conflict. An Israeli settlement sits right in the heart of the city, quite literally built amidst and on top of Palestinian houses, streets and market stalls. One Palestinian resident described it to me thus: 700 ideological settlers protected by 5,000 nervous police, surrounded by 200,000 scared Palestinians.

Hebron, or *Al-Khalil* in Arabic, is venerated by Christians, Jews and Muslims as the site of Abraham's resting place, and the holy sites there, including the Cave of the Patriarchs/Ibrahimi Mosque,[79] are now enclosed in an area known as H2 which lies within the Israeli settlement of Kiryat Arba. Access is strictly controlled, to the extent that entire Palestinian streets have been closed[80] while other alleyways in the winding labyrinth of the Old Town have had to erect solid coverings to stop settlers spitting, hurling abuse or, at times, dropping rubbish and rocks from above. It is one of the saddest places I have been.

Before I completed my journey I thought it important to visit a settlement, though I knew that one visit could never tell me everything I needed to know about these communities. The Israeli settlements in the West Bank contain a mixture of people who have moved for economic reasons (cheap rent), practical reasons (more space) and religious reasons (God-given land), and within those groups there are a wide variety of political and religious views. With this is mind, I took my chances with visiting a place called Tekoa, just 20 miles from Jerusalem. In fact, in a manner of speaking, I visited twice.

I first spent an evening in Tequ'a, which is a small Palestinian town located in the rolling hills south of Bethlehem, with beautiful panoramic views of the cone-shaped hill of Herodium where Herod the Great is said to be buried. There I stayed with Abu Nasim, a strong, broad-shouldered man with a permanent grin and a high-pitched laugh. We talked through the evening about his house and family, and about the land and the Byzantine church that he had discovered in the hills nearby. Before I slept, he told me that one of his sons was in an Israeli prison for throwing stones at the IDF; another son had also done time in jail, and his brother had been shot by the military. His life, he said, had been constantly shaped by the actions of the Israelis and their incursions in the West Bank. What did he do for work? I'd asked.

'I have a job as a builder on an Israeli settlement. It's the only place that I can get a job right now.'

The settlement that he worked at was less than a mile away, and it too was called Tekoa.[81] Through a friend in Jerusalem I arranged to meet a man called Fred Grossman, who had been an influential figure in the creation of Tekoa in 1977, helping the handover from members of a paramilitary IDF programme who had set it up as an outpost. He was one of the first civilian residents and, since then, had been responsible for the creation of at least two other settlements.[82] Tekoa is part of the Gush Etzion bloc of settlements which has grown up around Kfar Etzion, the first of the modern-day settlements, built just months after the end of the Six Day War. These days, Fred lives in a trailer on another small outpost a few miles south where he spends his days playing banjo, reading the Torah and writing articles about national security under the self-appointed title of 'intelligence analyst'.

We met on the roadside, and as his car pulled up I realised just how nervous and uncomfortable I was. I had no idea what to expect from a settler, especially one with Fred's particular history. I told myself to be prepared for anything. Even so, he managed to surprise me; as he stepped out of his car, I saw that he looked remarkably similar to my late grandfather. Jack – my grandpa – was an architect and artist and, in his older years, something of an eccentric who swam in the freezing cold Atlantic Ocean every day and drove around the north of Ireland in an old battered car wearing jazzy shirts. He was universally loved by those in the town, and whatever I know about being humble and generous in life, I learned from him. Fred – the settler – had the same craggy nose and lined face, with an easy smile underneath a bushy old-timer moustache. He was lean like Jack too, and wore a striped shirt, which smelt of mothballs, tucked into tight jeans. Because of the similarity, and because he was so wonderfully effusive as he shook my hand, I couldn't help but feel a warmth for him, against my better judgement.

Also in the car was someone else whom my friend in Jerusalem had put in touch with Fred. Lorrie was shy, with oversized glasses and a baseball cap, and there was nothing all that remarkable about her except that she was a pro-Palestinian Jewish lesbian novelist from New York. She too was interested in hearing more about settler life, and Fred took us first to his home where he made coffee and we chatted idly about music and life. He had grown up in the USA, but moved to Israel after the Six Day War. He was divorced, and rarely saw his children. He carried a gun on his hip, and liked his coffee black and his music folksy.

He held strong views, but he pressed them upon us gently. First, and perhaps most important, was his stance as a religious Zionist. Fred believed that the modern State of Israel is the manifestation of the prophecy that when the Messiah returns, the Jewish people will return to the Holy Land. Fred had unwavering faith that the West Bank, which he exclusively referred to as Judaea and Samaria, was part of this prophetic plan, and that the Jews should not wait for divine intervention. They must take matters into their own hands and begin the resettlement as soon as possible. As we drank coffee, he charted the history of the Israelites and the Jewish people, and made it clear that he did not believe there was such a place as Palestine.

'Do you know what Palestine is?' he asked.

'It's the country you're trying to destroy,' said Lorrie in a thick Brooklyn accent.

'No!' he said, looking distressed. 'No. Look, I don't want to destroy anything. Palestine is a geographical term, for a piece of earth that runs from Egypt to Syria. It was never a country, and so there is no right to land for the Arabs that we're calling Palestinians. This is how simple it is.'

We drove through Tekoa along broad avenues past identical, clean and spacious houses, each with a garden at the back and an allotment out front. The town seemed organised into pleasant cul-de-sacs so that children could run around safely, and it felt like the affluent suburbs of an American city. At the entrance was a large metal gate with a security guard, and all around ran a high perimeter wall to stop any unwarranted access.

Fred took us to visit his friend Avi. Avi was a surgeon from New York who had bought a large apartment in Tekoa where, when he wasn't working in the USA, he lived with his Mexican Jewish wife. He hosted us for more coffee and had indicated he was prepared to talk through the issues, but it was immediately clear that he would be more forceful with his opinions than Fred.

'This is Judaea and Samaria out here,' he corrected when I asked him about the West Bank.

'It was given to us by God, and it is the land of King David. The Arabs had a good run of it for a while, but we came back and we are reclaiming what is ours.'

'So where should they go?' I asked.

'That's interesting,' said Fred, jumping in with a more conciliatory tone. 'We don't want anyone to suffer, and there's so much suffering now. Look at Gaza. What a mess. Have you heard of Herbert Hoover?' he asked.

'The American president?'

'Yes! Well, he was known as the Great Humanitarian. And he had a solution, which he called the three-state solution.'

'What's wrong with the two-state solution?' asked Lorrie. 'Why can't the Palestinians just have some land and you live in peace?'

'Because it's not theirs,' snapped Avi. 'The Torah commands us to claim this land. We aren't giving it up for anyone. They can go to Jordan or wherever. That's not our problem. This is our land.'

I looked to Fred.

'Herbert Hoover,' he began, 'had a plan. He thought that Iraq, which also has so many problems, should be divided into three. They would have a Sunni state, a Shi'ite one and a Kurdish one. Once there are new borderlines, then other people, like the Palestinians, could move there safely to a new home.'

'You think all the Palestinians should move to Iraq?' I asked. I was genuinely surprised.

'Are you fuckin' kidding me?' asked Lorrie, articulating both of our thoughts with a little more clarity. 'You want to send the Palestinians to Iraq? What are you smoking, man?'

'Please,' said Avi, 'don't use words like that. What I'm saying is, it's not our problem.'

Fred looked into my eyes. I wasn't shouting at him like Lorrie was, and he appealed to me directly. 'Leon, you're understanding this, aren't you? The Palestinians' situation is terrible. Something needs to happen.'

That evening, Fred took Lorrie back to Jerusalem and I walked on to Bethlehem. In the Church of the Nativity, as a storm gathered overhead, I squeezed through the Door of Humility – built low to require all to bow as they enter – and climbed down stone steps to the grotto where a 14-pointed silver star proclaimed in Latin: *Hic De Virgine Maria Jesus Christus Natus* (Here the Virgin Mary gave birth to Jesus Christ). Three Nigerian men from Lagos, arrived shortly thereafter. One by one they bowed and prostrated themselves fully into the alcove, eyes shut and bodies shaking. Soon, all three were crying with joy. Or faith. Or something else – something powerful, that only they knew.

They left shortly after, quietly singing songs of praise to each other. I followed them up the steps and back through the church, out to the dark, cloud-covered skies of a rainy Bethlehem evening. The next day, I walked through a checkpoint, past queues of Palestinians waving their IDs, and retraced my steps through the Old City of Jerusalem to the entrance of the Jerusalem Hotel where, 2 million steps previously, I had begun in earnest almost half a year before.

There is a condition, apparently, that afflicts a few hundred people every year and is completely unique to this city. It is called Jerusalem Syndrome, and is caused when a person arrives with expectations – perhaps after a lifetime of dreaming, or believing that this axis of faith will solve all the insufferable problems of life – that are far beyond realistic. When they arrive into the dusty, noisy hustle and bustle of a Middle Eastern city going about its day, filled with all sorts of other believers, alternative believers and even (God forbid) non-believers, it is too much. The said pilgrim becomes psychotic. They will run off screaming, or begin preaching to strangers in the street. Often they are eventually found wandering the narrow alleyways of the Old City quietly mumbling claims of being a prophet; perhaps, they say, they are Jesus himself. At any given time, there are probably at least 50 self-professed Sons of God in the city. Most are scooped up and sent to a psychiatrist who specialises in the syndrome. Some return home, cured, while others who are beyond help are encouraged to take a more tranquil approach to their disposition. Perhaps they ultimately agree to disagree with the rest of the world as to whether or not they are the Messiah resurrected.

Upon my return, I happily avoided becoming the latest casualty, though I did see the appeal in the simplicity of believing oneself to be the Son of God. Instead, as I dozed in my hotel room and met friends for coffee and wandered along the streets buying baklava and halwa, I replayed in my mind the events of the previous days and months. My walk through Israel was not a fair investigation of either the country or of Jewish culture – in three weeks I could never hope to learn much, and it could certainly not be fairly placed against five months of travel in Arab countries. What it did reveal was that there was much in Israel that I needed to explore if I ever hoped to understand the challenges on both sides of this conflict. It also reaffirmed to me, however, that, for the most part, people are people, and they all share the same hopes, dreams and fears. This was apparent throughout my wanderings and on all sides of the religious and ethnic divides. The exceptions were Fred and Avi, who were the only true extremists that I met anywhere, alongside Haman in the West Bank, who wanted to expel the Jews from geographical Palestine. Perhaps I was attracted to moderates as I walked, and them to me, but no one else came close to Fred and Avi's – and Haman's – level of dogmatism. There is no reasonable conversation to have with someone who holds the unshakeable belief that 'God gave this to us, and we're keeping it.'

I write this closure to the book under something of a black cloud: in 2016 the UK voted for 'Brexit', the US elected Donald Trump as the de facto 'leader of the free world', and a wave of right-wing populism has swept across the West.

The Middle East is at a crossroads. The civil war rages on in Syria, now into its sixth year with little sign of a resolution. ISIS, or Da'esh, have been pushed back, but they continue to wreak havoc and their ideology still appeals to the vulnerable and disenfranchised. Saudi Arabia and Iran are at loggerheads, as always, and have found settings for their proxy wars in Syria and in Yemen; the latter is quietly being obliterated by war and famine. Iraq shows no signs of stability, and as the Kurdish region in the north pushes for independence, so too might Turkey make a play to absorb the land around the city of Mosul (if Iran doesn't get there first.)

In Israel and the Palestinian territories, things are equally worrying. Settlement expansion continues, and Donald Trump's pick as ambassador to Israel, David Friedman, seems determined to move the US embassy to Jerusalem, breaking with the tradition of every previous administration and putting any future peace negotiations into jeopardy. Meanwhile, factionalism within the Palestinian leadership continues to tear apart any sense of unity, denying the younger generation a chance to be the change they want to see in the future.

On my walk, I saw things changing in front of my eyes and beneath my feet. I saw the movement of peoples – of refugees and Bedouin and pilgrims and hikers – and I felt the slow adaptation to modernisation across the West Bank, Jordan and Sinai. Religion is still all-powerful in the Holy Land, and of the three Abrahamic faiths it is only Christianity that is fading, slowing being squeezed into smaller, tighter communities. In many places where the economy is poor, as Shai Yagel in the Negev noted, religiosity increases as people cling on to something that provides an eternal promise of hope.

But other values are shifting too. Globalisation has arrived – though not everywhere – and many of the next generation in the Middle East are tech-savvy, fashion-conscious and politically fluent. Perceptions of gender are changing, with women's co-operatives springing up and more women in positions of power than ever before. These things take place slowly, but they are happening alongside a parallel retreat into religious silos amongst others.

Along all the paths that I walked, I was struck more by what was similar than what was different. Those who rule a country can never answer or speak for those who live there, and the vast majority of people that I met were moderates within their own belief systems, simply looking for a way to make life better, easier, and more enjoyable. There was fear, of course, and bias, but only very occasionally was there real hatred. Mostly, it seemed like the people I met felt they were the objects of hate, rather than being purveyors of hate themselves. The Bedouin felt it from the Egyptians, the Palestinians from the Israelis. Israelis felt it from everyone. The increased impermeability of the boundaries and borders in the regions only accentuates this.

So what can we do from afar? Well, we can walk. To walk is to connect stories. It is a way to draw parallels that would simply not be obvious in any other way. It paints a picture that cannot be seen when remaining stationary or moving too fast. Trails, meanwhile, can bring life to a dying landscape, and can forge relationships between segregated communities. Walking on such trails illuminates hope, and peace, and hospitality, and it can often foster understanding. Perhaps there is only so much it can achieve in a fractured landscape, but perhaps not. It is an inherently positive activity, and a simple one rooted in equality and goodwill.

Let's be clear: I'm not suggesting that walking can bring peace to the Middle East. But I like it, and I don't have any other ideas. So why not? It seems like a good place to start, and with politics and security seemingly going backwards, walking may be a way to move forward while simultaneously offering opportunities and empowering development along the way. I can't think of anywhere better for a stroll than through the Holy Land because, for all its problems, it is one of the most spectacular, friendly and stimulating places that any of us could ever hope to visit.

# Acknowledgements

There are a significant number of people without whom this journey would not have been possible. Then there are yet more people without whom this *book* would not have been possible. For every step and word I owe thanks to a network of friends, new and old, spread across the globe who helped me plan, walk, talk and write. I am extremely fortunate to know such people, and even luckier that they lent their considerable skills and knowledge to making this work. The list below picks out some in particular. To all of those, and to the others not named, thank you – *shukran, toda* – and I hope you enjoy reading the story that you've been such a big part of.

Firstly, thanks to the staff and visionaries of the Masar Ibrahim, the Jordan Trail and the Sinai Trail, and to the many architects of those paths: William Ury, George Rishmawi, Mark Khano, Amjad Shahrour, Ben Hoffler, Musallem Abu Faraj, Tony Howard, Di Taylor, Josh Weiss, Stephanie Saldana, David Landis, Stefan Szepesi and all the others involved that there isn't room to mention, or that I didn't get a chance to know – the trails are wonderful, and they work, in practice as well as in theory. Additionally, all my gratitude to those on the staff and board of the Abraham Path Initiative for your support of this idea – you made the journey possible.

On the road, thanks to my guides and well-wishers and trail saviours (in vague geographical/linear order): Ahmad, Jameel, Um Fares, Anwar, Majdi, Mohammed Atari, the Mardawi family, Osama, Ahmad, Eisa, Jolanda, Sandra, Carmen, Mahmoud B'doul, Suleiman, Nasr, Musallem, Suleiman and Harboush, Shai, and Hani. I'm also enormously grateful to everyone who came to say hi, or offered me coffee or food or a place to sleep – you all exemplify the hospitality that I have come to see characterises the region.

To all of those that travelled to share long days on the road with me: Dave, Laurence, Sean, Pip, Tony, Di and Austin – you were the best of company. Also to Nicky, Joris, Nasser and everyone else who came for a day or two along the way. In Jerusalem and Bethlehem and Beit Sahour: Hannah, Martina, Aaron, David, Anna and the rest of the team – I'm sure Dave and I wouldn't have made it to the start line without you. And Raed – thank you for the room at the wonderful Jerusalem Hotel, where I was able to both begin and end this journey. In Amman, thanks to Matt Loveland and your wonderful family, to Jamie and Irina and family, and to Amjad, Ayman and the rest of the team at Experience Jordan. In Petra, thank you to Patricia and Eid for the idyllic room at 'Petra Bed & Breakfast', and also my appreciation to Nabil for letting me stay at the wonderful Feynan Ecolodge.

In particular, I'm extremely grateful to Matt Harms who was a regular troubleshooter and hiking companion through the journey, to Mark Khano for the many miles and conversations that we shared, and to Stefan Szepesi who helped orchestrate the whole idea and who, as well as fitting into most of the categories above, encouraged, guided and walked with me on the path. Thank you.

John and Zachary at Railriders Adventure Clothing – I appreciate the continued support and wonderful clothing. Also thank you to Osprey, Keen, BAM bamboo clothing, Marmot, Snow+Rock, SunGod, Leki, Powertraveller and Mophie for the equipment and assistance along the way.

To everyone who read early drafts of the book – I'm sorry. You were very patient. Tatiana at I.B.Tauris, and the rest of the team there – thanks for doing such a wonderful job in helping this come to fruition. To my agent Jo of Wolfsong Media – thanks for all your hard work over such a long time to make this happen.

Finally, to friends and family, who listened to me worry before, during and after the walk. Thanks all for the support: in particular to the Wynesses, Symonses, Heaneys and McCarrons. To Clare – neither the journey nor the book would have been possible without you, and I'm forever grateful for your care and understanding. To Aunt Diana (who did the maps) and Mum, who thought I'd probably die but was glad that I didn't.

# Trail Companions

T his journey was rarely a lonely one, and many of the miles that passed beneath my boots were walked in the company of friends, old and new. There is – sadly – not room to mention everyone that I had the pleasure of spending time with on the trail, but here are those who I travelled with for at least two days. Thank you, all, for the help and guidance and conversation.

Dave       Anwar       Laurence       Stefan

David       Matt       Hannah       Mohammed

Eisa

Mahmoud

Mark

Tony

Di

Nasser

Sean

Pip

Suleiman
(Wadi Rum)

Harboush

Austin

Musallem

Suleiman (Sinai)

Nasr (Sinai)

257

# Information on the Trails

Aquick note on all trails:

It is always useful to check the UK Foreign and Commonwealth Office advice before going anywhere, particularly in this region. Keep up to date with the local news and be alert to shifts and tensions in the geopolitical climate. That said, almost all of my most interesting journeys in life have been in places to which visits are not exactly encouraged by the Foreign Office. My advice is simply to make sure you're well informed; don't get caught up in the culture of fear of strange places, but equally don't go somewhere that is obviously not safe. (For example, trying to hike in most parts of Syria right now is neither clever nor appropriate.)

At the time of writing, it is perfectly fine to visit and hike on any of the trails below.

## Masar Ibrahim al-Khalil

If you are interested in walking on the Masar Ibrahim al-Khalil (MIAK) in Palestine, the best place to start is at their website: http://masaribrahim.ps/en.

The most useful pages on the site for practical purposes are under the 'Plan Your Trip' tab, which has information on, among other things: accommodation options, what to wear, climate, how to get there, safety and security, and how to contact local guides.

Bear in mind that it is advisable, though by no means compulsory, to travel with a local guide in much of the West Bank. It is not a good idea to wild-camp, more out of respect for the local communities than for your own safety. The accommodation on offer will be in Bedouin tents, homestays or small hostels and hotels. They are, as a general rule, very basic, so be prepared for this. Dress conservatively and appropriately for a journey through rural areas in a predominately Islamic country – covering knees and shoulders should do the job. Women do not have to cover their hair, and will be welcomed all along the trail, even in more traditional areas. The trail is accessible all year round, but I would caution against walking between May and September, simply because of the heat.

To get there from the West, Tel Aviv is the easiest entry point. It is generally inadvisable to tell Israeli immigration that you are heading to the West Bank, so it is best to say that you plan to visit Jerusalem (which you probably will be doing before you start the journey). Most Arab countries don't allow flights to Israel – that would somewhat undermine their stance that it doesn't exist – so if you're coming from somewhere within the region, Amman is the nearest airport. From there you can get a taxi or bus to Jerusalem with relative ease.

The MIAK is still a work in progress. I believe there are now some waymarkings in place, and as I found to my delight the route is beautiful and varied. In many areas, however, the trail is still developing, particularly in the areas of guiding, homestays, maps and tour operators. This will not be the same as walking along the Camino de Santiago. You should be proficient with a GPS and comfortable with navigation (this is less important if you have a guide, but still useful).

Finally, be respectful. The beauty of this trail is that you will have a chance to speak to Palestinians and, crucially, to listen to them. Feel free to talk with them on all sorts of topics, but don't push too hard on political or religious issues – you are a guest, after all. This is general travel etiquette, but its importance is accentuated in a place with certain sensitivities like the West Bank.

One last note – there are tour operators who offer journeys along the Masar Ibrahim. This can be a good option if you'd like someone to take care of the logistics for you and shuttle luggage between rest stops. All operators are equal, of course, but some are more equal than others – I can recommend Edge Expeditions, who run a two-week trip in the autumn, led by yours truly. Visit www.edge-expeditions.com to learn more.

# Jordan Trail

Much of the same advice as above applies here too. Start by visiting www.jordantrail.org, and look at the 'Plan Your Trip' section. It is simplest to fly into Amman and finalise the details of your trek from there – travelling within the country is relatively easy, with buses or taxis available to take you just about anywhere you might want to go. As with the MIAK, it's best to avoid trekking in high summer.

The Jordan Trail is more of a work in progress than the MIAK and thus requires a little more legwork on the part of the walker (pardon the pun.) It is essential here that you are competent with a GPS and have downloaded the maps from the website. I cannot emphasise this enough. You can camp anywhere along the route, and in many sections this is the only option if you travel independently, so you must also be comfortable travelling in this manner.

Jordan is a very peaceful and welcoming country. You are unlikely to run into any trouble. To be respectful, however, it is advisable to follow the same guidelines as above regarding clothing and cultural etiquette. It's also useful to learn a few words of Arabic – you might not be able to understand much, but saying 'Hello' and 'Please' and 'Thank you' in the local language is always nice.

There are a couple of sections of the Jordan Trail that are really quite tough for independent hikers. The three wadis area includes some very strenuous hiking, and will require carrying a lot of water. South of Petra, there is a large section of trail with no obvious water sources or resupply points. Your options here are to cache supplies beforehand or to arrange for a guide or support vehicle. The best place to get help with these logistics is via a company called 'Experience Jordan' – www.experiencejordan.com – who have been involved with the trail since its inception. They can also organise tours on the trail, and will be happy to help with any other queries that you have.

The Jordan Trail has also begun organising 'thru-hikes', which look to be an annual event, taking a group of people along the whole 40-day, 600+ km route. Follow them on Facebook – @TheJordanTrail – for the latest news on those if you're interested in seeing the country that way.

## Sinai Trail

The Sinai Trail is slightly different to those above in that it requires a guide and, for most journeys, at least one camel. Visit www.sinaitrail.org to get started. You can download the maps and study the route and read about the history and aims of the trail, but once again, logistically speaking, the most useful section is found on the sidebar that says 'Book a Hike'. This page provides phone numbers for guides directly, as well as a contact form where you can email your request.

Getting to Sinai is not as easy as it used to be, especially if you are coming from the UK. That said, it's still not hugely difficult. If you live somewhere that has a direct flight to Sharm el-Sheikh, then you're in luck. From Sharm airport, it's an easy taxi ride to the trailheads along the coast. The alternative method (at the time of writing, there are still no direct flights from the UK to Sinai) is generally to fly to Cairo, and from there to catch a connecting flight or bus. By sea, it's possible to cross from Aqaba in Jordan to Taba or Nuweiba, and there is a land crossing between Taba and Eilat, Israel.

If your entry point to the country is via any of the coastal towns and cities, you will automatically be offered a 14-day Sinai-only visa, valid exclusively for the eastern Gulf strip. This is not useful for the Sinai Trail, so it's better to get a full 30-day Egyptian tourist visa. Make sure you request this instead when you land/arrive.

The Sinai Trail is probably the one on this list that hikers might be most wary of in terms of security. As per the advice at the top of this section, it's crucial to keep up to date with the latest news, but I found Sinai to be incredibly safe and calm. Thousands of other visitors find the same. Don't let an unwarranted reputation put you off visiting.

Practically, you will need to be able to hike for consecutive days, of course, but you won't need to carry as much gear as for an independent journey on the Jordan Trail, for example. That's what the camel is for. As a final note here, the Sinai Trail recently won the prestigious 'Best New Tourism Award' from the British Guild of Travel Writers. It got it entirely on merit, and it is a sign that the trail has every chance of becoming a great success in the future.

## Abraham Path Initiative

I have not mentioned the Abraham Path Initiative in this book, but it is a very important part of the picture of trails in the region. The organisation is a non-profit that supports the development of the cultural route of Abraham, serving as a platform for experiential education in the Middle East and aiming to inspire people worldwide through stories, walking and hospitality. The initiative has supported the trails above, and is also in the process of creating a cultural corridor in Abraham's footsteps, so that from a distance the rest of us might walk virtually in places that are not currently accessible.

Visit www.abrahampath.org to learn more.

# Glossary

*adhan* – the Muslim call to prayer

*ahlan wa sahlan* – literally: welcome!

**Bedouin** – Arab desert nomad(s)

**Decapolis** – a confederation of ten city-states, founded in the Hellenistic period and which also later flourished under the Eastern Roman Empire, including Scythopolis (now Beit She'an), Pella, Gadara and, the most southerly city, Philadelphia (present-day Amman).

**djinn** – ghost, or invisible spirit, in Islamic tradition

*habibi* – an affectionate term for a friend or loved one meaning: my dear

**Hadith** – sayings not in the Qur'an but attributed to the Prophet Muhammad

**halwa** – a popular confectionery across the Middle East, often made with sesame seed paste and sugar. It is extremely sweet and quite sickly after a while

**haram** – designation for something that is forbidden in Islam

**Haredim** (singular: **Haredi**) – conservative Orthodox Jews who reject modern secular culture

**hijab** – headscarf worn by Muslim women to cover their hair in public and in male company

**imam** – leader of a mosque

*insha'allah* – a ubiquitous phrase in Arabic-speaking cultures, used at the end of almost every statement to temper any certainty. It means 'God willing' or, at various times depending on who is speaking: 'if we're lucky', 'if I can be bothered' or 'No, this will definitely not happen, but I'll say yes and use the *insha'allah* get-out to mitigate later why it all went wrong'

**intifada** – an Arabic term that translates directly as a 'shaking off' or 'shuddering', but which has become accepted terminology for resistance or rebellion against occupation

**keffiyeh** – an Arab scarf, worn around the neck or on the head. The Palestinian version is chequered black and white and was famously worn by the politician Yasser Arafat

*khalas* – meaning: enough! or finished! Used with regularity in conversation

**kibbutz** (plural **kibbutzim**) – a communal village, usually based on agriculture, and commonplace throughout Israel

*kippah* (plural: *kippot*) – a cap worn by religious Jews to show respect to God

**madrassa** – Islamic college

*makhteshim* (singular: *makhtesh*) – crater-like geological features, created by erosion and found mostly in the Negev Desert

*maqam* – the tomb of an Islamic holy man

*maqluba* – pot of rice, meat, vegetables and spices, flipped upside down to serve

**masjid** – mosque

*mensef* – a dish of lamb, dried yoghurt and rice

*merhaba* – hello

**muezzin** – the man in charge of making the call to prayer from the mosque

**Mukhabarat** – a catch-all Arabic term for the secret police

*mumtaz* – excellent or, more colloquially, awesome

*Nakba* – (literally 'the Catastrophe') the Arabic term for the exodus of Palestinians from their homes after 1948

**Operation Defensive Shield** – the IDF military operation in the West Bank in 2002

**Oslo Accords** – peace agreements signed between Israel and the PLO in 1993 and 1995

*payot* – sidelocks, or sidecurls, worn by some Jewish males, based on an interpretation of the Torah that forbids shaving the 'corners' of one's head

*qasr* – literally 'castle', but often in Palestine also used to refer to structures built in the hills by farmers to store crops

*rababah* – bowed string instrument played by the Bedouin

*shababah* – musical instrument, played in the manner of a flute

*shaheed* – martyr

**shalom** – (literally 'peace') the most common greeting in Hebrew

*siq* – canyon

*souq* – traditional marketplace

*Tanakh* – canonical collection of Hebrew texts that make up the Hebrew Bible

**tell** – earthen mound covering a site of archaeological significance

*thobe* – ankle-length gown-like garment worn by men across the Middle East (also called at times a *jelebiya*)

**wadi** – canyon or gorge, usually dry

**yeshiva** – Jewish institution for the study of religious texts

*za'atar* – spice mix used in Arabic cuisine, consisting of salt, oregano, thyme, and sesame seeds

# Notes

1. A term given to Catholics in Northern Ireland who subscribe to the ideology of returning to a United Ireland.
2. Northern Irish Protestants loyal to the crown and British rule.
3. Type 'Belfast City Hall Flag Protests' into Google for a perfect example of just how ridiculous it is.
4. Jack Sommers, '7/7 Bombings anniversary poll shows more than half of Britons see Muslims as a threat', *Huffington Post*, 6 July 2015. Available at www.huffington post.co.uk/2015/07/03/77-bombings-muslims-islam-britain-poll_n_7694452.html.
5. Matthew Taylor, 'Racist and anti-immigration views held by children revealed in schools study', *Guardian*, 19 May 2015. Available at www.theguardian.com/e-ducation/2015/may/19/most-children-think-immigrants-are-stealing-jobs-schools-study-shows.
6. Alexander Sehmer, 'Hate crimes against Muslims in London "up by 70%", police figures show', *Independent*, 7 September 2015. Available at www.independent.co.u-k/news/uk/home-news/hate-crimes-against-muslims-in-london-up-by-70-accord-ing-to-police-10489175.html.
7. 'The Holy Land' is something of a vague and catch-all term for the land mass that is sacred to the three major monotheistic religions: Christianity, Islam and Judaism. The most commonly accepted geographical definition of it incorporates Israel, the Palestinian Territories, Lebanon, western Jordan and some parts of Syria and Egypt (including the Sinai Peninsula). I will refer to the Holy Land with regularity throughout this book, not because my journey was a definitive exploration of the area but because all parts of my walk passed through regions that fall within the above definition, and it is the most appropriate and helpful term I could find.
8. Ezekiel 5:5 (New International Version) says, quoting the 'Sovereign Lord': 'This is Jerusalem, which I have set in the centre of the nations.' Medieval maps show the three known continents of Europe, Asia and Africa arranged in a circle, looking much like a shamrock, with Jerusalem in the middle. The most famous surviving example of this is the Mappa Mundi in Hereford.

9. It is thought that this was an entranceway to the city, which Hadrian called 'Aelia Capitolina'.

10. There is no certainty in the timeline here – even Jesus's birthdate is now presumed to have occurred around 3 or 4 BC in our modern calendar system.

11. F. E. Peters, *Jerusalem* (Princeton, 1985), p. 145.

12. In the Jewish Quarter the Kotel, or the Western Wall – a small section of the retaining wall of the Second Temple built by Herod the Great – is at the heart of this. It is the holiest place where Jews can pray, although not the holiest site in Judaism; that is the Foundation Stone, which lies within the Dome of the Rock/Qubbat al-Sakhrah but, due to the entry restrictions, Jewish (and Christian) prayer there is forbidden. Jewish tradition says that this was the location from where the world was created, and is also the spot upon which Abraham was asked to sacrifice his son, Isaac.

13. Muhammad, the central figure in Islam, is said to have received the word of God in a cave near his home in the city of Mecca in Arabia; he immediately began preaching this new religion, and most of the Arabian Peninsula was converted before his death. The Qur'an and other Islamic texts tell us of the Night Journey, or *Isra* and *mi'raj*, when Muhammad was transported, on a single night in 621, from his home in Mecca to Jerusalem, where he then ascended to heaven. The Al-Aqsa Mosque – the third holiest site in Islam after Mecca and Medina – is now built on the venerated spot.

14. Israeli citizens are allowed to buy firearms, but Palestinians are not.

15. I will talk about Palestine a lot in this book. There are three Palestines, to my mind. One is a geographical term, referring to the land mass between the Mediterranean and the River Jordan (named as such, probably, by Herodotus in the fifth century BC). Second is the Palestine that sits at the negotiating table: a future state, as yet unrealised, desired by many and already partially recognised. Third is the Palestine that is alive in the existing territories and through the many millions of Palestinians. We must guess at where it begins and ends to a certain degree, but this is the Palestine to which I will refer in this book (unless otherwise stated).

16. The name 'West Bank' is simply a reference to the land on the western bank of the River Jordan.

17. The phrase comes from a bill of law called 'Jerusalem Law', but it has since been trotted out regularly by politicians and supporters of Israel worldwide. In late 2016 Donald Trump's nominee for ambassador to Israel, hardliner and lawyer David Friedman, promised to move the US embassy from Tel Aviv to Jerusalem in recognition of its status as capital of Israel. The security ramifications of this in Palestine and throughout the Middle East are terrifying.

18. Names are important in Jerusalem. To call this area only the Temple Mount can be seen as diminishing its importance to the Arab people and the Islamic faith. It is therefore easiest to give it both names. Coming from Northern Ireland, I am used to this. As a child my nearest city was Derry/Londonderry, and from an early age I lived in a double-named world.

19. The most well-known is related in Acts I, where we are told that Jesus ascended to heaven from this spot.

20. H. Afflerbach and H. Strachan (eds), *How Fighting Ends: A History of Surrender* (Oxford, 2012).
21. B'Tselem – The Israeli Information Center for Human Rights in the Occupied Territories 'The Separation Barrier', 1 January 2011. Available at www.btselem.org/separation_barrier/map.
22. A popular dish in Palestine, Jordan and the surrounding countries. Rice, chicken, potatoes and spices are cooked together and the meal is served by upending the pot onto a platter, sandcastle-style.
23. The reliable availability of water made this route the definitive way not only to Jerusalem but also for those heading onward to Damascus, the coast or even Baghdad.
24. *Voyages and Travels of Her Majesty, Caroline Queen of Great Britain {...} by one of Her Majesty's Suite* (London, 1821).
25. United Nations Relief and Works Agency for Palestine Refugees in the Near East (UNRWA), 'Palestine Refugees'. Available at www.unrwa.org/palestine-refugees.
26. Mark Twain, *The Innocents Abroad* (New York, 1910), p. 502.
27. B'Tselem – The Israeli Information Center for Human Rights in the Occupied Territories, 'Background on the restriction of movement', 1 January 2011. Available at www.btselem.org/freedom_of_movement.
28. This was the same Pilgrim of Bordeaux who wrote about the Church of the Holy Sepulchre. His accounts were brought to light by the French antiquary Pierre Pithou in 1588.
29. In the Arab world, the word *Abu*, meaning literally 'father of', is often attributed as part of a *kunya*, a form of Arabic nickname. The name that follows is usually the bearer's first-born son. Hence Abu Hamed means 'the father of Hamed'. The same applies to females with the prefix *Umm*, or 'mother of'.
30. Later, in Tel Aviv, I asked a friend of a friend who was in the IDF during this time why the village would have been visited so often by the IDF. He told me that everything was very tense then, and the army couldn't take any risks anywhere with security. It was likely too, he said (though he couldn't be sure) that there was intelligence relating to militant activity somewhere in Kufr Malek, and the army were there to monitor the situation and occasionally raid houses when they thought they might get their man.
31. *Shaheed* is how the Palestinians refer to people who are killed by the Israeli military. The connotation of martyrdom is a difficult one for outsiders, as the term is used both for young men like Abdal Aziz, who were simply throwing stones, but also for those accused of leading suicide bomb attacks against Israelis.
32. Stefan wrote the first walking guide book to Palestine, called *Walking Palestine: 25 Journeys into the West Bank* (New York, 2011). I highly recommend it.
33. Ettinger remains under various restrictions, including a ban from the West Bank for a year, East Jerusalem for six months, and a curfew elsewhere. He is also barred from making contact with a list of just under 100 right-wing figures for six months.
34. 'Outposts' are deemed illegal under Israeli law, but settlements are not. By international law, both are illegal. In general, outposts are smaller and more basic, normally started by ultra-Orthodox Jews with a particular attachment to a

certain piece of land. They do not enjoy easy access to facilities like electricity and water. In time, a large number of them become settlements once support from the government is agreed upon.

35. Raja Shehadeh, *Palestinian Walks: Notes on a Vanishing Landscape* (London, 2008), p. xii.

36. This is actually true all over – the Christian population of the West Bank is around 2 per cent. There are just a few notable towns left where Christians form a majority.

37. Since we hiked the trail, waymarkings have been put in place in some of the West Bank. As with everything here, putting some paint on a rock is much more complicated than it ought to be, but the early experiments have been successful and, hopefully, the waymarkings will continue to be seen as a part of the landscape.

38. 'Shalom' is the usual Hebrew greeting, meaning 'Peace' or 'Hello'.

39. This has been the circular conversation for years regarding the future of the land. 'One state' would see Israel, the West Bank and Gaza exist as one country with equal rights for all. 'Two states' would give Palestine its own area, based on a to-be-confirmed boundary agreement. The Palestinian leadership have demanded a return to the 1967 borders, which Israel does not accept, and, given the growth and apparent permanence of the settlements in the West Bank, this arrangement would seem improbable both politically and logistically.

40. The West Bank uses the Israeli shekel as currency. Until 1950, it used the Palestinian pound. The 1993 Oslo Accords prohibited the Palestinian Authority from issuing its own currency. Many Palestinians that I met pointed to this as a flagship injustice, and a symbol of the occupation.

41. About £0.80.

42. These are, respectively, the Jewish Home party and Yisrael Beiteinu.

43. In March 2013 Adalah – the Legal Centre for Arab Minority Rights in Israeli – published the 'Discriminatory Laws database' with over 50 entries.

44. In 2016 The Pew Research Center in the USA released a study called 'Israel's Religiously Divided Society' (www.pewforum.org/2016/03/08/israels-religiously-divided-society/) which outlines these problems in great detail.

45. The 2014 census recorded figures of 69 per cent Muslim and 30.9 per cent Christian.

46. The Decapolis was a confederation of ten of the region's most prominent Greco-Roman cities.

47. François René de Chateaubriand, *Travels to Jerusalem* (London, 1835).

48. Dave's recovery did take months but, with his usual approach of enthusiasm and optimism, he found a place to stay in Bali for much of it and healed his bones in the sunshine of the islands. By the time I returned home from the trip he was fighting fit, and we remain good friends.

49. In the year 2000, Pope John Paul declared the site of Tell Mar Elias an official pilgrimage destination. As of my visit a decade and a half later, however, the word had not spread far and wide; I was the only tourist.

50. Saladin founded the Ayubid dynasty and led the Muslim campaign against the Crusaders. He is one of the most revered leaders and warriors of the Islamic world.

51. Cairo to Damascus is a distance of perhaps 600 miles.

52. In Arabic, *mumtaz* translates as 'excellent' or 'the best', and I found it most often applied in the way that 'cool' or 'awesome' are used in English. I found myself still using it long after I returned home.

53. 'Not enough water in the West Bank?' – visual by Visualising Palestine and EWASH. Available at http://visualizingpalestine.org/visuals/west-bank-water.

54. Nura A. Abboud (EcoMENA), 'Countering water scarcity in Jordan', 29 October 2016. Available at www.ecomena.org/tag/water-scarcity-in-jordan/.

55. Crown Prince Rudolph, *Travels in the East* (London, 1884).

56. In the local dialect of Arabic the phrase used to ask a male 'How are you?' is often shortened to *Kefak*. *Kefoo* had grown out of this and it was endearing to see the older, broad Bedouin men with hard faces crease into smiles as they cooed to each other in passing.

57. Gertrude Bell, *The Letters of Gertrude Bell*, 2 vols (London, 1927).

58. Lowell Thomas, *With Lawrence in Arabia* (London, 1924), p. 175.

59. After the events in Irbid, on 18 December 2016, a number of attacks occurred in the city of Kerak, where I had been hit on the head with a rotten aubergine. Eleven Jordanians and a Canadian were killed in a shoot-out in the castle, and the atrocity was subsequently claimed by ISIS. Fortunately, at the time of writing, this seemed to have impacted neither on the international perception of security in the kingdom, nor directly on visitor numbers in the following quarter.

60. I was told this by a Bedouin in Wadi Rum who had first said that across the Red Sea lay only 'God, and the Bedouin'. He then clarified the hierarchy of ownership in the above description. Interestingly, he also mentioned that he knew members of the Tarabine tribe in Jordan, and said there were more in Saudi Arabia. The Tarabine were the first tribe that I would meet in South Sinai and had been split by the contemporary borders; they still shared the same lineage and would, he said, help each other out in time of need.

61. Not long after I returned home in 2016, the UK voted narrowly in favour of leaving the EU after a campaign which, as far as I could see, garnered support to leave largely by scaremongering on these immigration issues.

62. International Organisation for Migration, 'Summary of arrivals to Europe 2015'. Available at – http://migration.iom.int/europe/.

63. British Red Cross, 'Refugee facts and figures'. Available at www.redcross.org.uk/What-we-do/Refugee-support/Refugee-facts-and-figures. Sources: Home Office immigration statistics, October to December 2015; UNHCR mid-year report 2015; Office for National Statistics, mid-2013.

64. The lack of a definitive number here is due to differing opinions on what constitutes a tribe, what makes a group of people a sub-tribe instead, and so on. I cannot pretend to have any understanding of the finer details, but it does seem like something that it is agreed to disagree upon.

65. Camels are even-toed ungulates and therefore do not technically have hooves. They bear their weight equally between the third and fourth toes on their feet (unlike horses, who carry weight primarily on one 'toe'). The feet, however, are covered in a hard nail that looks much like a hoof and, underneath, the two halves are joined by webbing. This soft sole is susceptible to piercing from sharp rocks or

similar hazards, and the feet can swell if the camel is forced to walk on hard, compact surfaces for too long; they have evolved for the soft sand and more forgiving terrain of the desert, after all. It is with this in mind that one would inspect the feet, toes, sole and legs of a camel before buying.

66. Galatians 4:25.

67. He was found, in a papyrus basket, floating in the reeds of the River Nile. His rescuer happened to be the daughter of the Pharaoh, and she raised him in the court.

68. There are many mysteries about this account, and a great deal of detective work required to decode it. An eleventh-century copy of a long letter – the *Itinerarium Egeriae,* addressed to a women's circle – was discovered in the late nineteenth century by an Italian scholar, and multiple theories of the author's identity were subsequently offered. The most popular is that the writer was Egeria, a woman who is written about in the seventh-century letter of a Galician monk called Valerio. It is he who speculates that she is a nun, because of the nature of her pilgrimage, and that she may have been middle-class in order to afford it.

69. M. L. McClure and C. L. Feltoe, *The Pilgrimage of Etheria* (London, 1919), pp. 3–4.

70. In George Manginis's wonderful book, *Mount Sinai: A History of Travellers and Pilgrims* (London, 2016), he describes how the Bedouin nicknamed these tourists 'Cookii', and were bemused by how they, 'opted for camping outside the monastery walls and enjoyed familiar delicacies like Yorkshire bacon and potted salad, usually included in the agent's fee'.

71. The Syriac Sinaiticus is the oldest translation of the Bible. The manuscript is from the late fourth century, and contains a Syriac translation of the first four canonical gospels of the New Testament. The Codex Sinaiticus, meanwhile, is a 1,600-year-old handwritten translation of the Bible in Greek. The majority of it is now housed in the British Library.

72. McClure and Feltoe, *The Pilgrimage of Etheria*, p. 6.

73. Edward Hull, *Mount Seir, Sinai and Western Palestine* (London, 1885), p. 52.

74. www.mmi.gov.il/static/HanhalaPirsumim/Beduin_information.pdf.

75. Conscription is mandatory for all Israeli citizens, men and women, who are over 18 and of Jewish, Druze or Circassian descent. Notable exceptions include Arab Israelis, and Yeshiva students who make a case to show that Talmudic study is their profession. The standard length of service is two years for women and two years eight months for men.

76. The movement of Palestinians is controlled by a series of Israeli-issued identity cards which dictates, based on where they are from, whether they are allowed to visit Jerusalem, Israel, the Gaza Strip or parts of the West Bank. Most Palestinians who want, and are able, to leave the country travel to Jordan to do so because they are rarely granted permission to fly out of Tel Aviv.

77. Mossad is the national intelligence agency of Israel. It is widely regarded to be one of the most effective – and is one of the most feared – in the world.

78. 'Midreshet' comes from the Hebrew word 'midrasha', meaning 'place of learning'. In Arabic the word is 'madrassa'. There are many similarities between the two

languages that, even with a rudimentary understanding of either, become clear as you begin to spend time there.

79. The Cave of the Patriarchs is a series of underground caves associated with Abraham – it is believed that he chose the spot as his final resting place. Because it is holy to both Jews and Muslims, and because of the tensions in the city, the separate prayer areas are strictly segregated. The Palestinians refer to the area as the Ibrahimi Mosque (Ibrahim is the Arabic form of Abraham).

80. The most notorious of these is Shuhada Street, which was once the main market street and a thoroughfare to the Ibrahimi Mosque. The shops have been entirely shut down, and a large impenetrable gate sits at the entrance; only Palestinians who live beyond the threshold can cross, and they must present their ID cards to soldiers inside every time they wish to come or go.

81. The Arabic spelling used for Abu Nasim's town, Tequ'a, is a transliteration of تقوع. The Israeli settlement is purposely called by the same name with the same pronunciation – I use the different spellings here mainly as a shorthand to distinguish between the Palestinian town and the Israeli settlement.

82. It is worth pointing out once more that settlements in the West Bank are illegal under international law. Israel disputes this and continues to support their expansion.